WHERE'S DAD NOW THAT I NEED HIM?

ASK MOM!

SURVIVING AWAY FROM HOME

9th printing, April 2000

Cover Design by: Bob Simmons
Illustrations by: Nancy A. McDonald

Aspen West Publishing Co., Inc.
8385 Allen St. Suite #129
Sandy, Utah 84070-6415
(801) 565-1370

Hardcover ISBN: 9615390-2-X
Paperback ISBN: 9615390-3-8

This publication is designed to be an informational guide in
regards to the subject matter covered. It is sold with the
understanding that the publisher is not engaged in rendering
medical or other professional services. Where professional
services are required, the services of a competent
professional person shall be sought.

CONTENTS

Being a good consumer is pretty complicated these days --you have to deal with the fine print in sales agreements and the complex terminology in all kinds of contracts. A guarantee isn't a guarantee unless you know the strategy to use if you're not satisfied. Even a trip to the store is rough: how can you tell a real "bargain" from a rip-off?

Like good common sense, a little good consumer sense can save you time, money, and a lot of frustration.

SHOP TILL YOU DROP, BUT DON'T TAKE THE BAIT!

The bait?

That's right: "bait and switch" is a common tactic used by unethical merchants to lure you into their stores. Even though it is illegal in many states, it's still done far too often. Here's how it works:

A merchant takes out an ad for a sale item that has an incredibly low price on it. So you rush to the store. What happens? The salesperson tells you that the store has run out of that item, but he offers you a similar one--at a higher price, of course. Since you had your heart set on making the purchase, you go ahead--even though the price isn't what you hoped.

Did the store really run out?

No way. The store never intended to sell that item at that price. It used the item (and the price) to lure you into the store. Once you're inside, merchants figure they can persuade you into buying something else. Unfortunately, it usually works.

Avoid falling into the bait and switch trap by insisting on the advertised item. If a sales clerk tries to lead you to a "similar" item, refuse. Purchase only what was advertised.

There are plenty of other "sale" tactics. Some merchants offer an extremely low price on a popular item--but they only have five or ten to sell. It's similar to the bait and switch tactic: customers rush in, only to be told the store has "sold out."

Is it ethical?

No! By law, stores have a legal responsibility when they advertise a sale item to stock a reasonable supply. If they don't have a reasonable supply, they are supposed to state something like "limited quantities available" or "only five available" in the ad.

By law, stores are also supposed to offer "rain checks" unless they specify in their ads that they won't (the ad should say something like "Sorry, no rain checks"). A rain check is a coupon that will allow you to come into the store within a specified period of time (usually thirty days) that allows for restocking; with a rain check, you can purchase the same item for the original sale price.

To avoid the "limited supply" trap, ask for a rain check if the store has sold out of an advertised sale item. If the store refuses to offer a rain check for the merchandise, leave. Don't spend your money on "something similar." Some merchants also advertise a "sale" that isn't really a sale. Why? Because they inflate prices on the merchandise the week before the sale and then "mark it down" for the sale. Obviously, the mark-down doesn't reflect savings--it reflects the usual price.

To protect yourself against the false mark-down tactic, become a wise shopper. Window shop occasionally, just to acquaint yourself with usual prices. If an item you are interested in is advertised as on "sale," do some comparison shopping. Call several other stores in the area and ask for their price on the same item. Take advantage of the "sale" only if it reflects true savings over what you could purchase the item for in another store.

Finally, you might be offered a certain incentive for acting quickly--for purchasing before you leave the store. A merchant might offer you a "free" gift if you make an expensive purchase-but the cost of the gift has been built in to the price of the expensive item. In essence, then, you've paid for the "free" gift, and the merchant is betting that you'll be enticed into making a major purchase without taking time to think it over.

To avoid costly mistakes, never purchase an expensive item without taking time to think it over. A salesperson is naturally eager to earn the commission on the sale, but you should be equally concerned about your own satisfaction. If someone starts applying undue pressure on you to make a major purchase, back off. Leave the store, walk or drive around the block for a few minutes, or even go enjoy some lunch or dinner. Call around to compare prices on the same item at two or three other stores. After you've had some time away, reconsider. If you still want to make the purchase, return to the store. As a courtesy, find the salesperson who worked with you earlier so that he or she can be credited with the commission.

You don't even have to leave your house to shop--but just because you're at home doesn't mean you are safe from consumer rip-offs!

Door-to-door sales can be especially difficult to resist-and by law, you have an "out" if you succumb and regret it immediately afterwards. Under federal law, you have a "cooling off period" that allows you to cancel any sales contract within three days as long as you bought the merchandise anywhere other than the seller's place of business. (That includes your own home, your office, a flea market, a swap meet, and so on.)

You don't need to give any reason: you just need to give the seller written notice that you want to cancel the contract. Salespeople are supposed to give you a printed form you can use to cancel the contract. If you didn't get one, write a simple note stating

How To Get Out Of A Contract

If you're sorry now that you signed on the dotted line, do you have any options?

Yes--if you can prove that you were unfairly victimized, have little legal experience, or have little bargaining power.

Generally speaking, you can get out of a contract if you can prove:

* that the salesman used a fraudulent statement to persuade you to sign
* that one of the clauses in the contract is unreasonably oppressive

If you buy something from a door-to-door salesman, of course, you have three days in which to change your mind.

that you want to cancel the purchase. Mail it to the seller by registered or certified mail, and make sure to do it within the first seventy-two hours after purchase.

What happens then? You're entitled to your money back. You can also get back anything you used as a trade-in. And you have to let the seller have the merchandise back. If the salesperson doesn't come to get the merchandise within twenty days after receiving your notice of cancellation (you'll have the date from the certified mail receipt), you get to keep it in addition to your refund.

If you decide to buy through the mail, deal only with reputable, established companies. If you have a question about a company's reputation, contact the Better Business Bureau or the Department of Business Regulation to see if there have been any complaints made about the company. The Department of Business Regulation in the state where the company is located can give you information about how long the firm has been in business--watch out for firms that are new or that move often.

Never send a check to a mail-order company you aren't sure of. Insist that merchandise be delivered C.O.D. ("cash on delivery"). That way, you won't pay anything for the merchandise until it is delivered to you.

If you receive something through the mail that you did not order, do not pay for it. By federal law, you are entitled to consider unordered merchandise as a "gift." You can use it, give it away, or throw it away--but you do not have to pay for it.

WARRANTIES AND GUARANTEES: FIGURING THEM OUT

Simply stated, a warranty or guarantee tells you by law the degree to which a manufacturer, distributor, or retailer must stand behind the products he sells you. That issue has historically been one of the most clouded--and, as a result, the warranties and guarantees it produced have been equally difficult to comprehend.

While laws vary from state to state, the basics regarding warranties and guarantees are pretty much the same.

To begin with, you need to understand the difference between the two kinds of warranties:

An implied warranty is just that--implied. It's not written down, but it nonetheless provides protection to you when you are

4

purchasing merchandise. An implied warranty basically says that you are entitled to a refund or replacement if the item does not work properly when used as intended.

Let's say you buy two molded plastic chairs. You take them home, plunk them down at your kitchen table, and start sitting on them during meals. After three weeks, the chairs start buckling and cracking.

Are you entitled to a refund or replacement?

Yes. Why? Because it is logical to assume that chairs are meant to be sat on. Therefore, it is logical to assume that chairs will bear the weight of an adult who sits on it (unless the label specifies a weight or age restriction). Since you were using the chairs to sit on, your implied warranty should protect you.

Now let's say you buy the same two molded plastic chairs. You take them home, but instead of plunking them down at your kitchen table, you use them to stand on so you can reach the high shelves in your closet. After three weeks, they start buckling and cracking.

Are you entitled to a refund or replacement?

No. Why? Because chairs aren't made to stand on. Therefore, you should not assume that a chair will hold up if you are standing on it. Since you were using the chairs to stand on (a use other than the one they were intended for), you are out of luck.

An implied warranty also protects you in some other situations. If you ask a salesperson for an item that will meet a specific need or use, but you get something else instead, an implied warranty protects you. If you specifically ask a clerk for a food processor that will also grind meat and the food processor he sells you won't do the job, you're entitled to your money back--or replacement with a food processor that will grind meat.

Practically everything you buy in a store is covered by an implied warranty: it's understood that the item will hold up for a certain length of time (the time varies from state to state, so check the law if you have problems). It's understood that what you buy will work--at least for a reasonable time.

An express, or written, warranty is a formal written warranty that tells you exactly what your rights are. Written warranties accompany thousands of different kinds of manufactured items, from computers and washing machines to pocket calculators and television sets. Warranties offer you certain rights, but they also spell out certain limitations and conditions. For example, many warranties specify that the item is no longer covered if you have tried to repair it yourself or if you have taken it to other than an authorized repair agent or dealer.

Written warranties may be limited or full, and are generally in effect for a specified amount of time. A limited warranty is one that covers only certain things (such as parts, but not labor) in case something goes wrong with the merchandise. A full warranty, on the other hand, covers all costs associated with repair or replacement.

You should know that warranties can be invalidated if you have abused an item or clearly used it in a way other than the way intended by the manufacturer. As a consumer, you have an obligation to use products in a careful, reasonable way.

In order to be legal, warranties have to meet certain standards. First, the warranty must be written in clear language that is understandable to any person who reads; the warranty can't be garbled up with legal or unfamiliar terms. The length of a full warranty has to be written in large, bold letters at the top of the warranty, and the length of a limited warranty must be spelled out at least in the body of the warranty. The warranty must be made available to you as a prospective buyer before you agree to purchase the item so you can review its provisions ahead of time.

The warranty, in order to be legal, must clearly spell out what you should do if problems arise. The warranty must contain clear directions on how to register a complaint about the product as well as where you should go for repair service. The warranty must also contain an "anti-lemon" clause that entitles you to replacement or refund if you have tried to have it repaired a "reasonable" number of times.

Finally, you can "transfer" a full warranty to someone else if you sell or give the product away while it is still protected under warranty. The new owner retains all the rights as though he were the original owner. A limited warranty may or may not be transferrable, but that distinction must be clearly made in the warranty itself so there will be no confusion.

If you have a problem with a product that is covered by warranty, start by sending a written complaint to the seller and manufacturer; the address will be on the warranty. The warranty should contain information on how to settle a dispute;

follow the procedure outlined by the warranty.

If you still don't get satisfaction, you are entitled to sue; if the product falls within dollar limitations, you can take the case to small claims court (see information that follows in this chapter). You can also file a registered complaint against the manufacturer or seller with the Federal Trade Commission, Sixth and Pennsylvania Avenues, N.W., Washington, D.C. 20580.

CONTRACTS: WHAT TO KNOW BEFORE YOU SIGN THE DOTTED LINE

If you've ever bought anything or done business with any kind of an establishment, you've probably signed hundreds of contracts without even knowing it.

Why?

Many businesses now include mini-versions of their sales contracts in microscopic print on sales receipts; they are sometimes even printed on ticket stubs. While many are so complex you can't begin to figure them out, there are some things you absolutely need to know before you sign on the dotted line.

First, what is a contract? Simply stated, it's a legal agreement between two people or businesses: one agrees to provide a product or service, and the other agrees to pay for it. Many contracts are written, but you should know that a contract can also be oral--a verbal agreement between two people that can be binding by law. You should also know that a contract does not have to be signed--if you accept the product or service, you have, in essence, "signed" the contract.

To protect yourself from getting something you don't want, there's something simple you can do: read the contract fully before you sign it. If you don't understand something, ask; if you want something changed, make an attempt; if you can't come to an agreement, don't sign. It's that easy.

Or is it?

Not always--because it's not always immediately obvious what you are signing. Before you sign anything, make sure you under-stand the following:

Payment terms of the contract. Federal law requires that any contract list clearly four different figures: the sales price, the annual percentage rate, the finance charges, and the monthly payment.

Look those things over carefully; make sure you know the exact extent of the commitment you are making. Having figures listed also enables you to comparison shop--you might be able to find a lower interest rate somewhere else, for example, or you might be able to arrange lower monthly payments at a different store.

The amount of the down payment. As a general rule, you should pay as little as possible for a down payment. Why? There are several reasons. First, some contracts specify that you will forfeit your down payment if you change your mind and cancel; you want to risk losing as little as possible. If the merchandise turns out to be defective for some reason, the seller has more to lose by not satisfying you immediately, too, if you have paid a small amount down.

A large final balloon payment. Read the contract carefully to make sure there is not a large payment due at the end of the loan or finance period. You don't want a sudden surprise at the end--nor do you want to risk repossession when you can't make the last payment.

A full description of the merchandise. The contract should contain a full description of the merchandise, including the color, size, serial or model number, and any other identifying characteristics. That protects you from having someone substitute inferior merchandise when the product is delivered.

Blank spaces. Never sign any contract that has blank spaces on it. The seller could fill in anything under the sun after you sign, and you'd be held legally liable. Insist that every blank line is either filled in or x'd out before you sign a contract.

Terms you don't agree with. If you don't agree with a term or clause in the contract, draw a line through it and sign your initials next to the line. Then ask the seller to initial the changes, too. Some will, and some won't--but it's worth a try. If you can't come to terms, don't sign the contract.

Documentation of verbal promises. If a seller makes you a verbal promise, check whether it's included in the contract. If it's not, write the terms of the verbal promise in ink, initial the addition, and have the seller initial it, too. Make sure that the addition is written on both your copy and the seller's copy of the contract.

Once you've agreed to everything and signed the contract, make sure you get a copy. Your copy should bear both your signature and the seller's signature, as well as any additions or changes made to the contract.

Unfortunately, there are some common "loopholes" that appear on many contracts that can seriously impair your rights. In general, you should not sign a contract that contains the following:
- Any blank spaces
- A clause requiring a substantial payment before you receive goods or services (such as making you pay for half the health club visits in advance)
- A balloon payment at the end
- A clause that requires you to ship an unmanageably large item (such as a washing machine) to an out-of-state dealer for repairs
- A clause that relieves the seller of responsibility for anything he does (even negligible or wrongful acts)
- A clause that assesses you an unreasonably large late fee for payments made after the agreed date (late fees are reasonable and fair, but they shouldn't exceed about 5 percent of the payment)
- An "acceleration clause" that says you have to pay the full amount left owing if you are late on a payment
- A clause requiring you to pay the seller's legal fees if he has to sue you for nonpayment
- A clause waiving your right to trial by jury if the seller sues you for nonpayment

NOT SATISFIED? HOW TO GET YOUR MONEY BACK

Feel cheated as a consumer?

You only need two things--a telephone and a pen--to make your voice heard and get the satisfaction you deserve if you only know how to go about it.

As a consumer, you have rights (usually under implied warranty), and the law will protect you. But it only happens if you make it happen by working some strategies in your favor.

Before you do anything at all, carefully review your problem. Make certain that it is not your fault. If you're satisfied that the fault lies with the seller or manufacturer, decide what you want done. Do you want the item repaired at no charge? Do you want the item replaced with a similar (but defect-free) model? Or do you want your money back? Would you accept a merchandise credit at the store where you bought the item--or would you simply rather not deal with that store again? Once you've decided exactly how you want the situation to be resolved, take these steps:

Start with a personal contact. If the business is local, visit; if it's some distance away, make a phone call. Ask for the customer-service representative or the manager. Write down the name of the person you speak with. Tell what you purchased, the date you purchased it, what's wrong, and what you would like done; make sure all your facts are straight. Be courteous, but be brief and to the point. Be firm, but don't get angry.

If the customer-service representative or manager agrees to your demands, restate what has been agreed to ("Then I can expect a store representative here on Wednesday morning to pick up the television set for repairs at your expense?"). Be sure to make a notation of the call, recording the date and time, the person you spoke to, and the outcome. If the person you speak with refuses help, simply inform him that you will have to speak to someone with more authority.

If things don't get straightened out, try one more call. Call the store again, ask to speak to the person you dealt with earlier, and find out the status of your complaint. What is being done? Why didn't someone arrive as promised? Set up another appointment for the matter to be resolved. Give the store a deadline (such as seven or ten days) in which to get the matter resolved. State firmly but politely that you will need to take further action if this commitment falls through.

If you still haven't been satisfied, write to the manufacturer. If the store fails to resolve the situation, write to the manufacturer. (Addresses are almost always on labels; if you can't find it, call the store and ask for it.) Again, make sure you have all the facts straight.

Your letter needs to look professional, so type it single spaced on a plain white sheet of paper (or on your company letterhead if it involves a product your business purchased). Don't lose your temper or make threats; keep the letter businesslike.

Begin the letter with a compliment; then describe what you purchased (include model or serial number). Tell clearly what the problem is. Then describe precisely what you have already done to try to get the problem resolved (who you talked to at the store and when, for example). Next, clearly outline how you want the problem resolved--and give the manufacturer a time limit in which to get the problem taken care of. Finally, let the manu-facturer know what you will do if the problem is not resolved to your satisfaction. Close the letter with a pleasant hope that the matter will be resolved quickly.

Mail the letter by registered or certified mail so you have proof it was received by the manufacturer. **Make sure you keep photocopies of all correspondence relating to the situation.**

Try one last time. Wait four to six weeks after mailing the first letter before you do anything. If six weeks pass and you've heard nothing, write again. This time, be firmer--and send a copy of the first letter you sent. Give a specific deadline and clearly outline what you intend to do if the matter is not resolved by that time.

As a last resort, sue. If you have tried all the above approaches and the matter has still not been resolved, sue the store and/or the manufacturer. For small investments, you can take the matter to small claims court (see the following section). Report the store and the manufacturer. Contact the Better Business Bureau, the State Licensing Division, and the Federal Trade Commission with details of your transaction. You won't get relief directly from these agencies, but your complaint will serve as a red flag to other consumers who are contemplating a similar purchase involving the same store or manufacturer.

Many television stations, radio stations, or newspapers have "consumer action" reporters who expose unsavory business practices in the community. If there is one where you live, take advantage of it. You'll not only do others a favor, but these reporters often exert tremendous pressure on businesses who are fearful of negative public opinion.

Finally, contact the closest consumer protection agency and register a complaint. The agency may be able to get some relief for you and will closely monitor the business for future violations.

If the problem involves mail-order merchandise, register your complaint with the Chief Postal Inspector, U.S. Postal Inspection Service, Washington, D.C. 20260-2100. If postal fraud is proven, you could get some or all or your money back.

IN YOUR OWN DEFENSE: TAKING YOUR CASE TO SMALL CLAIMS COURT

Minor legal problems and those involving a limited amount of money (the amount varies from one state to another) can be settled in small claims court--and it's a way for you to get legal relief without the expense of an attorney.

Basically, small claims court is an arbitrator--it allows two parties who disagree to come together, present their evidence, have it heard by a qualified judge, and have a judgment rendered. Small claims courts award money only; they do not have the authority to require a specific action. If the wrongful party refuses to pay up, most small claims courts will assist you by assigning law enforcement personnel to collect the money owed.

Here's how to make the system work for you:

First of all, make sure you have the right court. You'll find the courts listed in the yellow pages of your telephone directory; call the clerk and find out where you should file your complaint. Generally, you will need to sue in the city or county where the person you are suing lives or does business; the clerk can verify any local laws for you.

You'll need to pay a nominal fee (usually around $10), and you'll need to fill out a complaint. On the complaint, detail your problem, and be as specific as you can. You'll be assigned a court date, and the court will notify the person you are suing by mail.

Before you arrive at court, gather up all possible witnesses and evidence. Friends, colleagues, or others who have been involved in or who witnessed the situation are qualified to testify in your behalf. Collect any documents you can: photocopies of letters, cancelled checks, contracts, photographs, physician's bills, and so on.

You won't have an attorney to represent you: at small claims court, you represent yourself. In the week or two before your hearing, organize your thoughts. You'll have to stand before the judge and present your case; if you need a written outline to help you remember details, make one and take it with you.

Make sure you show up on time to your hearing. Dress conservatively, in business attire. Because you are the one suing, you'll be asked to present your case first. Tell your story in a clear, simple, straightforward way and explain any documents you brought to back you up. Introduce witnesses and ask that the judge give them a chance to speak. When you've finished, the judge may "cross-examine" you (ask you questions about the case). Your chances will be improved if you follow these guidelines during cross-examination:

- Don't joke around. Listen carefully to each question and answer it as best you can. If you're not sure what the judge is asking, request clarification in a polite way.
- Answer all questions politely and clearly.
- Don't lose your temper.
- Don't volunteer information you're not being asked.
- Don't get distracted or misled and start talking about unrelated matters.
- If you don't know the answer to a question, be truthful--say something like "I don't know" or "I forgot." **Never make up information to make your case sound better.**

After you've finished presenting your case, the judge will allow the person you are suing to answer the complaint. The judge will cross-examine that person, too. Then, depending on time and the judge's opinion, your witnesses may be given a chance to speak and may be cross-examined.

In some courts, judgment will be rendered at the end of the hearing; many courts mail you a decision within a week of your hearing. If you obtain a judgment but the person you sued refuses to pay, try writing him a letter. If that doesn't work, contact the court clerk and ask for law enforcement help in obtaining the payments due you.

AN ERROR IN YOUR BILL? HOW TO FIGHT BACK

If you regularly receive bills from credit card companies, loan companies, doctors' offices, or finance companies, you know by

now that you're dealing with a computer--not a human brain. And you also know by now that computers can make mistakes.

What if a mistake turns up on your bill? You're protected by federal law (under the Federal Fair Credit Billing Act), and you have the right to be heard--**not** by a computer!

As a first step, let the company know that there's a mistake on your bill. You need to inform the company in writing, explaining exactly why you think the bill is wrong.

If you pay for merchandise with a credit card and then discover that the merchandise is faulty or was misrepresented, you're protected by a special law. If you made the purchase in your home state (or within 100 miles of your home) or you were responding to an ad from the credit card company and the merchandise cost more than $50, you can simply inform the credit card company of the problem and that you will not pay the bill. If you have first tried unsuccessfully to settle the problem with the merchant, you are not required to pay the bill.

If the company finds that you're right, it must adjust the bill. When your next bill arrives, make sure the disputed amount--as well as any associated finance charges--have been taken off your bill.

If the company still thinks it is right, it has to tell you why.

What if you remain convinced that you are right? You have ten days in which to send the company another letter stating that you still dispute the bill. That's a critical step you shouldn't pass up: not only does it keep negotiations open, but the company is required by law to report to all credit agencies that the matter is still being disputed. As a result, you won't be reported as just casually making a late payment.

At that point, you need to produce documentation to prove your case. Make sure you keep copies of all correspondence with the company. Stand up for your rights, and keep fighting until you are satisfied with the decision.

A PENNY SAVED: WHEN IT PAYS TO BUY USED GOODS

You've heard the old saying, "They don't make it like they used to ...." Well, when it comes to some merchandise, that's true--and you'll be the winner if you can buy a used or secondhand item that still holds its value.

Become a keen and observant shopper at yard sales, thrift stores, flea markets, and auctions. You should keep an eye out not only for antiques (items more than fifty years old that have investment value), but for great used merchandise that has held its value, is durable enough to serve you well, and is a bargain to boot!

The following items are the best fare in used goods to watch out for:

- Typewriters (low-cost manual Underwood and Royal typewriters are usually the best buy)
- Tools (tools manufactured several decades ago often had better workmanship and are of higher quality than today's tools)
- Depression glass (the rose-colored glass was heat-tempered and will stand up to plenty of abuse)
- Silver flatware (older silver flatware is almost always of higher silver content than today's copies)
- Crystal (you can find patterns similar to goblets being sold new today for about half the price; make sure they're not cracked or chipped)
- Cooking utensils (most small appliances are made to last a lifetime, so you should get plenty of use out of second-hand ones)
- Swiss watches (most Swiss watches will last through several generations)
- Costume jewelry (much of today's costume jewelry is a copy of pieces made thirty to eighty years ago--but the originals are heavier and of better quality)
- Lace (look for handmade vintage lace in good condition)
- Books (older books are usually printed on heavier paper with higher-quality bindings; keep an eye out for the classics)

How to Shop at Auctions

Auctions--often held to dispose of an estate--can be especially good sources of real treasures. But there's a definite art to shopping at auctions--and if you know how to do it, they can be great fun as well as sources of great value!

Auctions are generally listed in the classified advertising section of the newspaper. There are different kinds of auctions: fund-raisers (people contribute items to be auctioned off for a specific charity); estate auctions (a deceased person's belongings

15

are sold and the proceeds split among heirs); art gallery auctions (pieces of art are sold); trade auctions (lost, unclaimed, and surplus items are sold); and country auctions (almost anything, working or not, is sold in a very informal atmosphere). The classified ad should describe what kind of auction it is, so select one you're interested in.

The best time to attend an auction? Midweek in summer. Why? Auction regulars tend to be on vacation, and dealers tend to be on buying trips. You'll usually get by with bidding less for the things you really want. If you're interested in the most spectacular offerings, the best time is on weekends and holidays at lunchtime and dinnertime.

Almost every auction has a presale exhibit a day or two before the actual auction; **always** attend the presale exhibit if you plan on going to the auction. Why? It gives you a chance to browse among the merchandise, inspect it close-up, and decide what items you are interested in bidding on. Remember that on the day of the auction you may be seated at the back of an auditorium, and it's practically impossible to see fine detail at that distance. If you find a real treasure you're interested in, too, you can avoid the temptation to bid on items displayed earlier since you know what's coming up.

Some auctions even print catalogs of what they are offering. The catalog should have a description of each item; if you pick it up before the auction, you can determine where the real values lie.

Take good notes at the presale exhibit; write down the number of the item so you don't get confused when a similar item is placed on the auction block.

Then do some homework before you come back to the auction. You might be interested in an oak desk, for instance; find out how much it will cost to get shipped to your home. You might discover that the shipping cost is so high that the desk won't be a good deal at all, even if you can snare it at a low price. Or you might find out that what you thought was silk upholstery really isn't.

The day of the auction, take the essentials: a folding chair (many auctions don't provide seats), your notes, a pen and notepad, and cash or credit cards. (Few auctions accept personal checks, but you should check with auction officials beforehand to find out what they will accept.)

At most auctions, you will register and receive a bidding number. In order to get a number, you'll need identification; a driver's license is usually sufficient. When you want to bid, wave your number in the air and call out the amount. To be on the safe side, attend a few auctions as an observer before you start bidding in earnest--you'll get the hang of it quickly.

What if you get caught up in the excitement of the auction and buy something you'll never use--or, worse yet, that you **hate**? Never fear--take advantage of another American institution, the garage sale!

HOW TO STAGE A BEST-SELLING GARAGE SALE

If you have an attic, a garage, a spare bedroom, or even an apartment loaded with things you no longer want, you can turn your unwanted belongings into cold cash--and it's easier than you think!

A garage sale--also called a yard sale, porch sale, or "tag" sale--has become an accepted way of dumping things you no longer want (and remember that your junk may be someone else's treasure!). With a few basic strategies, you can turn a substantial profit for a few days of work. The secret is to plan ahead (start at least a month in advance), get the word out, and run your garage sale like a business.

Figure Out What You're Going to Sell

Chances are, you have more to sell than you realize. Go through your home, room by room, attic to basement, and assess your goods. Go through closets and drawers; look under the beds. Leave no leaf unturned.

Having a hard time letting go of sentimental items? Establish

Making It Big: The Best-sellers at Garage Sales

Want to make the most possible money at your garage sale this year?

The following are proven best-sellers:
* Baby clothing
* Baby furniture and equipment
* Children's furniture (especially beds)
* Outdoor furniture
* Dressers and chests of drawers
* Bicycles
* Skis
* Assorted sports equipment
* Television sets
* Washing machines and clothes dryers
* Refrigerators
* Sales samples of assorted products

some guidelines: if you haven't worn the clothing, used the object, or played with the toy in a year, sell it. (Heirlooms and family keepsakes are obvious exceptions!) If you think your offerings look scanty, invite some friends or neighbors to join in. That's a good idea, anyway--sometimes the most successful garage sales involve five or six families.

Decide When--and Where--You'll Hold the Sale

Weekends are best; most people are off work and making the garage sale circuit then. Hours are important, too: the earlier you can start in the morning, the more earnest buyers you'll attract. Stop mid-afternoon, since most garage-sale enthusiasts know that the real bargains are gone by then, anyway--and they go on to other pursuits.

Where should you hold the sale? In your house! Why? First of all, you won't have to worry about the weather. But that's not the only reason--items look more attractive in a house than they do in a garage or on the front lawn. You'll lure buyers with a bed that is draped with a quilt in a pretty bedroom; the same bed looks dingy in a garage.

Don't let people roam at random through your house: group all the sale items in several rooms. Clear out furniture and objects that are not for sale. Arrange sale items attractively on tables. Hide or conceal valuables, and block off other rooms and hallways.

Spread the Word By Advertising

If you want lots of customers, you have to advertise!

Begin with word-of-mouth; tell everyone you see, and mention some of your "draw" items. Get people excited--and ask them to tell their friends. Other effective and inexpensive ways to advertise a garage sale include the following:

- Classified advertising in newspapers; don't forget neighboring towns as well as your own! Don't settle for the standard, minimum ad--write a longer ad that will attract attention and stand out in the crowd. List the address, the days, the hours, and mention some of the items for sale. Don't list specific prices, and don't include your phone number.
- Free advertising in "pennysaver" newspapers.
- Street signs. Check with city hall about ordinances, and then tack

up some sturdy, weatherproof signs wherever you can. Lettering should be large and easy to read. The best signs are big, bright, bold, and brief. It's best to use plywood or paneling scraps--they don't bend or blow over like cardboard and heavy posterboard can. Use black spray paint. Place signs strategically so drivers from all directions can see them and find their way to your house.

• Fliers. Include all pertinent information, and deliver them around your neighborhood. Post some to community bulletin boards. If local laws permit, tuck them under the windshield wipers of cars parked at grocery stores and shopping malls.

Determine the Price

One of the most difficult--and crucial--things about staging a garage sale is determining what price to mark on your merchandise. One method is to critically look at your items and decide what **you** would pay for them. Avoid the temptation of pricing similar items in stores--someone who will pay a department store price will just go to the department store to begin with. For the greatest success, use the following pricing formula:

• Unused items in original sealed container, two-thirds of the price for an equivalent item in a store

• Antiques, 60 percent of the price for an equivalent item in an antique store

---

Natives Getting Restless? How to Keep the Mobs at a Garage Sale Entertained

Okay. . .you just had things under control, or so you thought, when a virtual mob arrives at your garage sale!

For security reasons, you only want to let fifteen or twenty people in your house at a time. So what can you do with the ones who are loitering around outside?

Easy! Try some of these suggestions:

* Put some selected items along the driveway; customers can browse there first. Try for some large items that can't be carried away (like a refrigerator). And, of course, post someone outside to "keep watch."

* Offer a special "sale" outside on something you have dozens of (like books or record albums). Post a big sign boasting "Buy two, get one free."

* Sell goodies--coffee, lemonade, fruit punch, cookies, or pastries. Be sure to stock up on plenty of napkins, and provide a clean trash can for litter.

- Clothing that is in good condition and in style, 50 percent of the price for an equivalent item in a store
- Out-of-style clothing, ten cents on the dollar for what new clothing would cost in a store
- Used, working appliances, 50 percent of the price for an equivalent item in a store
- Wood furniture in good condition, 50 percent of what it cost new
- Upholstered furniture in good condition, 20 percent of what it cost new
- Yard equipment and tools, 30 to 40 percent of what they cost new
- Name-brand children's toys (such as Playskool, Tonka, and Fisher-Price), 25 percent of what they cost new
- Sporting goods, such as bicycles, skis, and tennis racquets, 25 percent of what they cost new

If you have significant antiques or collectibles, have them appraised. If you are selling antique clothing (such as a beaded Victorian wedding gown), try to find similar items in an antique store; list yours for about 20 percent less (remember that a store owner marks up prices to cover overhead).

Kitchen items, such as pots and pans, dishes, flatware, glasses, and serving pieces, usually sell for just a few dollars.

If you are in doubt, attend some yard sales yourself, and make note of what items similar to yours are selling for.

Mark prices on all your merchandise in large, easy-to-read numbers. An easy way to do it is with self-adhesive stickers available in stationery stores; you can get different colors if you are having more than one family participate in the sale. Use a black pen or felt-tip marker. For furniture and clothing, pin on larger tags. For special items (such as a stereo), you might want to use a larger tag that allows you to list specifications as well as price.

Remember that if you price things too high, you'll still have lots of things left over as the last buyers walk away!

Be prepared to dicker on price; most veteran garage sale enthusiasts won't buy something unless they at least try to get the price reduced. As a general rule, don't come down on price during the first several hours of your sale--that's when the most eager buyers are there, and you won't have to come down. After that, you can consider dropping your prices; as a rule, don't come down more than 20 percent.

Display Merchandise with Flair

Things heaped up on a cluttered table look like junk--so it's worth your time to display your merchandise with flair. Keep your garage sale merchandise looking great by doing the following:

• Use ping-pong tables, picnic tables, card tables, kitchen tables, or coffee tables to display your merchandise. Cover each table with something pretty--a sheet, tablecloth, or doily.

• Keep things neat and orderly. Tables can be crowded, but they should be organized.

• Group like items together: kitchen appliances in one place, sports equipment in another.

• Hang clean, pressed clothing on a portable clothes rack; if you have clothing of particular value (such as a nice man's suit), slip a plastic dry-cleaning bag over it. If you can't find a clothes rack, use a heavy clothesline or a heavy rope. Group clothing by size, and mark each section with a large sign.

• Tack quilts, afghans, shawls, lace runners, small tablecloths, and doilies to the wall. Small tablecloths and quilts can also be draped over a wooden clothes-drying rack.

• Display jewelry by pinning it on a piece of black or dark blue cloth (velvet shows jewelry off the best). It will look better, and it will be more difficult to shoplift.

• If you have items of particular value, display them on a raised cabinet or in a china hutch that is behind where you will be taking money. You'll be able to stand "guard," and the items will be set off, too.

• Display toys, games, and puzzles out of the reach of children. If you don't, they will be scattered all over within the first hour or two of your sale.

Here Come the First Customers!

On the day of the sale, follow these tips for the greatest success:

• Borrow flashing street signs from your city; section off an area where people can park.

• Enlist the help of friends and neighbors who can help you manage crowds. If more than one family is involved in the sale, assign tasks to everyone.

• Establish an official "checkout" station where at least two people will be sitting at all times to take customer money. One person

21

should remove price tags, state the price, and put the merchandise in bags; the second person should add up the prices (on a pocket calculator or adding machine), take the money, and give change.

- Make sure you have plenty of change (in coins as well as a substantial number of $1, $5, $10, and $20 bills), a calculator or adding machine, bags of various sizes, and a sturdy, secure money box to keep your change in.
- Unless you know a person well, insist on payment with cash. Accept personal checks only from friends and family members.
- Keep one "guard" in each room to discourage shoplifting and price tag switching.
- Designate only one door through which customers can leave, and locate the checkout station at that door. Keep a guard at the front door to welcome people and to keep customers from leaving through it (even if they purchased nothing, they should go through the designated exit).
- Have plenty of bright lights. Things always look better in the light, and customers like to be able to see what they're buying. Bright lights will also discourage shoplifting and price tag switching.
- If you are opening up a bathroom for customers to use (even if it is only to try on clothing), empty out your medicine cabinet beforehand.
- Try to keep the crowd down to about twenty at a time. You might try handing out numbers and giving people something to do in the yard until it's their turn to go inside (see the accompanying sidebar for some ideas). If you get too many people in your home at one time, you'll have chaos--and something is bound to get broken, stolen, or lost.
- Throughout the sale, periodically take a few minutes to straighten things up. Eager customers will make a mess; you need to keep things neat and organized. As items sell, fill in bare spots by condensing; take out tables if you have to. A garage sale with lots of bare spots looks as though all the good things are gone--and you want to give the impression that plenty of good things are still left.
- At the sale's end, make cleanup fun by having a pot-luck dinner or treats. Enlist everyone's help, and things will go quickly.

TAKING CARE OF THE INEVITABLE: WRITING WILLS AND ARRANGING FOR FUNERALS

No one likes to face the less pleasant facts of life, but as a consumer, you're most vulnerable at times of loss. With some basic knowledge, you can learn how to write your own will and arrange for a funeral.

How to Write a Will

Why is a will important?

Basically, it guarantees that your wishes will be carried out after you die. If you die without a will, a probate court will get all your assets--and it will divide them up among your heirs according to state law. The court won't give anything to charity, and it won't give a gift to a favorite friend. The only way you can ensure those things is if you have it written down!

To be legal and binding, your will needs to establish who you are, how you want your property divided, and how you want your financial and personal affairs handled. Unless you have an extremely complex situation, you can write your will yourself.

Where To Get Vital Records

Need a copy of your birth certificate--or proof that you are married?

It's easy! You need to make the request for vital records in writing, and you need to pay any applicable fees. And if you're trying to get vital records for someone other than yourself, you need to be related--and you need to state why you want the document.
Here's where to get those vital records:

Birth and death records. Write to the state department of health or the state bureau of vital statistics. Include the full name, sex, race, and the city and county where the birth or death occurred. If you can, give the exact date of birth or death, too.

Marriage and divorce records. Write to the state bureau of vital statistics or the city or county clerk where the marriage or divorce occurred. Include the full names of the couple (including the woman's maiden name), their birth dates, the city and county where the marriage or divorce occurred, and the date of the marriage or divorce.

Military records. Write to the Department of Defense, Military Records Center, 9700 Page Boulevard, St. Louis, MO 63100. Include the person's name, Social Security number, date of birth, and branch of the service. If you know them, include the dates of active service and the date of discharge.

Since your will explains how your assets will be divided, start out by listing them. Figure out where you want each to go. Now start writing your will. Paragraphs should be written in the following order:

1. Identify yourself, state that the document is your will, and state that it revokes all previous wills.

2. Name your executor (the person who will act as your personal representative after your death in paying your bills, paying your taxes, selling your property, distributing your property, and making a final accounting). In the same paragraph name a substitute executor in case your originally designated executor can't serve for some reason.

3. Name a guardian for your minor children in case your spouse does not survive you. If your estate is large, you should also appoint a "property guardian" who will manage your children's inheritance until they are of age.

4. List specific gifts you want to give to certain people (such as valuable jewelry or a special keepsake).

5. Specify how the remainder of your estate is to be divided.

6. Specify how you want debts and taxes to be paid (you may want them paid with cash from your savings account, or you may want the executor to sell your house and use the profit to pay obligations).

7. Give the executor the legal right to dispose of your property in order to execute your will.

To be considered legal, your will can be in any form--but if you want to eliminate mistakes and confusion, make sure it is type-written. Number the pages to indicate both the total number of pages and the sequence ("Page two of six"). Sign or initial the corner of every page but the signature page.

Sign your name on the last page, immediately below the last line of your will; don't leave room for anyone to be able to insert something above your signature. For your will to be legal, you need to sign it in the presence of three witnesses **who are not beneficiaries of your will;** they, too, need to sign as witnesses. (Witnesses should be adults who are well-acquainted with you; if you can, choose people who are younger than you--and therefore apt to survive you.) You don't have to let the witnesses read your will, but they must be informed that they are witnessing the signing of a will. Finally, if someone has illegible handwriting, ask him to print his name beneath his signature to avoid confusion and problems later on.

You should sign and date only one copy of your will. The signed copy should be kept in a safe place that is accessible to your survivors after your death. (A safe deposit box is not a good choice, since no one but you can open it.) If you want to make copies of your will, do it before the will is signed and clearly mark them as copies.

What if you change your mind or need to add something?

You can draft a "codicil," which acts as a written amendment. It should follow the same standards as your will. It should be separately signed and attached to your original. If you get two or three codicils attached to your will, you should go ahead and draft a new will to avoid confusion.

Making Funeral Arrangements

The death of a loved one is difficult--and it can be made more difficult by the confusion that can surround the "technicalities." For the least amount of confusion in making funeral arrangements, follow these guidelines:

- As soon as death occurs, contact a physician; he must pronounce the death and provide you with a death certificate before you can make any funeral arrangements.
- Notify a funeral director. The funeral director will take care of the body, usually by transporting it to the funeral home. If the person has made arrangements for a medical bequest, the funeral director will transport the body to a hospital or medical school.
- Talk to the funeral director briefly about how the body should be handled. Some religions have guidelines (for example, some do not want the body embalmed), and you should inform the funeral director immediately of any such requirements.
- If the deceased person made any arrangements or requests, they should be honored. If not, you are usually safe in following the traditions of the person's religion.
- If you decide on a funeral service, you need to arrange for music, someone to conduct, someone to deliver a eulogy, a procession, and pallbearers. You need to decide where the funeral service will be held; traditional places are funeral homes or churches.
- You need to decide what the deceased person will wear for burial.

Remember the details, such as jewelry. If there are heirloom pieces that you want to be worn in a particular place or way, let the funeral director know.

- Decide whether you want a "viewing" (the opportunity for mourners to see the deceased), and whether you want an open or closed casket. If there was an accident or chronic illness that resulted in disfigurement, you may want to consider a closed casket; some religions (such as the Jewish faith) also require closed caskets.
- Decide where you want the person to be buried. If there will be a traditional burial, you will need to arrange for a plot, a concrete burial vault (an oversized container that the casket fits into that reduces damage to the casket from moisture and other elements), and a marker for the grave. If there will be a cremation, you will need to arrange for the cremation, a container to hold the ashes, and possibly a monument where the container will be stored.

Funeral expenses are widely varied because of the different factors that can figure in. The casket, for example, can range all the way from a few hundred dollars to almost $10,000-depending on the style and what it is made of. Funeral directors are salespeople, so you should decide on what you want before you arrive at the funeral home. Then agree to only what you feel is appropriate.

BECOMING FINANCIALLY FIT:
WHAT YOU NEED TO KNOW ABOUT MONEY

I t all looks so simple: a few dollar bills, a handful of coins. But what you do with those bills and coins has tremendous impact--on your ability to get credit, your ability to pay bills, and your financial leverage in general.

GETTING ALONG WITH MONEY:
LEARN TO SPEAK THE LANGUAGE

When a financial officer opens his mouth and starts to talk, what comes out?

If you're like most people, it sounds almost like a foreign language! Money terms are really quite simple once you understand them:

Annuity. Simply stated, an annuity is a contract between you and an insurance company. You agree to pay the insurance company a sum of money; in exchange, the insurance company agrees to give you a guaranteed monthly payment every month for the rest of your life, starting at a certain age. Your payment might be made in a lump sum or in gradual monthly payments.

Balloon contract. A balloon contract states that your last payment (the "balloon payment") will be much larger than the previous monthly payments. Balloon contracts are dangerous: unless you will have the required amount, you'll either risk repossession or will face borrowing the money all over again somewhere else.

Beneficiary. When you buy life insurance, the beneficiary is the one who will receive the money from your policy when you die.

Discount rate. The discount rate is the interest rate that the Federal Reserve charges to banks that borrow from it. The discount rate dictates what banks have to pay, so it also dictates what banks charge their own customers (usually a few percentage points higher).

Earnest money. When you decide to buy a house, you will be asked to put up "earnest money"--a small percentage of the sales price of the house. Simply stated, it's a way of showing that you are "earnest" about going through with the deal.

Fannie Mae. "Fannie Mae" is the nickname for the Federal National Mortgage Association, an agency created by Congress to buy up mortgages from banks, thereby giving the banks money for new mortgages.

Government money market funds. These are considered the safest of the money market funds, because they invest only in securities of the United States government. Other money market funds make loans to banks and large corporations, which does involve some risk. Government money market funds, however, do not offer the tax advantages of other money market funds.

Government savings bonds. When you buy a government savings bond, you invest money in the United States government. You are issued a bond for a certain amount of money; you pay a certain percentage of that amount, and your bond "matures" later. After your bond reaches its maturity, you can turn it in and receive the full amount of the face value of the bond, plus interest figured from the date of maturity. If you turn in your bond before it matures, you will receive a prorated amount of the full face value.

Most savings bonds pay you nothing unless you cash them in. An exception is the HH bond: it pays you interest on the face value in the form of two semiannual checks for as long as you hold the bond.

IRA. An "individual retirement account" is a specialized account you open at a bank. In it, you deposit money that will be kept in the account until you retire. An IRA earns interest, and you are not required to pay income tax on the money you deposit in the account as long as you meet certain qualifications. In order to qualify for tax advantages, you are limited to the amount you deposit in one year.

KEOGH account. A KEOGH account works much the same way as an IRA, but it is specifically designed for self-employed people. A KEOGH offers a wider range of investment options (it can be in a savings account at a bank or in a stock, for example), and all offer big tax savings. Best of all, it is a good way for a self-employed person (who does not have the benefit of a corporate pension) to secure a retirement fund.

Over-the-counter stocks. While stock in the nation's largest corporations is traded (bought and sold) only on the floor of major stock exchanges (such as the New York Stock Exchange), stock in many smaller companies can be bought and sold "over-the-counter." What that means is that you can buy or sell your shares of stock over the telephone through a network of dealers. Over-the-counter stocks make it possible to participate in the stock market for people with a limited amount of money to invest.

Pyramid scheme. A pyramid is a selling organization that relies on recruits to do the selling. You earn a commission on what you sell--but you also earn a commission on what the people "under" you sell. You can make lots of money in a short period of time. The problem? Sooner or later, the company runs out of customers, because there are never enough customers to support a pyramid scheme. When that happens, all but the very few at the very top get hurt. (Pyramid schemes are against the law in some states.)

Registered stock representative. A registered stock representative is a person who has received training, passed tests, and become certified as a dealer with the New York Stock Exchange (or some other major exchange).

Tax-exempt bonds. Also called "municipal bonds," tax-exempt bonds are bonds issued by any government body other than the United States federal government (which issues U.S. savings bonds). They are called "tax-exempt" bonds because you don't have to pay tax on the interest you earn with these bonds.

Vesting. Vesting means that you have a right to collect your retirement benefits from a company even if you quit or are fired before you reach retirement age. When you reach retirement age (usually sixty-five), you can collect your pension even if you haven't worked for the company for years. (Vesting requirements vary with different companies.)

Wage garnishment. When you owe someone money and fail to pay, your creditor can get a court order against you. The court can order your employer to hand over part of your wages directly to your creditor every payday until the debt is satisfied.

BUILDING A SOLID FOUNDATION: HOW TO SET UP A BUDGET

What's a budget?

Simply stated, it's the foundation of all your financial planning. A good budget enables you to maintain control over your money. Once you have a well-designed budget, you can set priorities based on the things that are most important to you.

Budgeting takes time--a well-designed budget that accurately reflects your individual situation is not something you can do in an hour or two.

Designing a budget, in fact, takes a lot of homework. The first time you design it, you have to find out exactly how much money you earned during the previous twelve months and--this is the hard part--**exactly how you spent the money you earned.** (After your budget is initially designed, you can make additions or revisions without as much intensive labor!)

To find out how much you earned and how you spent it, you need to gather up all the necessary documents: paycheck stubs, canceled checks, utility bill receipts, credit card bills, medical or dental bills, drugstore receipts, tax returns, mortgage or rent receipts, and anything else to do with your earning or spending.

(A note for future budgeting and budget revisions: now that you know what kinds of things impact your budget, file these papers when you first get them. Making a revision to your budget will be a snap!)

Effective budgeting involves five steps:

Divide Categories By Priority

Now that you have all the necessary documents, divide them into separate piles (you can use shoeboxes if you want to): rent or mortgage, medical, food, utilities, and so on. Obviously, not everything you spend money on has equal importance in your life--some spending, like a mortgage payment, is clearly an essential, while other spending (such as what you spent on a health club membership) is clearly for extras.

Now put each pile into one of four categories: essentials (those things you **must** have in order to maintain life), necessities (those things you consider necessary), extras (those things you enjoy, but could do without), and one-time expenses (those things that occur only once and wouldn't be listed on a monthly budget).

Remember that this is **your** budget, so you should determine the priorities and list the specific items under each. Do it the way you are most comfortable with or the way that will help you control your money the best; you might want to have a general category of "utilities," for example, or you might decide to break it down into the money you spend on natural gas, electricity, water, and sewer.

While each budget should be individually tailored, your breakdown of categories should look somewhat like this:

ESSENTIALS
Mortgage or rent payments
Utility bills
Groceries
Taxes other than withholding
Insurance premiums (life, health, and automobile)
Gasoline and car maintenance
Debt repayment (includes credit card debt)
Expenses related to work (commuting, child care)

NECESSITIES
Savings (including IRAs and KEOGHs)
Medical and dental bills
Medications (prescription and over-the-counter)
Clothing
Home maintenance
Education (tuition, special fees, lessons)
Home furnishings (furniture, appliances, decor items)
Laundry and cleaning supplies
Personal care and grooming items
Family allowances
Spending money
Pledges or donations to a church or synagogue
Special-occasion gifts

EXTRAS
Meals at restaurants
Entertainment (such as movies and concerts)

Tickets to sporting events
Tobacco and alcohol
Candy and soft drinks
Toys and games
Videocassettes, albums, compact discs
Sports equipment
Club memberships
Books, newspapers, and magazines
Vacations
Contributions to charity
ONE-TIME EXPENSES
Washing machine
Reroofing the house
Furnace
New transmission
(Any other extraordinary, one-time expense)

Add Up the Totals

Time to dust off the adding machine or calculator. Add up what you spent in each category during the previous twelve months. List each category and its total on a sheet of paper.

Now add up all your income. Be sure to include **every** source of money, such as income tax refunds, interest from savings accounts, and stock dividends, in addition to your salary (including any overtime). List each category and its total on a second sheet of paper.

Now you need grand totals: total up how much you spent and how much you earned.

Now you've got a clear picture of what happened during the previous twelve months--but you need to design an income for the next twelve months! To allow for inflation, add approximately 5 percent to each category. Your targeted savings goal should be 10 percent of your estimated income.

Balance Income Against Expenses

How does your income compare with what you've spent?
If your income covers all your expenses, great!
What if you're left in the red?
You have several options:

1. You can reduce the amount you spend in some categories; you might decide to join a carpool instead of commuting to work, or you might buy only half the albums and compact discs you bought last year. Reduce in every other budget category that you can before you reduce the amount of money you are putting into savings; savings should be cut as a last resort.

2. You can completely eliminate some categories from your budget. You might decide to quit smoking, drop your health club membership, or stop taking music lessons.

3. You can figure out a way to produce more income. You might decide to get a part-time job or start making wooden toys to sell, for example.

Design the Actual Budget

Once you've achieved a balance between what you earn and what you spend, write it down: IT'S YOUR BUDGET!

You can divide it any way you want to, as long as it's easy to understand and keep track of. It's usually easiest to divide up the year by pay periods; you should have a new sheet for each pay period, week, or month, however you decide to divide it.

Write the Budget Down

On each sheet of paper, list the broad divisions (such as essentials and necessities) and the individual categories within each one. Write your budgeted amount next to each. Every time you spend money within that period, write it down on the line next to the appropriate category, subtract it, and come up with a new total representing the amount of money you have left.

(To make the process easier, you might want to prepare one master sheet that lists the divisions, categories, and amounts. Then have the sheet photocopied, and use a copy for each new pay period or monthly division.)

Are you finished?

Nope--you need to keep adjusting your budget to reflect what is happening in your life. If you suddenly start spending more or less in a certain category because of circumstances beyond your control (such as increasing gasoline prices), you need to be able to adjust.

Keep working on your budget--it's a constant that reflects your own personal situation. Stick to it, and you can achieve financial goals you may have thought impossible!

PAYING--OR NOT PAYING--BILLS IN AN EMERGENCY

No matter how carefully you have budgeted, the day may come when you encounter a totally unforeseen catastrophic event that may take every penny (and more) of your paycheck.

What can you do now?

Hopefully, you have an emergency savings account set aside to help with such problems (see following material). If you don't, you're going to be faced with some rough choices. You don't have enough money to pay all of your bills, and you have to decide which ones you will pay first.

How can you make that determination?

First, you need to realize that you're in a temporary, emergency situation. You **will** need to pay all of your creditors eventually. What you need now is a way to determine who gets paid now, and who will have to wait.

The basic rule of thumb is this: **pay your creditors according to how effectively they can collect from you.** Here's how:

To be paid first are creditors that can cut off an essential service to you. These include your landlord (who can evict you), the utility companies (who can shut off your utilities), the telephone company (who can shut off your phone), your auto loan company (who can repossess your car), your insurance company (who can cancel your insurance), and the person to whom you pay alimony or child support (who can have the amount withheld from your paycheck by court order).

To be paid second are creditors who could repossess or foreclose, but who will take some time to do it, or creditors whose collection practices are not as effective as those in the first category. These creditors include banks and finance companies where you have secured or unsecured loans for anything other than a car, the IRS (which takes up to ten months to begin collection procedures), and credit card companies (who generally try to avoid canceling your card because it means they lose their leverage to get you to pay).

To be paid last are those creditors who will ignore your deliquency or whose collection methods are very ineffective. These include hospitals, doctors, dentists, and retailers, who will usually work with you on an extended payment plan.

Obviously, you never want to be caught in this situation--and you can avoid it with some careful planning and savings.

WHICH ACCOUNTS ARE AVAILABLE?
SORTING OUT THE CONFUSION

If you've dealt with a bank at all, you know what a savings and a checking account are. But unless you've become a little more involved, you might not be familiar with the different kinds of accounts that are available to anyone wih a dollar to deposit.

Basically, the nuts-and-bolts accounts include the following:

Checking accounts. You deposit money and then pay a monthly "service charge" for the privilege of writing out checks against your deposits. Some banks offer overdraft protection to depositors who are creditworthy.

Passbook savings accounts. Passbook savings accounts have traditionally charged no fee and paid a lower interest rate, but they are a good, solid, no-frills account for someone who has less than $500 to save. Because of the development of new kinds of accounts, though, some banks are no longer paying interest on passbook savings--they simply keep your money in a safe place for you. If that's the case, you should move your savings to another bank.

Interest-paying checking accounts. Depending on the amount of your minimum balance each month, you will be paid interest on the money in your checking account. Banks vary in the way they figure interest, in the fees they assess, and in the minimum balance they require, so shop around. Interest-paying checking accounts usually don't pay off if you habitually write your checking account down to below $100 each month.

Money-market deposit accounts. Some banks are now letting depositors open money-market deposit accounts for as little as $100. Find out what the bank's restrictions are, though--a small money-market deposit may not earn the full money-market interest rate. Put a small amount of money in this kind of account only if it pays interest and charges no fees.

Certificates of deposit. If you have a large amount of money to deposit and you don't foresee needing a percentage of it in the near future, you should consider depositing part of it in a certificate of deposit. Certificates of deposit pay significantly higher interest rates, but there are stiff penalties for early withdrawal (depending on the bank, your money will be tied up for six months to five years or longer).

SAVINGS ACCOUNTS: HELPING YOUR MONEY GROW

Hopefully, you've budgeted at least 10 percent of your income for savings. Now, how do you go about making the best of your savings dollar?

There are a few basic rules you should always stick to. Put your money **only** in federally insured institutions; if something goes wrong, the government will back up your deposits. And, regardless of what you decide to invest in (a certificate of deposit, a money-market fund, or a bond, for example), tie your money up for as brief a period as possible. You need access to your money, and you don't want to have an emergency only to find out that you can't withdraw your savings for ten years!

How to Find More Money to Save

What if you just can't seem to budget enough for savings?

The answer is a simple one: get to work on some strategies that can help you trim money out of even a tight budget. Consider these:

• Pay off your credit card debts, and avoid using your cards for a while. You'll save about 20 percent--the amount you would pay in interest on your cards.

• Don't get a "gold" credit card. They do offer expanded services, but if you don't regularly use these services (such as free traveler's cheques), they're not a bargain. In the meantime, you pay a higher annual fee for the privilege of holding the card.

• Save on car insurance by raising the deductible on your collision insurance. You can save a significant amount by changing your deductible from $100 to $250. How can you tell if the risk is safe? Generally speaking, your deductible can equal about one week's take-home pay.

• If you can, avoid installment loans completely. If you wait until you have cash to pay for an item, you'll get a **real** "bargain"--no

36

interest!

- If you do need to borrow, shop around for the best possible interest rate. A difference in just a few percentage points can save you thousands of dollars over the life of a five year loan.
- Cancel service contracts on appliances and new cars. You don't need them--such merchandise is almost always covered by warranty--and you can pocket the money instead.
- Take full advantage of your health insurance plan. Many people don't use services they are entitled to because they don't want to bother with filling out forms. Find out how much your plan covers, and get reimbursement on everything you can (such as prescription drugs).

These are just a few ideas; use them to spark your own imagination. Then, of course, you can take another critical look at your budget. Could you live with going to fewer movies? Eating out only once a month? Settling for other than brand-name clothing? With some careful scrutiny, you may be able to squeeze a surprising amount of money out of a budget you think is already bone-dry!

Establish an Emergency Fund

Isn't an emergency fund the same as a savings account?

No!

Your savings account should be just that--money you are **saving**, not money you are dipping into every time the furnace needs to be repaired or the car needs new brake shoes. Your

How Much Does Your Credit Card Cost To Use?

The answer depends on how you use it!

Analyze your charge habits, and then use this guide to find a card that will be best for you:

If you carry an unpaid balance every month, look for a card with the lowest interest rate. Banks have gotten competitive, and you can save significantly by shaving off just a few percentage points.

If you pay your balance in full every month, look for a card that charges little or no annual fee, offers a grace period before charging interest (usually twenty-five days), and charges no monthly fee for card use. It's worth it to find a card that gives a grace period, even if it charges a little higher interest, because you won't be paying any interest anyway.

savings account is a way for you to accumulate enough money to eventually begin investing--and to realize tremendous returns.

What's an emergency fund, then?

An emergency fund is a **separate account** where you stash enough money to see you through an emergency. How much? Most agree that three months' gross salary should do it. It should be kept in a regular savings account that you can dip into on a day's notice. **Never** use a money savings instrument or plan that pays high interest but carries a heavy penalty for "early withdrawal." You need immediate access to the money in your emergency fund.

If you're starting from scratch, you need to budget in regular deposits until your emergency fund is established. If you can't come up with any extra in your budget, consider taking on a part-time job for five or six months, and devoting your entire take-home pay to your emergency fund.

There's only one steadfast rule for an emergency fund: **withdraw money only in the event of an emergency.** Poor planning is not an emergency. A trip to Disneyland is not an emergency. A new wardrobe for autumn is not an emergency. The furnace breaking down at the end of January is an emergency. A serious medical problem that is not covered immediately by insurance is an emergency. Transmission breakdown on the family's only car is an emergency. The family breadwinner losing his job is an emergency. Got the idea?

Shop Around For a Bank

Never heard of shopping for a bank?

With deregulation in the banking industry, banks are now in stiff competition with each other--and each one is trying to offer bigger and better service to customers as a result. What it boils down to is this: you have more and better choices than ever before when it comes to banking!

The sky's the limit when it comes to options. You can have a checking account at one bank, a savings account at another bank, and a certificate of deposit at a third bank--depending on where you can get the best deals on which services. Or, if you want to do all your banking in the same place, you can shop for a bank that offers what you need.

To find the best bank, consider these factors:

Which banking services are most important to you? If you never travel, free traveler's checks won't really attract your business. If you don't want a safe-deposit box, it won't matter that a bank offers

Automated Teller Machines: How To Guard Against Loss

Automated teller machines did for banking what drive-up windows did for the food industry-- but make sure you don't trade all that convenience for a big financial loss due to carelessness.

If you like the convenience of ATMs, follow these precautions to guard your card (and your cash):

* *Never give your PIN (personal identification number) to anyone,* no matter what. No one ever needs to know your PIN except you--and if someone finds it out, he has instant access to your bank balance.
* *If you are allowed to choose your own PIN,* make it a random number that's easy for you to remember. Avoid choosing a number that could be "guessed," such as your birth date, the last four numbers of your phone number, your house number, or the last four numbers of your Social Security number.
* When making a deposit to your account at an ATM, *never deposit cash.* You'll get a deposit receipt, but it does not hold up as proof of a cash deposit. If the deposit is erased for some reason (usually because of a computer malfunction), you're out of luck.
* *Choose the safest possible location* when you do your ATM transaction. The best is a drive-up machine that enables you to stay in your car; next best is an ATM in

a busy, well-lighted place. For best security, the ATM should have glass or plexiglass walls to prevent thieves from hiding inside. Avoid after-hours visits to isolated ATMs in dimly lighted areas or on the street.
* *Ask your bank how your PIN is verified,* and choose an ATM where verification is done within the machine (you'll avoid "electronic eavesdropping").
* *Choose an ATM that helps you guard your PIN.* Look for a machine with a frame around the key pad so other bankers can't watch you punch in your number. If others are waiting in the ATM booth, stand as close as you can to the key pad to obliterate their view.
* *If someone else enters the ATM booth while you are making a transaction,* finish up as quickly as you can, and leave. Don't strike up a conversation with anyone. Con artists often try to start a conversation in an attempt to distract you before you finish your transaction.
* *If you are short-changed by the machine,* telephone the bank immediately. Your chances of getting your money replaced are greater the sooner you let someone know about it.
* *If you lose your ATM card,* notify the bank immediately so it can cancel the card and invalidate your PIN. That way you reduce the risk of an unauthorized user getting money out of your account.

a free one to each depositor. Sit down for a minute and think about what you want most in a bank. Some of the options that are commonly offered include the following:

Low-fee or no-fee savings and checking accounts

High-yielding insured savings

Interest-bearing checking accounts

Overdraft protection on checking accounts

Free checks

Free traveler's checks

Quick credit for deposits

Numerous branches, with one near you

Extended evening and weekend hours for convenience

Drive-up windows

Automatic teller machines

Once you've got your list in hand, visit local banks. Determine whether they offer what you want. Find out the rates on savings and interest-bearing checking accounts. Compare all the services. (Most banks have a preprinted list of services and rates; simply ask at the information desk or ask a teller.)

Get to know the branch manager or an assistant. If you're busy, it's a real temptation to use the drive-up window. But make it a point to get out and walk into the lobby on a regular basis to take care of your transactions. Why? You'll be a familiar face. The bank employees will know and recognize you. Then if you have a problem or need help, you'll be more than a name on a deposit slip.

Make sure a good deal is really a good deal. A bank might significantly lower the monthly fees on a checking account in order to attract your business. Sounds good? Could be--but don't accept it at face value. The bank might be sharply increasing the fee for buying new checks or for using an automatic teller machine in order to cover its loss.

Use more than one bank. If you can get some good deals at one bank but some of the services you want at another, split up your accounts between two or more banks. You should have your savings account at a bank that pays the highest interest, and your checking account at the bank that charges the lowest fee and gives you the greatest banking convenience. Don't compromise on what you want and need just in an attempt to stick with a single bank.

Consider an out-of-town bank, especially for investments. If you can't get the rates or service you want locally, investigate what's available elsewhere. Go to your local library and brush up by reading several financial newsletters. They regularly feature banks that pay the highest going rates. If you can double your interest and don't need daily access to your money, it's worth it to bank by mail!

Even after you've opened an account, stay on the lookout. Large banks are constantly expanding, and chances are good that a new bank will open up eventually in your area. New banks are usually willing to offer real incentives to attract new customers--and you should be one of the first in line to take advantage!

USING CREDIT WITHOUT GETTING USED: HOW TO SAFELY BUILD YOUR CREDIT POWER

What is credit?

Simply stated, it's the practice of paying for something in installments while you are enjoying use of the item. It has become a way of life in America, and many people have come to rely so heavily on credit that they can't function without it.

Credit has definite advantages--you can pay for essentials over an extended period of time. You don't have to miss great buys because you're temporarily short on cash. You don't have to carry large amounts of cash or go through the inconvenience of trying to write personal checks. And you get a detailed record of all your monthly purchases with each month's bill.

But credit has definite disadvantages, too. It costs money, because you pay a fee to use your card and interest on your purchases. It makes you susceptible to theft. And, perhaps worst of all, it makes it very easy to overspend, buy on impulse, and sink way too far into debt.

Knowing what kinds of credit are available and how to handle consumer credit can enable you to enjoy the advantages of credit without being zapped by the disadvantages.

A New Breed of Plastic: The Kinds of Credit Available

There are two basic kinds of credit available. **Open-ended** credit allows you to make purchases on credit repeatedly up to a predetermined limit. You might have a limit of $1,000 on a credit card, for example; as long as you make your payments on time, you can continue to charge and pay for purchases on the card as long as you don't exceed $1,000 at any one time. **Closed-end** credit is given for a one-time purchase of a specific item (such as a car). You agree ahead of time to the amount of the payments, the number of payments, and the length of the loan.

Credit cards are available from many different companies. You can get a bank credit card (such as a Visa or MasterCard), a gasoline credit card, a retail credit card (good only at a specific retail store), or specialized credit cards available only to certain people (such as members of a specific club or organization).

Before you sign up for a credit card, look at how much it's going to cost you. Is there an annual fee for use? When do interest calculations begin? (Many cards offer a twenty-five-day "grace period" before they start charging interest.) How are the finance charges calculated? (You should only pay on the "adjusted balance," or the amount you still owe at any given time, instead of on a previous balance.)

Before you borrow money for an installment loan, look at it just as carefully. What's the interest rate? How are finance charges calculated? (You should pay only on adjusted balance at any given time, not on the original loan amount.) What is the length of the loan? (You don't want a three-year loan on an item that will be worn out or worse in two years.) What collateral do you need to offer? Is there a penalty for early payment?

In essence, take the time to find out what you're getting into before you accept credit of any kind--what you think is a great deal may prove to be a grave financial mistake.

How to Establish Credit

Whenever you apply for credit, the creditor uses a "credit scoring system" that is designed to be fair to everyone. In essence, it rates (or scores) your ability to repay and your willingness to repay. Your ability to repay is usually based on things like your income, the amount of debt you already have, and your assets. Your willingness to repay is demonstrated by your payment history on past loans.

The credit scoring system varies slightly from one financial institution to another, but most look at factors like whether you own or rent your home, how long you have been employed at your job, and how long you've been at your current address. It's all designed to determine your stability.

What if you've never used credit before, and you want to establish a good rating now? The key is to start small and gradually build your creditworthiness. Try the following approach:

1. Open a checking account at a local bank, and handle it responsibly. Guard against overdrafts or bounced checks. Try to keep a minimum balance in the account.

2. Open a passbook savings account at a local bank and avoid the temptation of dipping into it. Demonstrate to the bank that your account is growing steadily.

3. Apply for a small "passbook loan," a loan that is secured against your passbook savings account. Repay it promptly; guard against making any late payments.

4. Apply to a local retailer for a credit card. Handle the card responsibly, never exceed your credit limit, and make payments promptly.

5. After you have established yourself with the retail credit card for a year, apply for a national bank card (such as Visa, MasterCard, or American Express).

Find Out What the Credit Bureau Is Saying About You

Simply stated, a credit bureau is a central clearinghouse for information on consumer credit. Every time you apply for a loan, make a payment on a loan, or fail to satisfy a debt, a report is made to the credit bureau. There may be several different bureaus in one city, and one retailer may make reports to a different bureau than another retailer does. You can find credit bureaus listed in the yellow pages of your local telephone directory.

Your credit record is critical: it shows a potential creditor whether or not you pay your bills on time. You need to take it seriously, because negative information stays on it a long time. Bankruptcies stay on your record for ten years; other negative information will stay on for seven.

Periodically visit your local credit bureau and ask for a copy of your file; there may be a minimal charge, but it's worth it. You should review your file carefully to make sure all the information on it is accurate; if it's not, you have legal rights that allow you to challenge the information and have it removed from your record.

Safeguard Those Cards!

As mentioned, using credit cards opens you up to theft and fraud--so make sure you safeguard your cards, as well as yourself, when you use them to make purchases.

To minimize the chance of theft, follow these suggestions:

• Keep your credit cards in your wallet; never leave them in a desk drawer, a dresser drawer, a jewelry box, or a glove compartment.

• Carry with you only the credit card(s) you intend to use. You'll reduce the chance of losing other cards and will also cut down on the temptation for impulse spending.

• Know the laws. If your credit card is lost or stolen, your liability is limited by federal law to $50 per card. Once you notify the company that the card is missing, you cannot be liable for any purchases made after your notification.

• Safeguard your credit card numbers: all someone needs is your number in order to make purchases and have them charged to you. **Never** give your credit card number out over the phone to someone who calls you and says he needs it to verify certain information.

• Closely watch the clerk the entire time he has your credit card. If he makes a mistake and voids out a transaction, ask him for the spoiled receipt so that **you** can tear it up.

• After you sign the card receipt, make sure you have all the carbons (if you don't, ask the clerk for them). Then take the carbons with you and dispose of them somewhere else.

• Make a list of each credit card you hold, its number, and the name and telephone number of the company. Keep your list in a safe place. That way you can notify card issuers immediately if your card is lost or stolen.

• Scrutinize your monthly credit card bill as carefully as you do your monthly bank statement. Open your statement the day it arrives, even if you won't be paying it for a few weeks. Keep all credit receipts stapled together until you receive your bill; then check each one against your bill. If you find charges for purchases you did not make, you need to contact the card issuer immediately to dispute the charges.

Do You Have Too Much of a Good Thing?

Credit can be used well to enhance your buying power and

strengthen your financial position--or it can be used poorly to sink you hopelessly into debt.

If you've misused your credit cards and charged more than you can repay in a reasonable amount of time, **stop using your cards until you have paid the balance in full.** If the temptation is too great, get a pair of sharp scissors and cut your cards in fourths before you toss them into the nearest garbage can. Then work as quickly as you can to pay the balance due so you can minimize the damage to your credit rating.

How do you know when you're in trouble? The following are tell-tale signs of runaway credit card use:

- You owe more than 15 percent of your take-home pay on debts other than your mortgage.
- You always make only the minimum payment due (or pay only the interest owing on your amount due).
- You use your credit card to pay for essentials, such as groceries.
- You skip paying some bills some months in order to pay others.
- You have to dip into your savings account in order to pay credit card bills.
- You're not sure exactly how much you owe.

Each one is a red flag: stop using credit before you do serious damage. If you need help digging out of the hole, contact a local non-profit consumer credit counseling service; such a service can help you set up a strict repayment plan and can negotiate with your creditors until debts are satisfied.

Getting Back on Your Feet After Credit Mistakes

What if the mistakes have already been made? Is it too late?

No. There are a number of strategies you can use to resolve the situations in a better way and eventually reestablish your credit. Here's how:

- Don't ignore it, because it's not going to go away. Your creditors will be much more willing to give you a break if you contact them, explain the difficulty you're having, and try to negotiate. You still might damage your credit rating, but it will be less damaging than it could be.
- If you can, meet personally with your creditors and explain your situation. If your inability to make payment is due to something beyond your control (such as unemployment or an extended illness), your creditors may rewrite your loan or agree to lower

monthly payments.

- Get good consumer credit help as soon as you realize you are in trouble. A good counselor will help you set up a workable budget, will outline a strict repayment plan, will contact your creditors for you, and may even arrange for you to make a lumpsum payment to him. He'll then disburse your funds to your creditors for you.
- Shy away from debt consolidation loans. Why? They give you a false sense of security. When you are only making payment to one creditor and the payment has been reduced, it's easy for you to start charging again.
- Declare bankruptcy only as a last resort. Remember, your debts will be erased--but you'll lose your home and it will stay on your credit report for ten years, affecting your ability to qualify for car loans and mortgages. As a general rule, you should resist bankruptcy until your non-mortgage debt exceeds 40 percent of your annual income and you have no ability to boost your income.
- Set up a strict budget (follow the guidelines listed in this chapter). Look at where you can cut back. Then, no matter how difficult it seems, stick to your budget.
- One of the most important things you can do is **set up a savings account.** Even if you are still working to pay off debt, deposit something (even if it's a small amount) in a savings account every month.
- Start small in trying to get credit. If you have a bad credit rating and want to start over, you'll need to begin with a very small purchase for a very small amount of money. Make your payments on time, and you'll gradually be able to borrow more.
- Ask for a copy of your credit report, and make sure it's an accurate reflection. You are allowed to make explanations on the report; use that right if you have filed a bankruptcy or had a judgment filed against you. You may have had loans with good repayment record that are not reflected on your credit rating; contact those creditors and ask that they make a report.
- Check your credit report before you apply for an important new card or loan. If you're clearly not ready, don't apply yet; your ability to get future credit will be impacted if you are denied a number of times. (Each time a potential creditor asks for a copy of your file, the request is listed on your record.)
- Don't apply for several different sources of credit at one time; creditors may fear that you are plotting something.

- Shop around for a mortgage. Even if you have declared a bankruptcy or have poor past credit, there are mortgage companies who will work with you if your income is adequate.

What About Co-Signing a Loan?

If a friend or member of the family asks you to co-sign a loan, should you do it?

That depends--on what your responsibility will be and on who the borrower is. Co-signing a loan is a serious commitment because not only does it go on your credit report, but you may eventually have to repay the loan.

Before you ever co-sign a loan, ask some serious questions:

Who is the borrower? Do you know the person well? What is his situation? Why can't he qualify for credit without a cosigner? Is he reliable? Does he understand the importance of maintaining a good credit history? Do you have reason to believe that his situation will change or that he will not carry out his responsibilities for the loan?

Your answers are important, because they help determine what kind of a risk you're taking. It's one thing to co-sign a loan to help your own child start establishing a credit record; it's quite another to co-sign for an adult friend who just can't seem to qualify on his own (probably because of past poor credit).

What's your responsibility as a co-signer? Even though you are not the one receiving the goods, services, or cash, you are ultimately responsible to make sure that the debt is paid. If the borrower fails to pay, regardless of the reason, the lender can legally come after you and demand payment. If you have put up personal property as security or collateral on the loan, you could lose it if the borrower fails to pay.

If you decide to go ahead and co-sign, there are some things you can do to help protect yourself and to make sure you stay on top of the situation:

- Carefully read the co-signer's agreement before you sign anything. Look for specifics that spell out your exact responsibility. If you're uncomfortable about any of the clauses, don't sign!
- Insist on getting a copy of the papers between the borrower and the lender. Look at all the terms of the loan. Pay careful attention to the amount the borrower has agreed to repay, including all

interest and finance charges. Before you agree to co-sign, make sure that you could personally pay the loan in full.

- If you are planning on needing credit yourself in the period before the loan will be paid, you probably shouldn't cosign: you may be denied credit of your own until the obligation is taken care of.
- Insist that the lender notify you in writing **immediately** if the borrower misses a payment. Then you can immediately put pressure on the borrower. You will also have fair warning that there's a problem instead of suddenly finding out that the loan is three or four payments in arrears and must be paid within a week.
- Try negotiating with the lender to reduce your own liability. Not all lenders will agree to it, but you might be able to get some concessions. For example, you might be able to secure an agreement in writing that you will be responsible for the principle of the loan only and not the interest or any court costs that occur in an effort to collect it.
- Insist that you be responsible only for the original loan as agreed upon. You do not want to be liable if the borrower later refinances (adding more interest for a longer period of time) or tries to borrow an additional amount on the same loan.
- Know your rights under the law. If you don't, have the lender clarify them for you. If there is another co-signer, how much of the responsibility do you each bear? Would you need to repay all of the loan, or only part of it? What if the borrower declares bankruptcy before the loan is repaid? Will the debt be dissolved, or will you still have to pay it? And, finally, what if the borrower voluntarily turns the goods back to the bank before the loan is repaid? Will the lender come after you for the remainder, or will the lender accept the goods in settlement of the loan?

Remember that your credit rating is a precious commodity. If you can co-sign without substantial risk, you may be able to help somone out without hurting yourself--but always keep in mind that co-signing is a gamble!

KEEPING YOUR COOL AMID THE STORM: HOW TO DEAL WITH SUDDEN CHANGES IN INCOME

At some point in your financial life, it's bound to happen to you:

for reasons usually beyond your control and impossible to predict, you'll take a wild swing in income level. You might be suddenly laid off because of an unanticipated plant closure--or you might get a real windfall from an unexpected inheritance. Whether your income takes a nosedive, a giant leap, or just begins to vary considerably, you need to be **careful** in adapting to changes.

When Your Income Drops

In some cases, you'll know at least several months in advance that your income is going to be less--a two-career couple might decide that the wife will quit when an expected baby is born, for example. In those cases, begin early to plan. Boost your savings. Pay off some debt ahead of schedule so you won't be saddled with payments. Redesign your budget, and start to live now on the lower amount.

But in many cases, your drop in income will be sudden, unexpected, and beyond your control: you might get laid off, you might be permanently injured and unable to continue working, or budget cutbacks at your company may force you into early retirement.

How can you handle the unexpected?

Begin by taking immediate action to protect what you do have left. Follow these guidelines to minimize the effects of your drop in income:

- **Immediately** find out what benefits you're entitled to (such as unemployment benefits or food stamps) and apply for those benefits at the first possible chance. Many have a waiting period of a few weeks--and the waiting period starts the day you apply, not the day you lose your income. You can cut down on the period of time you are without income by applying as soon as you qualify.
- **As soon as you know how much your income will be,** redesign your budget. Start as quickly as you can to cut back and "live within your means."
- If you are currently making payments to creditors for installment loans and credit cards, **contact your creditors immediately** and explain the situation. They will appreciate the early notice instead of finding out about your drop in income after you have missed two or three payments. Negotiate and ask for some help. If you've been making payments on time and have been a reliable

49

borrower, your creditors will almost certainly be willing to make some adjustments for a few months. See if you can get the amount of the payment temporarily reduced, if you can refinance the loan to get the payment permanently reduced, or if some other arrangement can be worked out. If your creditors are stubborn, contact a consumer credit counseling service for help immediately.

- **Act quickly to guard and preserve your employee benefits,** such as health and life insurance. By law, you are entitled to continue a health insurance plan at group rates for a specified period of time if you continue making the payments--even though you are no longer employed by that group. You can usually continue coverage for eighteen months after resigning or being laid off or for three years after early retirement. Check the law and insist on your rights--you don't want to be saddled with a huge medical bill on top of your other problems.

- **Don't do anything drastic at first.** You'll be tempted to sell your car, sell your house, or do something else to get a quick wad of cash. Most situations are temporary, and you can bounce back from most of them within three to six months. With some careful planning and negotiation, you can adopt some temporary measures to see you through.

- If you can avoid it, **don't dip into your savings.** If you've followed the advice outlined in this chapter, you should have an emergency fund; use it to help see you through a period of lower income. Then replace it as quickly as you can. But don't disturb your established savings unless it is a last resort.

- While most drops in income are temporary, you may be able to see that yours will be permanent (due to permanent retirement or disability, for example). **If the drop in income is clearly a permanent situation,** start to regroup. Determine where you can make big changes in your monthly outgo. You might decide to sell your newer car and replace it with a reliable used one or sell your home and purchase a less expensive one. Keep on top of your expenses, and keep adjusting your budget until you find one you can live with.

When Your Income Increases

Lucky, right?

Right--if you handle it the right way. Too many people see an increase in income (even a one-time or temporary one) as license to abandon all financial restraint. Others start living on an increased budget right away without careful planning. Still others don't remember to budget, and end up getting into trouble.

Follow these suggestions to get the greatest benefit out of any sudden increases in income:

• If your income increased because you got a raise at work, **remember to figure in the increased taxes and expenses.** You might need to purchase a better wardrobe to reflect your new position, for example. And you will always pay higher taxes when you get a higher income.

• As soon as you know exactly what your new income will mean in terms of take-home pay, redesign your budget. **Figure in only the net increase,** not the gross amount of your raise. By redesigning your budget immediately, you'll know exactly how much extra you have to spend, and you can decide where you want to spend it. In other words, you can put your money to work for you right away.

Keeping Financial Records; When Is It Safe To Throw Them Away?

If you deal with many financial transactions, you could quickly get moved out of house and home by all the receipts and records--but it may make you nervous to toss them away, too!

How do you know what you should keep, and how long you should keep it?

In essence, you should keep documents long enough to avoid any danger from the IRS. By law, the IRS has three years in which to challenge your tax return, and you have three years in which to file an amended one. To be on the safe side, keep any documents that impact your tax returns or your standing with the IRS for six to seven years.

Some records are more critical than others, so they need to be guarded more carefully. While circumstances can vary, a good general rule follows.

Keep these in a safe-deposit box at the bank: mortgage deeds, car titles, property appraisals, a copy of tax returns for the previous five years, a household inventory, records of major expenditures on your property, records of paid-off debts, a list of debts owed to you (with supporting evidence), stocks and bonds, birth certificates, marriage licenses, military discharge papers, passport, citizenship papers.

Keep these at home in a fireproof and waterproof file: a copy of your most recent tax return, copies of any current leases, numbers of all credit cards, serial numbers of all securities, insurance policies, service contracts, warranty cards, medical records, copies of your will.

- **Avoid the temptation to "reward" yourself** by running out and making a bunch of purchases because you got a raise. Even small ones have a wicked way of adding up quickly--and, before you know it, all your "extra" is gone with little or nothing to show for it.
- If you're in debt, **use the extra money to reduce your debt load.** You should apply the extra to paying off bills instead of using it as an excuse to get even deeper in debt.
- If you are not in debt or are able to make all your payments comfortably on your old income, **put all your extra money in savings.** You might not see a change in your month-to-month standard of living, but you'll see a tremendous change in your long-term security.
- **If the increase is a one-time "windfall,"** you need to be much more conservative with it than if you got a long-term increase in earnings. If you decide to invest, do it carefully; stick with guaranteed investments. If you want to gamble on the stock market, use only a part of your money while the rest is in guaranteed investments. If you want to see an increase in daily spending, invest the money in an interest-bearing account **and spend only the interest you earn.** If you decide to use the money to purchase a new home, try to keep your mortgage what it is now by using the money for a large down payment; remember that you'll retain your current monthly income with which you make payments!

When Your Income Constantly Fluctuates

If you're in the kind of business where your income regularly changes (you're a freelance writer who lives on royalty checks or a plant worker whose hours change with the seasons), you need to plan carefully. These guidelines can help you live as rationally as possible:
- Devise a carefully thought-out spending plan **based on your lowest possible income.** That way, you'll be able to budget even if the money is slow in coming--and if you have a more lucrative period, you can exercise some options.
- **Strictly adhere to your spending plan.** When you do get money, put it in the bank immediately and spend it as designated. Don't get excited with a temporary "windfall" and decide you can pay

your rent in a few weeks. . .because you may be back to rockbottom by then.

- If you get an especially big check that you weren't planning on, **put the money in savings or in your emergency fund** instead of splurging on an impulse purchase. Then the money will be working for you and will be there later on if you desperately need some help.

- **Concentrate on building your savings;** you'll always have greater options if you can. If you suddenly have a slim period where money is extremely tight for several months, you won't be forced into drastic action (like selling your car or house) as a result.

ALL IN A DAY'S WORK: CHAPTER 3
HOW TO SUCCEED ON THE JOB

Y
ou've secured that all-important job interview. . .and
now you're not sure how to pull it off. Or maybe
you've been on the job awhile, and you think you're
entitled to a raise--but you're not sure how to ask. Or
perhaps you've been on the job all *too* long--and you
wonder if it's time to move on.

Need some quick answers? Some simple guidelines can help
you shine at an interview, get a good raise, and even figure out how
to gracefully leave when the time is right!

JOB INTERVIEWS: MAKING A GOOD IMPRESSION

You've heard the old saying, "It's the first impression that
counts"--and it counts at a job interview more than almost
anywhere else! If you want a great interview that will land you a
job, do some homework ahead of time and get ready for a winning
performance!

Homework? That's right! Once you've landed an interview,
find out all you can about the company you'll be interviewing with.
What kind of business is it? Who are its customers? How many
employees work there now? Will you be replacing someone, or will
you be filling a newly created position? What kind of competition
does the company have? How is it viewed in the community?

Knowing this kind of information will give you a real edge over
the competition. Why? First, you'll be able to talk knowledgeably
with your interviewer about the company. You'll look interested--
and that's impressive. And once you have all the facts about the
company and the position you're interviewing for, you can
emphasize the things about your own experience that make you
especially suited for the job.

When you're finding out about the company, find out what
"dress codes" are. Is it a very conservative office? One with a
relaxed atmosphere? Do employees wear uniforms? Find out how
the upper-level management dress--and make sure you dress that

well for your interview. Dress well, but appropriately. You probably wouldn't want to wear a three-piece business suit with a white shirt to an interview in a company that is trendy and upbeat --just as you wouldn't wear brightly colored casual clothing to an interview with a law or accounting firm.

Choose your interview clothing before the day of your interview--that will give you time for a trip to the dry cleaner if you need one. It will also give you time to launder, sew on buttons, fix hemlines, find matching stockings, polish shoes, and so on. Take care of the little things--carelessness with details can spoil your interview.

Choose clothing that is crisp and polished, but comfortable. It shouldn't be too tight anywhere, nor should it bind. Take a look in a full-length mirror. Does everything hang well? Are hemlines even? Make sure you have enough room through your shoulders, across your hips, and through the rise of your slacks. Sit down; make sure slacks don't bind and skirts don't creep up. Simply stated, you want to be able to concentrate on the interview--not on what you're wearing.

Keep jewelry understated; you don't want it to distract from *you*. Wear a watch that keeps accurate time. Go light on cologne or perfume. And absolutely do not chew gum.

Obviously, spend some time on personal grooming--above all, you should be clean. Hair and makeup should be understated but attractive. Fingernails should be clean and shaped; if you wear polish, keep it subtle and make sure it's not chipped.

Before the actual interview, stage a full "dress rehearsal." That means more than dressing in your interview outfit. If you've never been to the office where you will be interviewed, go there a day or two ahead. You'll be sure of the address, and you'll be able to allow plenty of time for commuting and parking.

Which leads us to the day of your interview: *make sure you are on time.* Many employers judge the work habits of a potential employee by whether or not he's on time for an interview. Build in plenty of time to get to the interview, to park, and to get to the office. If you plan to arrive a few minutes early, you'll be able to relax and wait for the interview instead of arriving out of breath.

Even if you mailed or delivered your resume ahead of time, take another copy with you. A professionally prepared resume should be typed on white paper and should include your name, address, telephone number, professional experience, education, membership in professional organizations, civic or volunteer work, and several references.

During the interview, sit in a relaxed but professional posture. It's best to cross your legs at the ankles or to tuck both ankles to the side. Keep your hands relaxed, in your lap. Keep good eye contact with your interviewer, and, above all, smile!

Finally, here's a tip that might surprise you: besides answering all the interviewer's questions in a positive, forthright manner, *you* should ask some questions, too! You'll seem much more motivated, intelligent, and interested in the job and company if you ask some well-thought-out questions at your interview. There's another bonus, too--you'll find out more about the job you're seeking, and you might be able to spot some potential problems that could serve as red flags.

Try some of the following:

How do you see the company's future? Obviously, you don't want to get placed in a dead-end job or in a department that will be phased out during the next year. You're looking for a solid, competitive company that has a bright future. Asking about the company's position in the marketplace can alert you to problems and will let your interviewer know that you are aware of the company's product line.

Why are you looking for someone outside the company to fill this position? Maybe the company is expanding, and needs to bring in new employees. Or your position might have been filled by someone who was promoted. Or the company might have created a new slot that demands skills present employees don't have. Those are all legitimate reasons for seeking outside employees. You might be a little cautious, however, if you are replacing someone who was fired or who left because of difficulties with a supervisor or the company.

What kinds of job skills are you looking for in an applicant? As soon as you find out, you'll be able to emphasize the ones most important to your interviewer. You'll also get a better sense of whether you are qualified and can meet the company's expectations.

What would my typical assignments be on this job? Try to pin the interviewer down to specifics. You want to get a feel for what the job will be like and whether it's something you'll enjoy.

Will I be in charge of other employees? If so, how many? In what capacities? Will you simply be supervising their work, or will you be responsible as a "team leader" for the work that comes out of your area? Will you also have some responsibility for hiring and terminating the employees you will be responsible for?

What kind of benefits does the company offer? At the interview, you should find out whether the company offers health insurance, life insurance, profit sharing, stocks or options, and a pension plan. Find out what the vacation and sick leave policy is and any other pertinent policy information.

You should also look for clues as to how structured your position is, how much direct supervision you will have, what kind of training or on-the-job support you will receive, and to whom you will have direct responsibility. Find out what working hours are and how long the lunch break is. Close the interview with a firm handshake, a smile, and a statement that lets your interviewer know that you're looking forward to being part of the team.

To extend your good impression, follow up the interview with a brief letter of thanks addressed to the person who did the interview. The letter should be typed in business letter format on plain white paper or your own letterhead. Thank the interviewer for taking time with you, and make one or two positive statements about the company. Close by letting the interviewer know when you will check back. Keep the letter brief (no more than two or three paragraphs), positive, and complimentary.

What if you encounter a real stumbling block during the interview? Maybe you're clearly not qualified for the position, or you can see that the company is barely surviving. Or there might be some other situation--hours, pay scale, no chance for promotion--that keeps you from wanting to pursue the job.

There *is* a graceful way out! In a courteous way, let the interviewer know that you are probably not the right person for the job. You might say something like, "I can see that a strong public relations background would be vital to success in this position. I don't have those skills, and as a result I wouldn't be able to meet the company's expectations." Or, "I am hoping to affiliate with a company that I can make a strong career commitment to. While your company is certainly an outstanding one, I am concerned about not being able to grow with the company." Then follow up with a short note thanking the interviewer for taking the time to talk to you and wishing him success in finding a suitable, qualified applicant.

YOU GOT THE JOB--NOW WHAT?

Congratulations!. . .but it doesn't stop there! To get ahead (or even stay where you are), you need to be a top-notch employee. Build your career and avoid pitfalls by using common sense and following these tips:

- Be dependable. Get to work on time--*every* day. Meet deadlines. Follow through with assignments. Be the kind of employee your boss can count on.
- Don't plan your social life at work. Make personal phone calls on breaks or on your lunch hour, away from your desk. Ask friends who want to drop in to confine it to your break or lunch hour. Planning a party, a barbecue, or a dinner? Do it at home, not at the office.
- Don't let your personal problems or a crisis at home bog you down at work. Don't talk about your personal problems; limit your conversations to business plans. Mingle with your colleagues, but steer the conversation away from your personal life. If you start to get moody or lose control, excuse yourself and visit the restroom. Take a few deep breaths, splash some cool water on your face, and regain control.
- Brush up on your job skills. Improve your typing, shorthand, or

accounting skills. Keep up on the latest trends. Visit the library and read any trade magazines or journals that apply.

- Join any professional organizations that apply. You'll learn more about how to do your job, plus you'll have association with others who can give you pointers. An added bonus: some of the best jobs are advertised through professional organizations, not through the want ads of your local paper.
- Don't make excuses for why something can't be done. Instead, take on the challenge and find out how it *can* be done!
- Be a good member of the team. You're likely to get both raises and promotions based on your ability to work well with other people. Acknowledge the help you get, take credit only where it's due, and work hard to hold up your end of the workload. Above all, avoid office gossip and squabbles like the plague.
- Respond quickly to requests. If your boss needs some figures, compile the figures--the same day. If you can't get the actual figures together that day, deliver a memo that day outlining when you will have the requested information.
- Be positive. Like what you're doing, and let it show.
- Accept criticism in a positive way. Instead of leaping in to defend yourself, ask, "How can I do it better? I'd really appreciate your suggestions."
- Keep yourself challenged. If you are not being challenged on the job, do something to improve yourself. Take a class in a new subject or learn a new job skill.
- Grab the chance for on-the-job training, special schooling, or leadership seminars.
- If someone in the office makes inappropriate sexual advances, you *can* maintain your respect without jeopardizing your job status. Politely ask the offender to stop hugging you, calling you "honey," or commenting about your anatomy. If that doesn't work, tell the person that you are not comfortable with the behavior and that it is affecting your work. Tell the offender that you want to be professional associates, that you enjoy that association, and that anything more would ruin it. If someone in a position to prevent your promotion or to impact your job insists on sexual performance as a qualification, take appropriate action to file a complaint or report the individual. Make sure that you have kept careful notes on the offender's behavior so that you can report time, dates, and specific incidences to back you up.

- Always be neat. Keep your work area cleaned up. If you work at a desk, clear it off every night before you leave to go home.
- Always be well groomed. Avoid clothes that are too tight, too baggy, soiled, stained, or wrinkled. Never wear clothing that needs to be repaired (missing buttons, ripped seams, sagging hemline). And never get sloppy about personal grooming on the job.

BACK FROM VACATION? DON'T BE OVERWHELMED!

It happens to everyone: you get back from a relaxing vacation only to find an avalanche of mail and phone messages and crises waiting for you at work!

Don't despair! There's an easy, organized, efficient way to get back on top of things. Approach things in this order:
- Before you do anything, meet with your boss. Find out what went on while you were gone and what things are priority now.
- Check your calendar with your boss or coworkers. Find out if there have been meetings scheduled that you need to be aware of.
- Quickly sort through phone messages and mail, looking for emergencies. Take care of any emergencies then and there, setting other messages and mail aside for later.
- Once emergencies have been taken care of, return all phone calls in the order in which they were made. If someone isn't in, leave a message for them to return *your* call. You've then placed the responsibility back on that person, and you won't have to worry about remembering to place another call.
- Open all your mail. Answer, file, or route each piece until all mail has been taken care of.
- If you had unfinished projects when you left on vacation, check on their status. Review deadlines and make any necessary adjustments.
- Plan your calendar for the rest of the week, allowing for time to review projects and get everything back to pace.

THINK YOU'RE WORTH MORE? HOW TO ASK FOR A RAISE

Few things are more delicate in the workplace than the dread proposition of asking for a raise. With a little advance preparation, though, you can make a convincing case to your boss!

Where do you start?

In your own mind! Are you sure you deserve a raise? No? Then you shouldn't be asking for one! Before you approach your boss about a raise, you need to wipe any doubt out of your mind. Be convinced of the salary you should be getting. Remember that it has nothing to do with your personal worth, but with the work you are doing for the company.

Once you've resolved that in your mind, get ready to "sing and dance and do a commercial for yourself." Think back over your accomplishments during the last year; recall projects that went well. Then make sure your boss is aware of your good work. If you receive a compliment from a client or customer, pass it on. If you solve a particularly difficult problem, mention it to your boss. Don't brag, but matter-of-factly pass on the details.

For several months before you plan on asking for a raise, ask your boss for regular feedback. You need to know how he sees you--and what he thinks you could be doing better. React to all feedback in a positive, action-oriented way. If you can't get your boss to offer verbal feedback, ask for several written evaluations.

Get ready to present your case. Gather up all your information ahead of time--review your successes, rehearse some specific plans you have that make you an ongoing value to the company.

When you're ready to move, make sure the timing is right. The optimum timing is three to four months before the budgets are prepared for the next year; if you wait until the budgets are done, your chances of getting a raise are slim.

Set up an appointment with your boss at a time when you can both be relaxed. Avoid an appointment first thing in the morning when your boss is coping with all the pressures of the day's schedule; steer clear of periods just before important meetings, too. An afternoon meeting toward the end of the week, when things are winding down, might be best. Ask for the meeting in your boss's office so that it will be on a professional level; don't go to a restaurant or other place away from the office.

Be relaxed, friendly, and forthright. Open the meeting by saying something like, "I asked for this meeting to talk about my raise." Realize that your boss will probably be uncomfortable, and will probably initially turn you down. Don't take it personally--it's his job to save the company money and keep expenses down.

Summarize your achievements while on the job; talk in specifics, and remind your boss of what you've done for the company while you've been on board. Then, to cement your value to the company, hint at some things you have planned to improve your department or to accomplish certain goals.

After you've spelled out your achievements and sketched your plans, tell your boss what kind of a raise you have in mind. Don't ask for "a raise"; instead, tell him exactly how much you would like to have. Asking for a raise involves negotiation, and you need to spell out exact figures.

What if your boss says no?

There are a number of strategies you can try to defuse the situation. Whatever happens, remain friendly, confident, and firm; don't get angry or defensive. Try the following:

- Your boss says you need to improve in a certain area. If you agree, say: "I appreciate your feedback. I'll get back to you as soon as I have polished my skills in that area."
- Your boss says he can't make the decision, but has to defer it to someone else. You say: "I'll be happy to make some notes to strengthen our position with your superior." (Saying "our position" lets your boss know that you are confident he is on your side and will fight for you.)
- Your boss says the company isn't making enough money to give out raises this year. You say: "I understand that money is tight, but I'm sure the company will want to use its available resources on people who really produce in areas that count. That will profit everyone."
- Your boss hesitates, citing several past mistakes or shortcomings. You say: "Those things are in the past. I think my raise should be based on my ability to produce good results, which I have been doing."
- Your boss listens to your arguments, presents the request to his superior, and gets turned down. You say: "I appreciate your support. I'll think more about it, and will come up with a new approach we can use. When the time is right I will get back together with you, and we can try again."

READY TO MOVE ON? HOW TO TELL
When It's Time to Quit

The reasons are endless. . .and, whatever your reasons, maybe you've decided it's time to quit a job.

What should you do now?

First, you need to make an important--and basic--decision. Are you going to quit the job you have now before you find another job? Or are you going to start looking for another job while you are still employed?

Your resources will undoubtedly have something to do with the decision. If you quit one job before you have another one secured, you will need a way to support yourself. You may qualify for unemployment benefits after a certain length of time. If you will not qualify for unemployment benefits, you should have enough in savings to cover your needs for three to four months--the average time it takes to find a job. You also might be able to save your vacation days so that you can be paid for two or three weeks while you look for another job. If you have enough money to meet your needs, you'll have less tendency to panic and settle for a job that is wrong for you.

Money's not the only issue, though. You need to consider your self-esteem: how will you feel about yourself if you are not employed? How will you feel about yourself if you stay at your present job? You also need to consider the way others will view you--will you be looked at unfavorably if you don't have a current job?

In general, avoid making any kind of job decision when you are emotionally upset. If something has happened at work that has upset you, wait until you have calmed down before you make a decision to leave. You need to wait until you can make a clear, rational decision.

All situations are different, but in general, you should stick with your job if the following are true:

• Your salary and benefits are good.
• Your job provides opportunities for growth.
• You enjoy both challenge and reward on the job.
• Your job is in the field for which you are qualified.
• You are learning new skills or improving old ones on the job.
• You know about future growth plans that involve you.
• The things that bother you are also bothering most of the other employees.
• The new job would simply be a lateral move--same salary, same responsibilities, same benefits.

If you've decided the job is one that you should quit, you need to decide whether the time is right. Should you quit now, before you have something else secured, or should you wait?

Again, every situation is unique, but in general, you should probably consider quitting before you have another job lined up if the following apply:

• The nature or hours of your job make it impossible to schedule job interviews or make follow-up phone calls while at work.

• Your workload is so heavy or your responsibilities are so great that you can't possibly take any time off to hunt for a new job.

• Your self-esteem is suffering by staying on the job.

• Your boss and/or coworkers are convinced you are a failure and don't seem to want to give you a chance to prove otherwise.

• You work in a group where phone conversations are periodically monitored or in an office environment where phone conversations are easily overheard, making it impossible to discreetly set up appointments or make follow-up calls.

• You may be able to get a good reference from your boss if you leave before things get worse.

• If you end up leaving one job before you have another, don't let it reflect poorly on you. If you are questioned by a potential employer, just say, "I've always thought it was dishonest to look for employment on my company's time. I felt I owed it to the company to devote all my time and energy to my job as long as I was still on the payroll."

In general, you should stay at your present job if the situation is a tolerable one and if you have a little flexibility that allows you to make job contacts. You must remain honest and fair in your dealings with your current employer, though: set up job interview appointments for your lunch break, and make appointments or follow-up phone calls on your designated breaks.

There are some things you can do in the weeks and months before you leave to make the transition smoother for you and for your employer. In general, try the following:

• Review your files, and gather samples of non-confidential work that you can compile into a portfolio to show to potential employers. Obviously, you should never take anything of a confidential nature or anything that would betray a company's standing with its competition.

• Go through your telephone file or phone book, and copy out the names and phone numbers of any personal contacts you established while working for the company. Ethically, you should not take with you any contacts that "belong" to the company.

- Give your boss at least two weeks' notice to allow time for the company to replace you. Offer to do whatever you can to make the transition smooth, including an offer to help train your replacement.
- Don't go over a list of grievances or gripes when you announce your resignation. Be brief and matter-of-fact; if your boss presses for details, simply state that it's time for you to move on and pursue some other interests. Remain professional and positive.
- Ask your boss and any influential colleagues for letters of recommendation *before* your last day at work. Even if you are leaving under difficult circumstances, your boss may agree to write a letter about some of your successes or about some areas where you did a good job.
- Ask your boss and any department heads you have worked with if you can use their names as references when you search for a new job.

- Do what you can to help your company as you leave. The people you leave behind will have better feelings about you, you'll have a greater chance of getting a positive recommendation, and you'll feel better about yourself.
- If you can, start making contacts before you leave. If it's not possible or if it would be too awkward, wait until you have left to start setting up job contacts.
- No matter how awkward it seems, attend farewell lunches or parties. You'll leave on a positive note, and will be remembered with greater fondness.
- After you have left, drop a personal note to your boss, any influential colleagues, or any department heads you worked with. Thank them for the chance of working with them, comment on one or two positive things you learned or accomplished, and wish them the greatest continued success.

CHAPTER 4

ON THE GO:
TRAVEL AND VACATION TIPS

I t's that time of year--and you're ready to head for the beach or hit the slopes!

You're not alone--according to the U.S. Travel Data Center, 69 percent of all Americans over the age of eighteen take at least one trip of more than 100 miles each year. Almost eight in ten drive to wherever they're going; most of the rest travel by plane, with a slim number taking a bus or train. Almost half stay with relatives or friends when they reach their destination; another third stay in hotels or other commercial lodging. Only about 3 percent own their own vacation home or cabin; about 4 percent rent vacation homes or cabins, and about 5 percent use campsites or trailer parks.

And, according to the Travel Data Center, the typical vacationer is married, between the ages of twenty-five and forty-four, a college graduate, and a white-collar worker.

Want to have the best vacation ever? Then start by doing a little advance work, follow some simple travel tips, and maybe even consider something a little unusual (like a night at a bed-and-breakfast, or a day on a train). But, most important of all, have fun!

DUST OFF THOSE SUITCASES:
PACKING FOR A TRIP

- In between uses, store your suitcases standing on end, not laying flat.
- To keep suitcases from picking up musty odors, fill them with crumpled-up newspapers between uses. To give them a sweet scent, toss in a fabric softener sheet, a bar of perfumed soap, a sachet, or a small tin of cinnamon.
- When you pack your suitcase, pack a large, collapsible canvas bag in the bottom of your suitcase to hold any treasures or souvenirs you pick up while shopping. That way you won't be forced into cramming your finds into an already-full suitcase!
- Make a detailed, itemized list of everything you pack. If your luggage is lost or stolen, you'll have a much easier time documenting your insurance claim.
- Make sure you pack a large plastic garbage bag (or two) to store dirty laundry in--it will keep your dirty clothes from soiling your clean ones.
- Pack shoes in medium-sized plastic bags (bread bags work well) to keep them from soiling your clothing.
- Pack anything that could leak or spill--such as shampoo, hair-spray, fingernail polish, liquid makeup, perfume, or liquid medications--in ziploc-type plastic bags. You'll protect your clothing and other packed items from leakage and soil in case a lid comes loose or a container splits open.
- Before you pack anything in a plastic bottle, loosen the lid, squeeze the bottle gently to force out some of the air, and replace the lid tightly. You'll create a vacuum effect that will help to prevent spills or leaks.
- To keep sweaters and other knits from creasing or crumpling, roll them instead of folding them.
- If you can, use a garment bag for clothing you want to hang. If you don't have access to a garment bag, place tissue paper between the folds on clothing to keep wrinkles to a minimum.
- Put an identification tag on both the outside and the inside of your luggage if you are flying or staying in hotels or other commercial lodging.
- If you are flying or leaving your luggage in commercial lodging, make sure you lock it. If your luggage does not have locks, you can

purchase locking straps that wrap around and secure your luggage.

- If you are flying, taking a train, or taking a bus, arrive early and check your luggage in as early as possible. Statistics show that most lost luggage is checked in less than half an hour before departure time.
- If you are flying, put some kind of bright, unique marking on the outside of your luggage (such as wrapping bright orange tape around your suitcase handle) to prevent someone else from picking up your luggage by mistake at the baggage claim area.
- If you are visiting a foreign country, take along an extra suitcase or collapsible canvas bag. Pack all your purchases in the same bag to speed your trip through Customs.
- If you need to carry prescription drugs, make sure they are in the original containers. If you are traveling far, ask your pharmacist for a copy of the prescription in case your medication is lost or stolen. Since brand names differ in foreign countries, ask the pharmacist to list generic names for your prescription drugs if you will be traveling abroad.
- If you are flying, never pack film or a camera loaded with film in your suitcase; airline security x-ray scanning devices ruin film. Carry your film in hand luggage and offer it to security personnel to inspect by hand. Make sure your camera is empty, since security personnel may insist on sending the camera through the scanner.
- Pack things you can't afford to lose--eyeglasses, prescription drugs, passport, tickets, and so on--in hand luggage, and keep it with you at all times. Remember: if it's in your suitcase, you may never see it again!

ON A SHOESTRING?
TRIMMING THE COST OF YOUR VACATION

- The best general tip for cutting the cost of a vacation is to **start planning early.** The best discounts on rental cars, hotel rooms, airline seats, and train seats are generally for those who make reservations early--and the most economical cars, rooms, and seats are generally the first to go.
- Try working with a travel agent if you will be flying or spending time in commercial lodging (such as a hotel, vacation home, or

condominium). Let the agent know you are interested in discounts, package deals, or special offers.

- If you don't use a travel agent to line up your airline reservations, be prepared to do some homework. Call every airline that serves your destination and ask about rates--and be sure to ask for discounts for advance reservations, supersaver rates, or excursion rates.
- If you are flying, consider using a charter flight. These usually leave late at night or early in the morning--but if you can accommodate unusual hours and can make your reservations early, you can generally save a significant amount.
- Whenever making reservations, ask about any available discounts. You might be able to save money if you pay cash instead of using a credit card, for example--or you might save significantly if you stay for a week instead of five or six days.
- If you are employed, ask about corporate discounts. Some hotels and motels offer discounts to employees of certain firms, even if they're obviously on personal vacation.
- Check with your credit union to see if it offers discount tickets to attractions where you will be visiting. A number of credit unions, for example, offer discount passes to Disneyland and Sea World.
- If you will be traveling often and can travel on short notice, consider joining a travel discount club. These often purchase blocks of tickets on airplanes or cruises or in hotels in popular vacation spots--which you can in turn get for less.
- Sit down ahead of time and make a careful budget of your travel expenses. Remember the seemingly-small details, like toll roads, tips, and taxi fare--they can add up in a hurry. Look like more than you can spend? Go over your proposed budget item by item, and decide where you can cut back. Then determine ahead of time to stick with your budget and avoid impulse purchases.
- After you've made up your budget, establish an "emergency fund." The amount will vary, depending on where you are going and how far you are traveling. (You will need more, for example, if you are visiting a large city across the country than if you are staying in a rural area several hundred miles away.) **Never** carry your emergency funds in cash; it could be stolen, you could lose it, or you might be tempted to spend it. Ideally, it should be an unspoken-for amount on your credit card, a stash of traveler's checks that can be replaced if lost or stolen, or an amount left in

your bank at home if you have access to it through electronic banking.

BEING TRAVEL-SMART: PREVENTING VACATION WOES

There are some things you can't do anything about--like a week of rainy, overcast skies. But there are plenty of travel woes you can prevent by doing a little careful planning and taking some common-sense precautions.

• Travelers are a favorite target of thieves and pickpockets, so take extra care while on vacation. To foil hotel-room burglary, hang the "do not disturb" sign outside your door whenever you leave-- thieves will think the room is occupied.

• Never carry large amounts of cash or unnecessary credit cards in your wallet. Do carry most of your money in traveler's checks, which can be replaced if they are lost or stolen; make sure you record the serial numbers from the checks and keep them in a separate, safe place.

You can reduce the amount of cash you need to carry by paying for rooms in advance with personal checks; most businesses ask that you simply allow enough time in advance so the check will clear.

If you have a major credit card, you will probably be able to use personal checks at many businesses in the United States. You will also be able to charge purchases, gasoline, lodging, and other necessities with major credit cards.

To be on the safe side, have an extra stash of cash in a separate, safe place, such as in a cosmetic case or tucked in the bottom of a garment bag.

• Keep careful guard while you are in airports, train stations, or bus terminals. Keep your luggage firmly between your feet and your briefcase or handbag tucked firmly beneath your arm at all times.

• When walking, carry your briefcase or handbag on the side away from the street; a favorite ploy is for passing motorcyclists or bicyclists to snatch bags.

• Whenever you are seated in a restaurant, keep your handbag on your lap and your briefcase firmly between your feet.

• Never put your handbag or briefcase in an empty seat next to you on an airplane, train, or bus; keep it in your lap or firmly between your feet.

- Avoid wearing expensive jewelry while on public transportation or while walking on the street. If you do decide to wear gold chains or other expensive jewelry, conceal beneath your clothing or coat until you reach your destination.
- Avoid carrying an expensive camera in open while sightseeing. If you can, keep your camera concealed in a canvas bag, oversized handbag, or other bag while you aren't using it--an expensive camera will attract thieves.
- If you are driving your own car or a rental car, keep valuables out of sight--ideally, locked in the trunk. Never leave suitcases, cameras, or other bags where people can see them, even through the windows of your locked car. Leaving these things in open view advertises that you're from out of town and acts as an enticement to thieves.
- If you use credit cards while traveling, consider asking your bank to temporarily raise your credit limit in order to enable you to cover emergencies, such as stolen cash or luggage. (Then, of course, avoid the temptation to use the "extra" funds on souvenirs or sightseeing.)
- Take two major credit cards if you can, and alternate their use.
- Whenever you make a credit card purchase, ask the clerk for all the carbons from your receipt--you'll prevent the clerk from tampering with the amount and pocketing the change.
- If you have secured a hotel room or rental car with a credit card, make sure you ask the clerk to release the hold on your card as soon as you settle the bill. Forgetting to ask the clerk for a release can result in a three- or four-week hold on your card for the maximum amount you could have spent, impacting your ability to make charges elsewhere.
- To avoid getting caught without a room at a hotel where you have reservations, guarantee the room on your credit card and ask the hotel to mail you a written confirmation. If you don't have a credit card, send a personal check in advance for the first night's charge and ask the hotel for a receipt and a written confirmation.
- Arrive early in the day. If the hotel has overbooked, you'll have a better chance of getting a room--and many hotels won't guarantee a room after 6 p.m. If you get delayed en route and can see that you will be late, call the hotel and request that they hold the room for you.

- If a hotel where you have guaranteed a room overbooks and refuses you a room when you arrive, stand firm. By law, the hotel will have to make certain concessions for you if you have already secured the room with a credit card or personal check. Generally, the hotel will have to find you comparable accommodations somewhere else, pay for your transportation to the new lodging, and reimburse you for any long-distance calls you need to make to inform associates of your new location. If the hotel is a member of a chain (such as a Hilton, Marriott, or Sheraton), it will probably try to relocate you within the chain.
- To avoid getting bumped from an airline, request "advanced check-in" when you purchase your ticket; you'll get a boarding pass (complete with your assigned seat) with your ticket. If you will be changing flights in the middle of your trip, ask for all the boarding passes at your first check-in point.
- Arrive at the airport early--at least forty-five minutes before departure time (ninety minutes before departure time for an international flight). Check in as soon as you arrive at the airport to assure your seat assignment.
- If you travel during holiday seasons, try to fly on "off" days (Tuesday, Wednesday, and Thursday). Fly as early in the day as you can, and schedule any connecting flights at least one hour apart to allow for unforseen delays.
- If the worst scenario occurs and your flight is overbooked, you *do* have some options, by law. The airline will probably ask for volunteers who are willing to wait until the next flight; in return, they will offer free tickets, cash incentives, or other rewards. If you're not pressed for time, you can get a good deal by volunteering to wait.

  Airlines are also required to compensate you if they cannot get you to your destination within an hour of the original flight's arrival time; most are required to give you the price of a one-way ticket (a maximum price may apply). Find out your rights before you leave home, and stand up for them!
- If the airline loses your luggage, it is required by law to compensate you. You'll need to submit receipts or an itemized list of what was in your luggage. There are limits on required reimbursement; your homeowner's or tenant's insurance may pay the rest.
- If the value of your luggage contents exceeds $1,200, you should

take out additional valuation coverage when you check in at the airport. If your luggage is lost or damaged, you will be compensated by the insurance company.

FLYING THE FRIENDLY SKIES: MAKE THE BEST OF AIR TRAVEL

With an increasing number of Americans taking to the air, the country's major airlines are responding by offering more flights, better prices, and other consumer enticements. If you know the lingo, you can take advantage of these offers--and make the best of your flight dollar!

To start, learn the basic types of flights and airfares. In general, most airlines offer the following:

Nonstop flights. A nonstop flight leaves one city and does not stop until it reaches its destination.

Direct flights. A direct flight means that you will stay on the same plane throughout the flight, but you may land many times between the city where you board the plane and your destination. On a direct flight, however, you will not be required to change planes during a stopover.

First class. First-class seats are generally located in the front of the plane, separated from the rest of the seats by a curtain or other divider. Most planes have only eight or ten rows of first-class seats available. The seats are wider--there are only four seats to a row instead of six--and there is more leg room between rows. Various amenities are offered (such as in-flight movies or free champagne), and meals are usually nicer. But you pay a price for the service: first-class seats usually run 33 percent higher than coach seats on the same flight.

Coach. Coach seats are the "regular" seats, comprising the majority of the available seats on the plane.

Super-saver. Super-saver rates are available on many flights and on many airlines, but certain restrictions apply. You generally have to buy your ticket in advance--at least a week before departure, but sometimes as long as two or three weeks. You generally have to stay at your destination for a specified period of time--and most airlines require that you stay for at least one Saturday. And most super-saver flights depart in the middle of the week and during slow travel times. But the savings can be substantial: super-saver tickets are usually only half of what regular coach tickets cost.

Promotional fares. If you're planning on air travel, watch for promotional fares--they are often offered by an airline when it starts traveling to a new destination, opens a new terminal, introduces a new type of aircraft, or even when it responds to stiff competition. Promotional fares can be as much as 50 percent less than regular coach, but they are generally for a limited time and apply only to a limited area. There will usually be only a few dozen seats on the flight available at promotional fare, so you need to act quickly when promotional fares are announced.

Children's fares. Not all airlines offer children's fares, but those who do usually offer a 25 to 40 percent discount to children under the age of twelve. On some airlines, children under the age of two fly free. If you are traveling with children, be sure to ask whether the airline offers a discount.

There are other ways you can save money on air travel, too, if you are willing to meet the restrictions or put up with some inconvenience. Depending on your circumstances, you might consider the following:

Standby. Basically, "standby" passengers do just that--they stand by until all ticketholders have boarded the flight. If there are seats left over, they board; if not, they wait for another flight. All standby seats are given on a first-come, first-served basis, so if you decide to fly standby, get to the airport at least two hours in advance of the flight's departure time. Standby is obviously most successful during slow travel times, early in the morning, late at night, and on weekdays. You run the risk of getting stuck in an airport for hours, but you can save 65 to 75 percent on your flight if you're willing to gamble.

Night fares. Some airlines offer discounted prices to people who are willing to travel very early in the morning or very late at night; some airlines dub these their "red-eye" flights.

Charter flights. While charter flights are not widely available, you may be able to find one booked by a group that has some available seats. Generally, these are available to popular tourist areas (such as Las Vegas) and fly at irregular hours. If you are interested in finding a charter flight, contact a travel agent.

Unlimited mileage passes. Some airlines offer unlimited mileage passes: you purchase a "pass" for a specified price that enables you to go anywhere the airline flies during a specified period of time.

Frequent flyer programs. Some airlines offer "free" tickets to customers who total a certain number of air miles within a specified period of time. If you have to fly frequently on business, you may be able to "earn" free tickets for vacations.

Off-season fares. During months of the year when air travel is traditionally slow, some airlines offer reduced rates to attract customers. You might be able to get a real bargain if you're willing to vacation in an off-season.

Changing planes en route. You might be able to save substantially if you are willing to fly one airline partway to your destination and another the rest of the way. You'll have the hassle of changing planes midway, but you can sometimes save hundreds of dollars.

Avoiding major airports. You can sometimes save money by flying to a nearby smaller airport rather than a large city's major airport. Even after you pay for additional ground transportation, you might be able to save substantially.

Flying between major cities. If you're traveling cross-country, you'll almost always be able to save substantially if you fly between two major cities. Why? The competition is stiffest on these heavily traveled routes, so airlines lower their fares to attract customers. Again, you may have to pay for additional ground transportation to get to your destination, or you may have to ask friends or relatives to travel a little out of their way to pick you up--but the savings may be worth it!

A few tricks of the trade can make airline travel more comfortable. If you'll be flying, consider these tips:

- Chew gum during takeoff and landing to help your ears adjust to changes in pressure.
- If you are traveling with a baby, offer the baby a bottle or pacifier during takeoff and landing to help compensate for pressure changes.
- Avoid drinks that contain caffeine while in flight.
- Cabin air is pressurized and very dry. Carry some lip balm or petroleum jelly to soothe your lips. If you have dry skin, you might also consider a light moisturizer or body lotion.
- The pressurization on airplanes causes your body to swell if the airplane exceeds an altitude of 5,000 feet (which almost always

occurs on flights of over one hour). To be your most comfortable, wear loose shoes and loose clothing made of natural fibers (such as cotton, wool, or linen).

- Airline cabins tend to be cool; even if you are traveling during warm weather, you should carry a light jacket or sweater on the plane so you can stay comfortable. (Almost all airlines provide a few light blankets, but not all passengers will be able to have one.)
- If you will be traveling on a long flight and want to sleep, avoid caffeinated beverages or alcohol. Carry earplugs, an eyeshade, and a light jacket or sweater. Ask the flight attendant for a pillow early in the flight.
- If you can manage it, pack all your items in carry-on luggage; most airlines allow you to have a cosmetic case, a small carry-on suitcase, and a garment bag. To meet flight restrictions, these usually must be small enough to fit under your seat or in the overhead compartment; flight attendants will usually hang your garment bag in a compartment at the front or rear of the plane. Check with the reservation clerk when you purchase your ticket to find out what the airline's specifications are. If you can possibly do it, you will save yourself time at the baggage claim area and will prevent the possibility of lost luggage.

GOING BY RAIL: THE JOY OF TRAIN TRAVEL

Train service is not available in all states, but if you have the time to travel by train and service is available to your destination, you'll discover a wonderful, relaxing way to see the U.S.A.!

Obviously a train can't speed you to your destination as quickly as can a plane--but you'll discover all kinds of benefits from train travel if it suits your schedule. First and foremost is the scenery: nothing can compare to winding through the heart of America with an unhampered view from a relaxed vantage point. Attendants are specifically trained to pamper riders. And you'll find a variety of extras, like hospitality hours, bingo games, free newspapers, and so on.

Most trains feature dining cars, snack cars, or cafe cars where you can select from the menu--but if you're traveling on a budget, you are welcome to bring picnic fare aboard.

Like planes, trains offer a variety of accommodations and a

broad range of fare plans to meet different budgets. Depending on the train you board, you may find the following:

Family bedrooms. These small, private rooms generally sleep four (sometimes five) in upper and lower bunks. Each room has a window, so you can watch the scenery go by as you lay in bed.

Economy bedrooms. Economy bedrooms, which sleep two to three, feature one upper bunk, one lower bunk, and one hideaway bed. Like family bedrooms, these feature privacy and a window for a view.

Slumbercoach seats. The most economical way to get a comfortable bed on a train is with a slumbercoach seat--a seat that converts into a bed. Slumbercoach seats are available in single and double size. You lose privacy--you sleep in the seat you sit in all day--but prices are considerably less than for a bedroom.

Reclining seats. Almost all other seats on the train are reclining--if you can't afford a slumbercoach seat, you can still recline your seat and tuck a pillow beneath your head when you're ready to sleep.

Point-to-point fares. These are the simplest, but most expensive, tickets. You purchase a full-priced ticket that enables you to travel any time between two points, making as many stopovers as you want. Some train lines offer only point-topoint tickets, so check when you make reservations.

Round-trip excursion fares. If you're making a round trip (traveling both ways by train), you should check into round-trip excursion fares. Restrictions will apply--you generally have to travel at certain times, for certain periods, and you have to have a certain number of stopovers en route. As with airfare, however, the savings can be worth it: tickets are generally 25 percent less.

One-way-plus fares. This is like the "buy one, get one free" deal you see in some retail ads. In essence, you purchase a one-way ticket to a certain destination, and the train offers you your return ticket at a fraction of the price--usually between $1 and $10. These are promotional fares that apply only to certain routes at certain times of the year, so watch for these specials.

Family-plan fares. Family fares are generally available year-round with no stopover or other restrictions. Generally, one adult pays full fare. The second adult and children aged twelve to twenty-one each pay half fare. Children aged two to eleven each pay one-fourth fare, and children under the age of two travel free.

Sleeping accommodations are extra.

Children's fares. If you're not taking advantage of a family-plan fare, you can still generally get special children's fares. In most cases, children under the age of two ride free; children aged two to twelve who travel with an adult pay half the adult fare. Children over the age of twelve generally pay full fare.

Before you make reservations, check to find out whether the train is offering any special fares. During certain times some train lines offer a single fare that allows you to travel without restriction within a certain geographical area for as long as thirty days.

To make the most of train travel, follow these guidelines:

- Before you make reservations or decide on your trip details, get the necessary materials: the latest timetable (which lists schedules), a list of applicable fares, information about on-board services, and a system map. Plot out your trip and decide whether you can make the necessary connections economically.
- Pay for your ticket in advance, ideally when you make your reservations. If you have already purchased a ticket, you won't have to pay any fare increases that occur before you actually board the train.
- Before you make reservations, consider the timing of the train along its route. You won't want to pass through an area with breathtaking scenery at midnight!
- Always make reservations. Some trains have small cars or areas where people without reservations can travel, but many trains will not accept passengers who do not have reservations. *All* sleeping accommodations require reservations. If you fail to make reservations and want to travel anyway, arrive at the train station early--at least one hour before departure--and tell the station ticket agent to alert you in case of cancellations.
- If you need to cancel a ticket you have paid for, you can generally receive a refund if you cancel it at least thirty minutes before departure time.
- If you can afford it, purchase sleeping accommodations if you will be on the train overnight. You'll be better rested and relaxed when you reach your destination.
- Avoid baggage hassles by compacting into carry-on luggage. On most trains, each ticketed passenger can carry on two pieces of luggage--and they don't need to be as small as on a plane. You'll save the risk of lost or stolen luggage and will save time on the

other end as well.

- If you are traveling long-distance and need to check baggage, plan to arrive at the station at least thirty minutes before departure. Most trains will allow each ticketed passenger to check three pieces of luggage.

- Remember that trains, like planes, can run behind schedule. If you are making a connecting train, allow at least one hour between connections--more if you can.

- Try to avoid extremely long layovers in train stations-many are small, and most of the smaller stations are open only during the hours the trains actually arrive and depart. If you do get stuck with a long layover, plan to take a cab to town and relax at a restaurant or take in a movie.

- As with planes, avoid holiday travel if you can. The year-end holiday season is the busiest for the nation's trains, and you'll naturally have greater difficulty staying on schedule, getting prompt service (such as meals), keeping track of luggage, and so on. When you can, make other travel arrangements.

HOME AWAY FROM HOME: THE BED AND BREAKFAST INN

If you want a personal, homey experience with a cozy bedroom and a mouth-watering breakfast served by a friendly host, you'll want to try a bed and breakfast inn next time you travel!

What are they?

Simply stated, a bed and breakfast is usually a private home that has opened its doors to paying customers. No two bed and breakfasts are alike--and that's part of the charm, say those who like to stay there. One bed and breakfast might be a basic home with a shared bathroom; another might be a luxurious mansion complete with a sauna and pool. Generally speaking, a "bed and breakfast" is a private home that has been opened to guests; a "bed and breakfast inn" is a small hostelry (usually consisting of only four to six rooms) that is run more like a warm, informal hotel.

Regardless of what the accommodations are like, bed and breakfasts are famous for their old-fashioned hospitality. Many hosts provide hand-stitched quilts, good-night mints, or a pot of steaming tea to make guests feel welcome. Breakfast the next morning is always included in the price of the room, making it a great deal. Because you'll be sitting around the breakfast table with other guests, a bed and breakfast is for you if you enjoy meeting other people.

There are a few disadvantages to bed and breakfasts. Obviously, the quality will be inconsistent--you might stay at a real gem one night, and at something less than desirable the next. You can increase your odds by phoning ahead and asking about accommodations, but even homes that have been inspected and listed in directories can vary substantially in quality.

In some bed and breakfasts, you have limited privacy and independence. In a private home, you will probably have to share a bathroom--and you may have to keep the same hours the family does.

You may find that the advantages outweigh the disadvantages, however. If you like a cozy, homey atmosphere, bed and breakfasts are for you! Typically, your host can advise you about local shopping, restaurants, entertainment, and cultural attractions--and you'll get the kind of personalized advice you'll never get elsewhere. And, best of all, they're a bargain: a night at a bed and breakfast costs about half what a hotel in the same town would cost.

For the most successful bed and breakfast experience, follow these suggestions:

- Do your homework ahead of time. Before you make reservations, invest in a call to the bed and breakfast you're considering. Find out where the bed and breakfast is located--is it in a safe neighborhood? Is it close to your planned activities? Is a private bath available? If not, how many guests will share the bathroom? Will you have use of the telephone, television, kitchen, and living room? Is there a swimming pool? Is parking available, and is it free?
- If you are traveling with pets or children, make sure you understand the policies regarding each.
- Always make reservations. Since bed and breakfasts have only a few rooms, they are often booked. If you show up unannounced, you likely won't get a room.
- Find out ahead of time what payment policies are. Are credit cards accepted? Personal checks? What's the per-night rate? Is there a deposit required? Is there a minimum required stay? (Some bed and breakfasts require a minimum of two nights.) If you should have to cancel your reservations, what is the refund policy?

- Remember that you are sharing someone's private home, so rules of common courtesy apply. Keep noise to a minimum, especially late at night and early in the morning.
- Keep reasonable hours. You shouldn't be traipsing in and out of someone's home at all hours of the night. Try to arrive in the late afternoon or early evening; if you can see that you will be delayed, phone your hosts and let them know when you'll be arriving.
- If you share a bathroom, leave it clean each time you use it. Never monopolize a shared bathroom.
- You're staying in a private home, so remember to return the house key before you leave.

VACATION TIME-SHARE: CAN IT WORK FOR YOU?

What is vacation time-sharing?

In this country, vacation time-sharing had its beginnings during the mid-1970s housing slump, when developers were having a difficult time selling their resort condominiums. What had been a popular concept in Europe for decades caught on here. Simply stated, an owner sells fifty-two weekly "shares" in each condominium, resort home, or apartment.

Since the concept started, developers have sold time shares in luxury hotels, condominiums, resort lodging of all kinds, cabins, campgrounds, ski lodges, cruise ships, yachts, and houseboats.

Here's how it works: you pay one lump sum (usually at least several thousand dollars) to buy your "share." That share entitles you to spend a certain number of weeks (usually one or two) a year for a specific number of years (current time-share packages vary anywhere from two years to several generations) at the condominium, beach house, ski cabin, or whatever you have purchased into. In addition, you pay an annual "maintenance fee" that takes care of any required repairs, remodeling, yard maintenance, and so on.

How do developers decide who gets the lodging at what times of the year? Requirements vary, but most time-share plans require you to submit your request about a year in advance. You are usually asked to submit your first three preferences, and then developers work to hopefully give everyone at least one preferred time slot. In some time-share programs, you have the choice of several different condominiums or resort areas, so you can vary your vacation from one year to the next, depending on availability of sites.

Time-sharing is a good concept that works well for many people--but, unfortunately, there have been some abuses by developers who are not ethical. To avoid getting into a bad situation, do your homework before you sign the dotted line! You should check out the following before you sign any contracts or pay any money:

- Consider your personal style. Will you want to stay in the same place year after year--or would you rather visit different places? Are you the type who can schedule your vacation up to a year ahead of time--or does your schedule change too frequently?
- Insist on visiting the resort and seeing the actual condominium, cabin, apartment, boat, or unit you are buying. You might be promised a beautiful natural lake with sandy beaches, only to find a small man-made lake in the middle of an industrial section with a skimpy strip of sand along one side. If you can arrange it, spend a weekend at the resort before you make any decisions. Most time-share companies will agree to rent a unit to prospective buyers.
- Look for signs of substantial investment--quality construction, well-maintained units, carefully planned landscaping, and so on. No one can guarantee how the units will be maintained ten years from now, but if the developers are building a quality resort, they will likely be more careful with their investment.
- Find out ahead of time whether the time-share is deeded. In essence, a deeded time-share gives you actual ownership interest in the real estate. Non-deeded time-share, on the other hand, simply gives you the right to use the property for a certain number of years.
- Find out ahead of time what the annual maintenance fee covers; insist on a detailed breakdown. Find out whether the fee is "open-ended," which means the fee can be increased without limit from one year to the next.
- Get a complete detailing of the total cost, including finance charges, travel expenses, and annual fees. Then compare the weekly cost of your time-share with the weekly cost of renting a similar property in the same area. If you're paying substantially more, you might want to reconsider.
- Find out what your cancellation rights are--and then make sure they are outlined in the written contract.
- Find out whether you can sell your time-share. If you do decide to

sell, who dictates the price? Some contracts state that you can sell your time-share for no more than the price of your original investment. Is there a transfer fee if you sell?

- Find out what your rights are if the developer decides to sell the development. You should retain the rights to your property for the specified length of the contract, no matter what.

- Find out what your rights are if the developer or management company has financial problems. Your contract should give you the right to use your property even if a bank or other third party buys out your contract or takes over the property. One item to watch for is what's called a "non-disturbance" clause--it protects you from being liable if someone makes a claim against the developer or management company.

- If the property is still under development, you should get a written commitment that the property will be developed as promised, as well as a commitment for a completion date. You should also insist that your money be held in escrow until the property is completed as agreed.

- If you can, find out who the other owners are; the developer should be willing to give you some names. Call them and ask whether they have been pleased with the property and the management company.

- If you are seriously interested, check out the developer's reputation. The local Better Business Bureau, local real estate agents, the state licensing division, or the state attorney general's office should be able to alert you to any complaints that have been filed about the time-share or the developer.

- Make sure any oral promises you have been given are included in the written contract. Remember: if they aren't written down, they don't exist!

- Before you sign any contract, have an attorney review it. You'll have to pay a fee for the attorney's service, but it may save you thousands of dollars over a period of many years.

- Finally, refuse to be pressured by a salesperson. A reputable developer will allow you time to check out the property, contact other owners, and think over the decision. The law in many states also requires that the developer give you a "cooling-off" period after you sign the contract during which you can change your mind. Find out the law, and insist on your rights. Never try to make a decision under the pressure of a time limit.

All recipes yield 2-4 servings.

BEVERAGE RECIPES

Strawberry Nog

2 eggs

3 T. honey

1 C. apricot nectar

1 C. orange juice

1/2 C. nonfat dry milk

1 T. lemon juice

1 C. strawberries (partially
 thawed, if frozen)

strawberry slices for garnish

In a small bowl, beat eggs until thick. Gradually add the honey, beating constantly. Set aside. In a blender combine the apricot nectar, orange juice, milk powder, and lemon juice; cover and blend until well mixed. Add the strawberries and blend until smooth. Pour into four glasses; garnish with strawberry slices. Store in refrigerator if desired by covering container; stir well before serving.

Berry Milk

2 C. milk

1 C. fresh strawberries

4 T. sugar

2 T. orange juice
 (not concentrate)

Pour all ingredients into blender; blend until smooth. Serve immediately. Makes two servings.

Orange-Pineapple Cooler

1 6-oz. can frozen
 orange juice concentrate

1 C. pineapple juice

1 1/2 C. water

1 C. lemon sherbet

In a large pitcher, combine frozen orange juice, pineapple juice, and water; stir until orange juice is thawed. Pour orange juice mixture into four glasses, dividing evenly; top each with one scoop sherbet. Stir.

Three-Citrus Punch

1 quart orange juice

1 6-oz. can frozen
   lemonade concentrate

1 6-oz. can frozen
   limeade concentrate

2 C. water

1 1-liter bottle lemon-lime soda

Orange, lemon, and lime
   slices for garnish

In a large container or punch bowl, combine orange juice, lemonade, limeade, and water; stir until frozen concentrates are completely thawed and well blended. Chill until ready to serve. When ready to serve, stir in lemon-lime soda and float fruit slices on top. Makes eight 8-oz. servings.

Orange-Vanilla Frosty

1 quart orange juice

1 C. vanilla ice cream

1 12-oz. can cream soda

Pour equal parts of orange juice into four glasses. Top with one scoop ice cream; drizzle approximately 1/4 C. soda over each. Stir and serve immediately.

Minty Lemonade

1 C. sugar

1 1/4 C. water

1/2 C. orange juice
  (juice of 1 orange)

3/4 C. lemon juice
  (juice of 3 lemons)

1/2 C. fresh mint leaves

In a saucepan, combine sugar and water; bring to a boil, reduce heat, and cook for 5 minutes. Cool. Add fruit juices, and stir in mint leaves. Cover and let stand for 1 hour. Strain into a glass jar, screw on lid tightly, and store in refrigerator. To serve, pour 1/3 C. mixture into each glass, and fill with crushed ice and water. Makes five to six glasses lemonade.

24-Hour Root Beer

2 C. sugar

2 T. root beer extract

1 tsp. dry yeast

1 gallon warm water

In a plastic or glass gallon jug or bottle, combine sugar, root beer extract, and yeast. Fill jug half full with warm water, and shake well to dissolve sugar. Continue filling container with warm water to within 1/2 inch of the top. Cap tightly, and put in the refrigerator for at least 24 hours. Serve over crushed ice.

Home-Style Root Beer

2 C. sugar

1/3 bottle root beer extract

1 quart water

1 1/2 tsp. yeast

Combine all ingredients in a blender and mix thoroughly. Pour into a glass.or plastic gallon jug and finish filling with lukewarm water. Cap tightly and let stand at room temperature for 8 hours. Refrigerate; serve when well-chilled.

Raspberry Slush

2 C. sugar

3 1/2 C. water

1 C. orange juice

1 16-oz. can crushed
  pineapple with juice

2 10-oz. pkgs. frozen
  raspberries, thawed
  and drained

In a saucepan, heat sugar and water until sugar is dissolved; cool. Stir in orange juice, pineapple, and raspberries. Stir until well mixed. Freeze in covered container. To serve, place a scoop of slush in a glass; pour in ginger ale or lemon-lime soda. Makes enough to fill 12 glasses.

Hot Mulled Cider

1 1/2 quarts cranberry juice

2 quarts apple juice

2 C. unsweetened pineapple
  juice

1/2 C. brown sugar,
  firmly packed

1/2 tsp. salt

4 cinnamon sticks

1 1/2 tsp. whole cloves

1/4 C. butter or margarine

Pour cranberry juice, apple juice, and pineapple juice into a large kettle. Tie cinnamon sticks and whole cloves in a cheesecloth bag, and add to the juice mixture. Stir in brown sugar and salt. Heat to boiling; reduce heat and simmer 30 minutes. Remove spice bag. Add butter just before serving. Makes enough to fill 35 to 40 punch cups.

Sunny Citrus Slush

1 1/4 C. sugar

1 1/2 C. water

1 6-oz. can frozen orange
  juice concentrate

1 6-oz. can frozen lemonade
  concentrate

1 24-oz. can pineapple juice

1 1/2 C. cold water

2 quarts ginger ale or
  lemon-lime soda, chilled

Orange, lemon, and lime slices
  for garnish

In a large kettle, combine sugar and 1 1/2 C. water; bring to a boil and cook until sugar is dissolved. Remove from heat. Stir in juice concentrates, pineapple juice, and cold water until well blended. Pour into a 9 x 13 baking dish, cover, and freeze overnight. Cut frozen mixture into 24 squares; place squares in bottom of a punch bowl, and pour chilled soda over squares. Stir until the mixture is slushy, and serve by ladling into glasses. Garnish each glass with a slice of orange, lemon, or lime. Makes about 1 gallon, or 16 servings.

Banana Fruit Punch

2 1/2 C.sugar

2 1/2 C. water

1 24-oz. can pineapple juice

Juice of 2 oranges

Juice of 2 lemons

3 bananas, mashed with a fork

Ginger ale or lemon-lime
   soda, chilled

Crushed ice

In a saucepan, heat sugar and water together until sugar is completely dissolved; remove from heat. Stir in pineapple juice, orange juice, lemon juice, and bananas; mix well. Pour into a container, cover, and freeze, stirring occasionally during freezing process. When ready to serve, fill a glass 1/3 full with fruit slush, 1/3 full with chilled soda, and 1/3 full with crushed ice. Makes enough to fill 25 glasses.

Lemon-Lime Quencher

2 quarts cold water

1 6-oz. can frozen orange
  juice concentrate

1 6-oz. can frozen lemonade
  concentrate

1 6-oz. can frozen limeade
  concentrate

1 32-oz. bottle ginger ale, chilled

Fresh mint leaves for garnish

Combine all ingredients until well mixed; pour over crushed ice and garnish with mint leaves. Serves 12.

Chocolate Eggnog

1 1/2 quarts chilled eggnog

3/4 C. chocolate syrup

3/4 C. whipping cream

4 tsp. sugar

1 1/2 tsp. cocoa

1/2 oz. semisweet chocolate,
  grated as a garnish

In a large punch bowl, combine eggnog and chocolate syrup. Set aside. In a small bowl, combine cream, sugar, and cocoa. Whip at high speed until stiff. Spoon cream onto eggnog and sprinkle with chocolate. Makes 12 servings.

Cranberry Eggnog

3 eggs, separated

1/2 C. sugar

1 pint cranberry juice

1/2 pint whipping cream

Beat egg yolks with a fork or wire whisk until lemon-colored and thick. Add half the sugar, and blend thoroughly. Add cranberry juice slowly and gradually, beating until blended. Add remaining sugar, and stir until dissolved. Set aside. Whip egg whites until stiff peaks form. Whip cream until stiff. Fold cream into egg whites, then into cranberry juice mixture. Ladle into cups. Serves six.

Orange-Grapefruit Nog

1 C. orange juice

1 C. grapefruit juice

1/2 C. orange sherbet

1 1/2 C. cold milk

Combine all ingredients in blender; cover and blend until smooth. Chill, or serve immediately over crushed ice. Serves four.

Fruited Slush

2 6-oz. cans frozen orange juice concentrate

2 C. fresh or frozen fruit (raspberries, peach slices,
   strawberry slices, or blueberries)

1 pint orange sherbet

Prepare orange juice according to directions on can. In each of six glasses, place a generous spoonful of fruit. Pour in orange juice until glasses are three-fourths full. Top with a scoop of sherbet, and garnish with additional fruit. Serves six.

Spicy Apple Cooler

6 C. chilled unsweetened
   apple juice
3 T. lime juice
3 T. lemon juice
2 T. honey

1/4 tsp. cinnamon
1/8 tsp. ground cloves
Lemon-lime soda or sparkling
   water, chilled

Combine juices, honey, cinnamon, and cloves in a blender; blend for one minute, or until smooth. Fill 6 tall glasses with ice; pour juice mixture to fill glasses two-thirds full. Fill with soda or sparkling water and stir gently. Serves six.

Hot Spiced Tomato Juice

2 1/2 C. tomato juice
3 T. brown sugar, firmly packed
3 whole cloves

1 stick cinnamon
2 lemon slices

In a saucepan, combine all ingredients; bring to a boil. Reduce heat and simmer 5 minutes. Serves four.

Easy Eggnog

2 eggs, well beaten
1 15-oz. can sweetened
   condensed milk
1 tsp. vanilla

1/4 tsp. salt
1 quart milk
1/2 pint cream, whipped
Dash nutmeg

Mix eggs, condensed milk, vanilla, and salt until well blended; gradually blend in milk. Fold in whipped cream, and sprinkle with nutmeg. Ladle into cups.

Fresh Fruit Slush

Juice from 2 large oranges
1 C. sliced strawberries
1/2 C. seedless green grapes

2 medium bananas, sliced
1/2 6-oz. can frozen lemonade
   concentrate, softened

In a large bowl, combine ingredients. Stir until mixed. Spoon into four plastic cups; cover with foil and freeze until mixture is slightly icy (about 1 1/2 hours). Eat as is, or pour chilled lemon-lime soda over slush.

Strawberry-Pineapple Cooler

1 pint strawberries, sliced	1/2 C. pineapple juice
1/2 C. sugar	1 quart milk
1/4 C. orange juice	1 pint pineapple sherbet

Mash strawberries; stir in sugar. Add orange and pineapple juices. Blend in milk. Pour into four chilled glasses; top each with a scoop of sherbet. (You can use 1 10-oz. pkg. of frozen strawberries instead of fresh ones; eliminate the sugar in the recipe.)

Cantaloupe Shake

1 1/2 C. water	2 T. wheat germ
4 T. nonfat dry milk powder	1 C. diced cantaloupe
4 T. honey	4 ice cubes

Combine all ingredients but ice cubes in a blender; blend at high speed until smooth. Add ice cubes, one at a time, while blender is still running. Pour into tall glasses. Serves two. (You can use almost any fruit for this shake: try substituting for the cantaloupe 2 peaches, 1 banana, 1 C. strawberries, 1 C. raspberries, 1 C. blueberries, or 2 oranges.)

Apple-Cranberry Drink

2 small oranges, peeled with pits removed	2 T. honey
2 C. water	2 medium apples, cored but not peeled, cut into chunks
1/2 C. cranberries, stems removed	

Put oranges in blender; process until liquified. Add other ingredients, one at a time, and blend until smooth after each ingredient. Serves four.

Strawberry Lemonade

1 6-oz. can frozen lemonade
concentrate

Water

1 C. fresh strawberries

Sugar to taste

Mint leaves for garnish

Prepare lemonade according to directions on can, stirring in water as indicated. Slice 1/3 of the berries; set aside, covered, in the refrigerator. Puree remaining berries in blender; add sugar to taste. Add strawberry puree to lemonade, stirring to mix well. Pour into tall glasses to serve, garnishing with mint leaf and fresh sliced strawberries. Serves four.

Spiced Mocha

1 C. non-dairy creamer

1 C. instant chocolate drink mix
(5 envelopes)

2/3 C. instant coffee

1/2 C. sugar

1/2 tsp. cinnamon

1/4 tsp. nutmeg

Mix well and store in a covered container. To serve, put 3 heaping teaspoons of mix in a coffee mug; add 6 ounces hot water. To add even more spice flavor, stir with a cinnamon stick.

Hot Spiced Grape Punch

4 C. water

3/4 C. sugar

2 sticks cinnamon

8 whole cloves

4 C. grape juice

2 C. orange juice

In a saucepan, combine water, sugar, cinnamon, and cloves. Bring to a boil, boil for 10 minutes, strain, and cool. Stir in grape juice and orange juice; heat through and serve hot, garnished with lemon slices. Serves eight.

Jamaican Citrus Punch

2 oranges

40 whole cloves

1 46-oz. can orange
   Hawaiian punch

2 C. grapefruit juice

1/2 C. light corn syrup

Wash oranges well, and stud each orange with 20 whole cloves. Bake in a 400-degree oven for 1 hour; oranges will turn dark brown. Place oranges in the bottom of a deep bowl; mix remaining ingredients, and pour over oranges. Chill for 8 hours. When ready to serve, remove oranges; peel and section. Ladle drink into sugar-rimmed glasses, and garnish with orange slices. Serves eight.

Marshmallow-Peach Shake

1 1/2 C. milk

1 7-oz. jar marshmallow creme

1 C. ice cubes

2 C. peeled peach slices

Put milk and marshmallow creme in blender; cover and process until smooth. Add ice cubes and peach slices; process until smooth. Pour into two tall glasses and garnish with additional peach slices if desired.

Orange-Mocha Cooler

2 C. orange juice

1 C. milk

3 T. chocolate syrup

1 C. coffee-flavored ice cream

1 1/2 C. lemon-lime soda, chilled

In large pitcher, combine orange juice, milk, and chocolate syrup; stir to mix well. Pour, dividing evenly, into four tall glasses. Top each with a generous scoop of ice cream, and finish filling with soda. Stir and serve.

Pineapple Pick-Me-Up

4 scoops vanilla ice cream

1/4 C. sugar

1/3 C. chilled pineapple juice

4 C. milk

8 pineapple chunks

In a large mixing bowl, combine ice cream, juice, and sugar; beat until thoroughly blended. Gradually add milk, beating until blended and smooth. Pour into four glasses. Thread two pineapple chunks on each of four toothpicks; garnish drinks. Serves four.

Fruited Ice Cube Drinks

3 C. orange juice	3/4 C. pineapple juice
3 C. sugar	3/4 C. lemon juice
6 C. water	Lemon-lime soda

In a large pitcher or kettle, mix orange juice, sugar, water, pineapple juice, and lemon juice until well blended. Pour into ice cube trays and freeze. When ready to serve, place 4-5 cubes in each tall glass; fill with chilled lemon-lime soda. If desired, garnish with orange slices or pineapple wedges.

Hot Pineapple Punch

1 C. apricot nectar	4 C. pineapple juice
2 C. apple cider	3/4 C. brown sugar
1 C. orange juice	6 whole cloves

Combine all ingredients; heat to boiling. Reduce heat and simmer for 10 minutes. Strain out cloves. Serve punch hot.

Make It Healthy . . .

Want your drink to be healthy, as well as delicious?

It's easy: make it with orange juice!

Just one six-ounce glass of orange juice gives you all the vitamin C you need for the day. What does that mean to you? It means healthy gums, strong bones and teeth, a plentiful supply of blood, and speed in healing from injuries. That's not all: if you make your drink with frozen orange juice concentrate, it will be low in sugar, sodium, fats, and calories.

Bottoms up to good health!

Orange-Peach Delight

2 large ripe peaches, peeled, pitted, and sliced

1 C. orange juice

1/3 C. lemon juice

1/2 C. sugar

1/4 tsp. cinnamon

Crushed ice

Combine all ingredients in a blender; blend until smooth. Serve immediately.

Orange Julius

1 6-oz. can frozen orange juice concentrate

1 C. milk

3 C. water

1/3 C. sugar

1 tsp. vanilla

12 ice cubes

Combine all ingredients in a blender; blend until smooth, about 60 seconds. Serve immediately. Serves four.

Dad's Specialties

EGG RECIPES

Crab-Stuffed Eggs

6 hard-cooked eggs	1 C. chopped celery
1 tsp. dry mustard	2 T. chopped green pepper
1/2 tsp. salt	1/4 C. mayonnaise
1 C. flaked, cooked crab	Dash paprika

Peel eggs, cut into halves crosswise, and remove yolks. In a medium bowl, mash yolks and mix with mustard, salt, crab, celery, green pepper, and mayonnaise. Blend well. Fill egg whites with crab mixture; sprinkle with paprika. Makes 12 egg halves.

How to Buy Great Eggs

You'll find that eggs come in three "grades"--and translating an egg's report card is easy, once you know how!

Grade AA eggs are the most expensive--but they're also the best quality. If you break an AA egg on a plate, the white won't spread very much and the yolk will stand high.

Grade A comes next--it's still a high-quality egg, but the white will spread a little more. Grade B eggs are the lowest in quality; they are still fine to use in cooking and baking, but not the best for fried, hard-cooked, or scrambled eggs.

What about the color of the shell? It makes no difference! Whether the shell is white, brown, or speckled, the contents are the same. Never choose an egg with a shell that is cracked or broken, because bacteria can invade the contents.

Fluffy Ham and Egg Nests

6 eggs, separated

6 slices hot buttered toast

6 slices cooked ham

Salt and pepper to taste

Dash paprika

Separate eggs. Season whites with salt and pepper to taste and beat until stiff enough to form sharp peaks. Place a slice of ham on each piece of toast. In the center of the ham, heap a mound of egg whites. With a spoon, make a hollow in the center of each egg white mound; slip an egg yolk into each hollow. Season with salt and pepper to taste. Bake at 350 degrees until white is browned and yolks are firm. Garnish with paprika. Serves six.

Egg and Tomato Breakfast Soup

1/2 C. diced onion

2 T. butter

1 quart whole tomatoes

1/4 tsp. oregano

1/8 tsp. pepper

1 clove garlic, minced

6 eggs

In a large saucepan, melt butter; saute onions until transparent. Add tomatoes and seasonings and bring to a boil; drop in eggs while mixture is boiling. Reduce heat, cover tightly, and simmer for 10 minutes or until yolks are set. Serve in soup bowls; serves six.

Scrambled Eggs Shouldn't Really be "Scrambled"

This is a case when words play tricks: if you really "scramble" an egg, you'll get a pretty tough customer!

For tender scrambled eggs, mix eggs, milk, and a dash of salt in a bowl. Beat lightly with a fork *only until mixed.* Pour into a hot skillet that contains 1 T. melted butter. Turn the heat low and let the eggs cook, stirring only occasionally.

How To Fry An Egg

To fry an egg, break it gently into a hot skillet that contains 1 T. melted butter or margarine. Immediately reduce the heat, cooking the egg slowly and spooning the hot butter over the egg until the white is set and a film forms over the yolk. That's a "sunny side up." For a "fried egg over easy," quickly turn the egg over in the skillet as soon as the white is set. Sprinkle with salt and pepper and remove.

Deviled Eggs

6 hard-cooked eggs, shelled

1/3 C. mayonnaise

1 T. white vinegar

1/2 tsp. dry mustard

1/2 tsp. worcestershire sauce

1/4 tsp. salt

1/8 tsp. white pepper

Halve eggs lengthwise; remove yolks with a spoon, being careful not to break whites. In a small bowl, mash yolks; add remaining ingredients and mix until smooth and fluffy. Spoon mixture into egg whites, filling centers. Serve immediately or refrigerate.

Deviled eggs can be garnished with the following:

Tomato rose. With a vegetable peeler, peel a continuous strip of skin off a ripe tomato. Coil skin to form a rose. Place in center of deviled egg and garnish with watercress or celery leaves.

Shrimp. Place a cooked, shelled, and deveined baby shrimp on each deviled egg. Garnish with watercress or celery leaves if desired.

Salmon. Chop smoked salmon into fine pieces; heap 1/4 to 1/2 teaspoon chopped salmon on each egg. Garnish with sprigs of fresh dill.

Olives. Place a slice of ripe pitted olive on each deviled egg. In the center of the olive, place a thin strip of green pepper and a thin strip of sweet red bell pepper.

Radish pinwheels. Trim a small radish; cut into thin slices. Cut each slice into quarters. Arrange radish quarters on top of deviled egg in pinwheel pattern. Garnish with a sprig of fresh parsley.

How To Poach An Egg

Pour 1 inch of water, 1 T. melted butter, and a pinch of salt into a skillet. Heat the liquid, but don't boil it. Break the egg into a saucer or small bowl; carefully slip the egg into the hot liquid. Remove from heat, cover the pan, and let the egg stand in the hot liquid for 5 minutes or until the white is firm. If not firm enough, let stand another minute. Serve hot on a slice of buttered toast.

Baked Scrambled Eggs

6 eggs, beaten

1/2 C. heavy cream

Salt and pepper to taste

2 T. chopped sauteed
mushrooms

2 tsp. minced onion

1 C. broken shrimp

In a large bowl, beat eggs with heavy cream; add salt and pepper to taste, mushrooms, onion, and shrimp. Pour egg mixture into four buttered custard cups. Place custard cups in a shallow baking dish, and pour about 1/2 inch water into baking dish. Bake at 350 degrees for 15 minutes, or until eggs are set. Serves four.

Basic Omelet

2 T. butter or margarine

6 eggs

6 T. milk

1/2 tsp. salt

Pepper to taste

In a large frying pan, melt butter over medium heat, tilting pan to coat bottom. In a bowl, beat eggs, water, salt, and pepper until well mixed; pour into frying pan. Reduce heat to low and cook without stirring. As edges set, lift edges carefully and allow uncooked egg to flow to bottom of pan, tilting as necessary. Cook until mixture is set but top still looks moist. Spoon desired filling onto omelet. With spatula, loosen edge of omelet and fold in half as you slide omelet from pan to plate. Serves four.

Try the following ingredients, alone or in any combination desired, as omelet fillings:

--Sauteed mushrooms

--Cooked crumbled bacon

--Chopped cooked ham

--Shredded cheddar, Monterey
Jack, mozzarella, Swiss,
or colby cheese

--Warmed cottage cheese

--Sauteed onions

--Diced ripened tomatoes

--Diced yellow, red, or
green bell peppers

--Diced avocado

Oriental Omelet Filling

2 T. onion, minced

1 T. chopped green pepper

1 T. butter or margarine

1/2 C. drained bean sprouts

1/2 C. cooked chopped chicken

1/2 tsp. soy sauce

1/8 tsp. ginger

Melt butter in skillet; add onion and green pepper, cooking until tender. Add bean sprouts, chicken, soy sauce, and ginger; heat through. Spoon onto omelet before folding.

Ham Omelet Filling

1 T. butter or margarine

1 T. flour

1/2 tsp. instant chicken
   stock base

1/4 tsp. celery salt

1 C. milk

1 C. cooked cubed ham

1/2 C. shredded Swiss cheese

1/4 C. sliced toasted almonds

To make a sauce, melt butter in medium saucepan; stir in flour until well blended, and cook for 2-3 minutes. Stir in chicken stock base and celery salt. With a wire whisk, gradually add and beat in milk. Cook until thickened, whisking constantly. Set aside. Before folding omelet, sprinkle on cheese and ham; ladle half of sauce over cheese and ham. Fold omelet. Ladle remaining sauce over the top of the omelet and garnish with almond slices.

How to Store Eggs

You should refrigerate eggs from the time you get them home until you use them. Never wash your eggs before you put them in the fridge; eggs have a protective coating that keeps out bacteria.

If your recipe calls for separated eggs, keep the whites at room temperature for about 30 minutes before you use them.

If you don't use the yolks at the same time, place them in a small jar, cover them with cold water, screw on a tight-fitting lid, and store them in the refrigerator. They'll keep for about three days that way. To use, simply drain off water.

Egg whites can be kept in the refrigerator for about ten days if they are kept in a tightly covered container.

Mexican Omelet Filling

3/4 C. chopped avocado

1/4 C. sour cream

2 T. chopped green chilis

1 T. chopped green onion

1 tsp. lemon juice

1/4 tsp. salt

Dash tabasco sauce

1 C. shredded Monterey
   Jack cheese

In a large bowl, combine avocado, sour cream, chiles, green onion, lemon juice, salt, and tabasco sauce. Set aside. Before folding omelet, sprinkle with cheese. Spread half the avocado mixture on omelet; fold. Dollop remaining avocado mixture on top of omelet and serve.

Quiche Lorraine

1 unbaked 9-inch pie shell

1 tsp. butter or margarine

3 slices Canadian bacon, diced

1 medium onion, finely chopped

1/2 C. grated Swiss cheese

4 eggs, slightly beaten

1 C. milk

1 C. heavy cream

Dash nutmeg

1/2 tsp. salt

1/4 tsp. pepper

Place pie shell in 9-inch pie plate. In a small heavy saucepan, heat butter until melted; add bacon. Cook 5 minutes. Remove bacon and set aside. Add onions to butter in pan and cook for 5 minutes; remove onions and set aside. Cover bottom of pie crust with bacon and onions; sprinkle with 1/4 C. of the grated cheese. In

Don't Boil Those Hard-"Boiled" Eggs!

Boiling makes eggs tough--so a hard-boiled egg shouldn't really be boiled!

For a tender hard-boiled egg, place the egg in a saucepan and cover with cold water. Bring the water slowly to a boil. *As soon as* the water boils, remove the pan from the heat. Cover the pan and let the egg stand in the hot water. For soft eggs, let stand 3 minutes; for medium eggs, 6 minutes; for hard eggs, 20 minutes. Immediately after cooking, plunge eggs into cold water: they'll be easier to peel, and the yolks won't have a dark coating.

a mixing bowl, combine remaining cheese, eggs, milk, cream, nutmeg, salt, and pepper. Mix well. Pour over bacon and cheese mixture. Bake at 450 degrees for 15 minutes. Reduce heat to 350 degrees and bake 15 minutes longer. Serve hot.

Herbed Quiche

1 unbaked 9-inch pastry shell	1/8 tsp. pepper
2 eggs	1 1/3 C. shredded Swiss cheese
1 C. heavy cream	1/2 tsp. basil
	1/4 tsp. marjoram

In a medium bowl, combine eggs, cream, salt, and pepper; beat until well blended. Sprinkle cheese, basil, and marjoram evenly over bottom of pie shell. Pour egg mixture over cheese. Bake at 400 degrees until knife inserted in middle comes out clean. Let stand 5 minutes before serving.

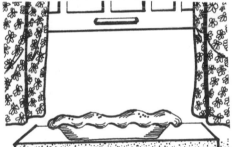

Scrambled Egg Casserole

1 1/2 doz. eggs	1/2 can cream of mushroom soup
2 T. butter	1/4 C. sherry
1/4 C. milk	1/2 C. fresh-grated parmesan cheese
1/4 tsp. salt	Paprika
1/8 tsp. pepper	
1 C. fresh mushrooms, sliced	

In a large bowl, combine eggs, milk, salt, and pepper; beat lightly until combined and pour into a greased non-metal baking dish. In a small bowl, combine mushrooms, soup, and sherry; stir until well mixed. Pour over eggs. Sprinkle with parmesan cheese and paprika. Cover and refrigerate overnight. Bake at 350 degrees for 30 minutes or until bubbly. Serves six to eight.

Dad's Specialties

BROWN-BAGGING IT:
LUNCHBOX AND PICNIC RECIPES AND IDEAS

What It Should Contain

To pack the greatest nutrition punch, your brown-bag lunch-whether at school or the office--should contain the following:
- --Protein
- --Starch
- --Fresh fruit or canned fruit
- --Raw or lightly steamed vegetables
- --A nutritious drink (fruit juice, vegetable juice, milk, nog, and so on)

Obviously, a sandwich with meat fills the protein and starch category--but don't get stuck on sandwiches. Try a pasta salad with meat in it, for example--or a taco salad, or some cold chicken strips with salad fixings. If the weather is nippy, take along a thermos filled with steamy meat-and-potato stew or meat and pasta soup. Roll up sliced meat and cheese in tortillas. Or pack a bag with a variety of low-salt crackers and some delicious spreads. Remember: you're limited only by your imagination!

Sandwich Ideas

--Plain old peanut butter can make a gourmet sandwich if you get imaginative about it. Try mixing peanut butter with equal parts of honey, jam, jelly, or marmalade. You can garnish a peanut butter sandwich with sliced bananas, cooked crumbled bacon, chopped dates, or chopped pitted prunes. And don't forget the bread: peanut butter is especially delicious on raisin bread!

--Want a hot sandwich in your brown bag? No problem--carry your heated sandwich filling in a wide-mouthed thermos. At lunchtime, assemble, using bread and various condiments that you've packed in separate containers.

--Instead of a plain cheese sandwich, shred the cheese. Mix it with mayonnaise, chopped walnuts, chopped olives, and chopped green pepper for a crunchy, tangy sandwich. Garnish with lettuce and tomatoes, if desired.

--An egg-salad sandwich is generally made with hard-cooked eggs, mayonnaise, and mustard. Try adding some variety to yours by mixing in one or more of the following: chopped green pepper, cooked crumbled bacon, pickle relish, chopped ripe olives, chopped stuffed olives, or minced pimentoes. Or try mixing the hard-cooked eggs and mayonnaise with mustard, chili sauce, and deviled ham for a delicious change of pace.

--To add crunch to a tuna salad sandwich, stir in chopped celery and chopped nuts.

--Instead of lettuce, garnish your sandwich occasionally with sprouts. Bean sprouts and alfalfa sprouts work especially well; simply rinse in water and pat gently dry. If you can, pack the sprouts in a separate plastic sandwich bag and wait to garnish your sandwich until you're ready to eat it.

--If you've got a sandwich filling that's soggy, pack it separately and assemble your sandwich when you are ready to eat it. It's a good idea to pack tomatoes and lettuce separately, too. If you can't do that, help prevent your sandwich from getting soggy by buttering your bread all the way to the edges.

--For a change from the regular lettuce and tomato garnish, try garnishing your sandwich with a fresh, raw vegetable--sliced green pepper, cabbage, celery, or carrots work well. Pickles and olives on sandwiches are great for a change, too, as is a sliced sweet red onion.

--For variety, change the kinds of breads you use for sand-wiches. In addition to ordinary white bread, you can try whole wheat, multi-grain, French, rye, pumpernickle, sourdough, raisin, or even a fruit bread (like banana or cranberry). For a real switch, put one kind of bread on the top of the sandwich and another on the bottom. And don't limit yourself to sliced bread, either: sandwiches are delicious on rolls, buns, English muffins, croissants, popovers, rice cakes, onion rolls, or bagels. Don't forget pita bread (pocket bread), corn bread, or flour tortillas.

--For an occasional change, try a vegetable sandwich instead of a meat filling. Combine shredded raw vegetables with a little mayonnaise to make a crunchy filling. As a sample, try mixing shredded carrots, well-drained crushed pineapple, and shredded cabbage.

--Don't forget last night's supper. Roast beef or chicken can be sliced for sandwiches; baked beans can be spread on thick slices of sourdough. Dollop a little chili sauce on sliced meatloaf.

--Instead of spreading mayonnaise on bread in your sandwich, get creative with various bottled salad dressings. Creamy onion dressing, Russian dressing, thousand island dressing, or bacon and tomato dressing are just a few you can try. To keep your sandwiches from getting soggy, carry the dressing in a small jar or container with a tight-fitting lid and spread it on your sandwich when you're ready to eat.

--Still another variation on mayonnaise could include ricotta cheese, farmer's cheese, or cream cheese. For an even more flavorful sandwich, choose cream cheese with chives, pimentoes, or green onions.

--Buy some unusual mustards to add variety to your sandwiches, or make your own spreads by mixing herbs and butter. Even a little lemon juice in butter gives your sandwich a fresh taste.

--If you've got a busy schedule, you can make enough sandwiches for the week and freeze them ahead of time; in the morning, toss your frozen sandwich in the bag and leave for school or work. By noon, the sandwich will be thawed. Follow these guidelines, though: don't freeze sandwiches made with mayonnaise, because the oil will separate. Don't put lettuce and tomatoes on the sandwiches before you freeze them; tote them in a separate plastic bag and assemble when it's time to eat. Don't freeze sandwiches made with hard-cooked eggs. And, finally, make sure you butter the bread all the way to the edges to keep fillings from soaking in as they thaw. Wrap each sandwich in foil and seal the edges by folding them over; place each foil-wrapped sandwich in a plastic sandwich bag, label, and freeze. Keep the sandwiches away from the sides and bottom of the freezer so that ice crystals won't form.

--Don't get caught in a rut with tuna salad. Other fish makes wonderful sandwich fillings, too. Try crab salad, salmon salad, shrimp salad, or any white fish filet.

Low-Fat Tuna Salad Sandwich

8 slices bread

2 T. diet margarine

1 6 1/2-oz. can water-packed tuna, drained and flaked

1/4 C. plain, non-fat yogurt

2 tsp. lime juice

1 tsp. poppy seeds

1 T. chopped green onion

Dash of salt

Dash of pepper

Dash of garlic powder

Lettuce leaves or alfalfa sprouts

1/2 cucumber, peeled and sliced thin

Spread bread slices with margarine. In a mixing bowl, combine tuna, yogurt, lime juice, poppy seeds, onion, salt, pepper, and garlic powder. Mix well. Assemble sandwiches, using lettuce or sprouts and tuna mixture. Makes four sandwiches.

Popovers

2 eggs

1 C. milk

1 C. flour

1/2 tsp. salt

1 T. vegetable

1/2 C. grated parmesan cheese

In a large mixing bowl, combine eggs, milk, flour, and salt. Beat until smooth. Add oil, and beat again until well blended. Sprinkle parmesan cheese in a thin layer in the bottom of wellgreased muffin tin; pour batter to fill tins half full. Bake at 475 degrees for 15 minutes; reduce heat to 350 degrees and bake for an additional 25 minutes. Remove from tins and let cool. Split and fill with sandwich fillings.

FRUIT AND VEGETABLE IDEAS

--For a change from raw vegetables, try lightly steaming your veggies instead. As soon as the cooking time is up, rinse with cold water to stop the cooking process and keep the vegetables bright and still slightly crunchy.

--Get creative with your vegetable choices. Besides carrot and celery sticks, go for the exotic: try raw zucchini, snow peas, purple cabbage, lightly steamed asparagus, and other finds from your local grocery's produce department.

--Do the same thing with fruit. To make fruit easier to tote, wash, peel, remove pits, and slice at home. Dip fresh fruit slices in lemon juice before you pack them to keep them from turning brown before lunchtime.

--For a fun change from sandwiches, use an apple as a "cup" for your sandwich filling. Simply wash the apple, slice off the top fourth, and carefully scoop out the core and seeds, being careful not to puncture the bottom. Sprinkle with lemon juice to keep the apple flesh from turning brown. Then fill with tuna salad, creamed cheese filling, or the filling of your choice. Replace the top, and wrap tightly in plastic wrap.

- Don't be limited to fresh or canned fruits. Dried fruits can be a delicious change of pace and a great way to include nutrition in your lunch. Try apricots, peaches, pears, apples, plums, or a combination served with cream cheese.

--Try a dip made out of yogurt, cream cheese, or marshmallow creme (see below) with your fruit.

--For a change from potato chips, try baked potato skins. Simply peel raw potatoes into thick peelings, arrange on a cookie sheet, and place under the broiler until the skins turn golden and start to curl. If desired, you can sprinkle them with shredded cheese, garlic salt, seasoned salt, paprika, salt, or pepper.

--Stuff a green pepper with your lunch fare, and you have a crunchy, nutritious "bowl." Wash the pepper, slice off the top, and pull out the core, seeds, and membranes. Sprinkle the inside very lightly with salt, if desired. Then fill with chicken salad, tuna salad, Waldorf salad, or other filling. Replace the top and wrap tightly with plastic wrap.

--For a delightful change, make fruit and cheese kebabs. Simply thread wooden skewers with bite-sized pieces of fruit and cubes of cheese: you could alternate Swiss or cheddar cheese with grapes, pineapple chunks, strawberries, cherries, melon balls, or other fruits. For the best success, choose fruits that don't brown when exposed to air (apples and bananas are not good choices).

--Make a delicious and easy vegetable salad with chilled cottage cheese. Simply chop raw vegetables into bite-sized pieces and stir into a single-serving container filled with cold cottage cheese. Tomatoes, cucumbers, green peppers, sweet red peppers, and zucchini all work well. Sprinkle with parmesan cheese or seasoned salt and enjoy!

--For a change, try marinated vegetables. You can purchase them bottled, or marinate your own with bottled Italian salad dressing overnight in a covered container in the refrigerator. Drain and carry in your lunch in a covered container.

--Make a crunchy vegetable sandwich by stuffing pita bread with raw vegetables. Try a variety, like chopped celery, carrot, broccoli, green onions, cherry tomatoes, raw green beans, or Bermuda onion slices.

Fruit Dip

8 oz. cream cheese, softened

8 oz. sour cream

1 8-oz. jar marshmallow creme

1 T. lemon juice

1/8 tsp. nutmeg

Combine all ingredients and mix until well-blended. Chill. Serve as a dip with fruits.

Dill Dip

1 C. sour cream

1 T. dill weed

1 T. dried minced onion

1 C. mayonnaise

1 T. Bon Appetite

Combine all ingredients and mix until smooth. Let sit for 1 hour. Stir again and serve as a dip for raw vegetables or chips.

Fruit-Filled Muffins

1 3/4 C. flour

1/4 C. sugar

2 tsp. baking powder

1/2 tsp. salt

1 egg, slightly beaten

3/4 C. milk

1/3 C. vegetable oil

1 C. bran flake cereal

12 flat-bottom wafer-style
    ice cream cones

1/2 C. chopped fruit (such as
    apples, pears, peaches, raisins)

In a bowl, combine flour, sugar, baking powder, and salt. In a small bowl, combine egg, milk, and oil; beat until well blended. Pour egg mixture into flour mixture and stir just enough to moisten all ingredients. Stir in bran flake cereal. Spoon enough batter into each cone to fill halfway; top with 1 T. chopped fruit, and fill the remainder with batter. Place cones on a cookie sheet and bake at 400 degrees for 20-25 minutes, or until golden brown on top. Makes 12 muffins.

BEVERAGE IDEAS

--To keep your entire lunch cool, freeze fruit juices that are packaged in single serving-sized cans or boxes. Put one in your lunch when you leave home, and it will be thawed (but still cold) at lunchtime.

--For fresh-squeezed juice, cut a hole about the size of a dime through the top of an orange. Insert a straw and squeeze firmly as you drink.

--Water can become a delicious and different drink if you get creative with the ice cubes. Pour grape juice, apple juice, lemonade, cranberry juice, or some other pure fruit juice into ice cube trays and freeze. Dump the cubes in your thermos, fill with water, and enjoy!

--Another fun twist with ice cubes is to freeze a "treat" in each one. It's simple: place a washed and trimmed strawberry, raspberry, grape, cherry, maraschino cherry, cranberry, or mint leaf in each compartment of the ice cube tray; fill with water and freeze. As the cubes melt, they add subtle flavor to your water.

--Don't forget vegetable juices. You can buy them, or if you have a blender you can make your own out of almost any vegetable. Try vegetable combinations, too.

--Get daring enough to combine fruit juices for unusual but delicious beverages. Then garnish your drinks with slices or wedges of fresh fruit.

--For a creative "stir," use a fruit straw-kebab. Thread firm fruits (such as strawberries, grapes, or pineapple chunks) on your drinking straw and submerge in your fruit juice, water, or soda.

--If you've mixed two or more ingredients in a drink, make sure to shake your thermos jug well before you open it at lunchtime.

--When the weather is chilly, don't forget that you can take hot drinks in your thermos. Hot drinks will keep that way longer if you fill the thermos to the top; pack lunch in a container that can be kept separate from the thermos. If you're toting a hot drink, season it with a few whole cloves or a few slices of fresh orange for a tasty change. Hot apple cider is even more delicious if you toss in a cinnamon stick.

--To perk up ice water, float a few slices of fresh lemon in your thermos.

--Your thermos will do its job better if you give it a head start. If you are packing a hot drink, pre-heat your thermos by pouring boiling water in it and letting it heat for 5 minutes before emptying and filling it with your drink. If you are carrying a cold drink, pre-chill your thermos with ice water for 10 minutes before emptying and filling it with your drink.

Banana Nog

1 banana	2 T. honey
1 C. milk	Dash nutmeg

Combine all ingredients in a blender; blend until smooth. Pour into pre-chilled thermos. Makes two servings.

Orange-Banana Frosty

6-oz. can frozen orange juice concentrate	2 bananas
2 juice cans cold water	12 ice cubes

Combine all ingredients in a blender; blend until smooth. Pour into pre-chilled thermos. Makes four servings.

DESSERT AND SNACK IDEAS

--Try for as much nutrition as possible in your desserts and fruits. Try granola or trail mix for a snack. Cookies and bars can be made with fruit and honey; you can savor a slice of sweet melon instead of cake for dessert. Or try using wedges of fruit dipped in plain non-fat yogurt that has been sweetened with honey and nutmeg.

--Plenty of delicious snacks and desserts can start out with plain, non-fat yogurt. In addition to sweetening with honey, try stirring in fresh fruit, frozen fruit, fruit juice, cereal, or nuts.

--For a cool treat during hot weather, enjoy a frozen banana. To prepare, heat chocolate chips in the top of a doubleboiler until smooth. Peel a banana; dip in the chocolate chips until covered, and roll in chopped nuts. Wrap tightly in plastic wrap and freeze. You'll need to keep this treat cold in your lunch.

--Make the most of your baking by planning ahead. Whenever you bake cake, bars, or cookies, wrap individual portions tightly in plastic wrap, then in foil. Label and freeze for use in lunches. Cakes, bars, and cookies should only be kept frozen for two to three months.

--If you can keep your lunch cold, try toting pudding. Make pudding at home, and pour into individual containers. Refrigerate and use in lunches.

--For a healthful "cupcake," spread peanut butter on a fruit muffin.

--For a sweet but healthy treat, try stuffed dates. Split each date, stuff with peanut butter, and top with a walnut or pecan half.

--You can make a nutritious dessert by combining a variety of dried fruits (apples, pears, peaches, apricots, raisins, and so on) with several kinds of nuts. Make up a big batch, store in a tightly covered container, and tote in sealed plastic sandwich bags as needed.

--Don't overlook popcorn as a nutritious dessert: it's low in calories and rich in fiber. Try a variety of toppings or seasonings to spice up your popcorn without adding fats and calories (see popcorn recipe section and the recipe below).

Meal in a Cookie

1 C. butter or margarine	1/2 tsp. salt
1/2 C. dark molasses	2 tsp. cinnamon
1/2 C. brown sugar, firmly packed	1/2 tsp. nutmeg
	1 C. wheat germ
4 eggs	1 C. rolled oats
2 C. flour	1 C. raisins
1 tsp. baking powder	1/4 C. water
1 tsp. baking soda	1 C. chopped walnuts or pecans

Beat butter, molasses, brown sugar, and eggs until fluffy and well mixed. Stir in flour, baking powder, baking soda, salt, cinnamon, nutmeg, wheat germ, and rolled oats; blend thoroughly. In a small saucepan, combine raisins and water; bring to a boil, and boil for 2 minutes. Stir raisin-water mixture and chopped nuts into batter. Spread evenly in a greased 9 x 13 pan. Bake at 375 degrees for 30 minutes. Cool and cut into 2-inch bars. If desired, drop by teaspoons onto cookie sheet; bake at 375 for 10 minutes. Bars or cookies can be frozen if wrapped tightly in plastic wrap.

Nutty Popcorn Surprise

2 1/2 quarts popped popcorn	1/4 C. butter or margarine, melted
1/3 C. raisins	
1/2 C. almonds	1/4 C. grated parmesan cheese
1/2 C. sunflower seeds	

In a large bowl or kettle, combine all ingredients until well mixed and until popcorn is evenly coated with butter and cheese. Store in a tightly covered container. Makes 12 individual servings.

Healthy Apple Snack Bars

1 C. whole wheat flour

1 C. quick-cooking oats

3/4 tsp. baking soda

1/2 tsp. cinnamon

1 C. applesauce

1/2 C. honey

1/3 C. vegetable oil

1 tsp. vanilla

1 6-oz. pkg. mixed dried fruit, chopped

1/2 C. chopped nuts

3/4 C. bran flakes, crushed

2 T. butter or margarine, melted

In a large mixing bowl, combine flour, oats, soda, and spice. In a separate bowl, combine the applesauce, honey, oil, and vanilla; stir into the flour mixture. Stir in fruits and nuts. In a small bowl, combine crushed bran flakes and melted butter. Sprinkle half the bran flake mixture over the bottom of a greased 9 x 13 pan; spoon batter over bran, spreading evenly. Sprinkle with the remaining bran mixture. Bake at 350 degrees for 25-30 minutes. Cool and cut into bars. Makes 24 bars.

Banana Carrot Cake

1 C. sugar

1 C. mashed ripe banana (about 3 bananas)

1/2 C. vegetable oil

3 eggs

1 1/2 C. flour

2 tsp. baking powder

1 tsp. salt

1/2 tsp. baking soda

1 tsp. cinnamon

1/4 tsp. cloves

1 C. quick-cooking oats

1 C. shredded carrots (about 3 carrots)

1/3 C. chopped nuts

In a large mixing bowl, beat together sugar, bananas, and oil; add eggs, one at a time, beating well after each. Combine flour, baking powder, salt, baking soda, cinnamon, and cloves; add to banana mixture and mix well. Stir in oats and carrots. Pour into greased 9-inch square baking pan; bake at 350 degrees for 40-45 minutes. Makes 8 servings.

Honey-Crunch Snack Mix

3 C. high-fiber whole wheat and bran cereal with dried fruit and nuts

1/2 C. peanut butter chips

2 T. honey

1/2 C. raisins

In large bowl, combine cereal and peanut butter chips; spread evenly in a greased roasting pan. Drizzle honey in a thin stream over the cereal, covering the entire length and width of the pan. Bake at 325 degrees for 5 minutes. Remove pan from oven, stir well to distribute honey throughout cereal, return pan to oven, and cook for 3 additional minutes. Remove from oven; sprinkle raisins over cereal and let mixture cool completely, stirring once or twice while it cools. Store in a covered container at room temperature. Makes 3 1/2 cups.

Granola

2 1/2 C. old-fashioned oats

1 C. wheat germ

1/4 C. dry-roasted sunflower seeds

1/2 C. coconut

1/2 C. raisins

1/2 C. nuts

1/2 C. dried bananas

1/2 C. dried apricots

1/4 C. sesame seeds

1/2 C. honey

1/2 C. vegetable oil

In a large bowl, combine oats, wheat germ, sunflower seeds, coconut, raisins, nuts, bananas, apricots, and sesame seeds; toss to mix well. Pour in honey and oil; stir until well blended. Bake in a shallow pan at 300 degrees for 20 minutes, stirring once or twice during baking. Cool. Stir again and store in a covered container in the refrigerator. Makes 8 cups.

Frozen Bananas

1 large banana, peeled and sliced

1/2 C. fruit-flavored yogurt

1/4 C. chopped nuts

Using a toothpick, coat each banana slice with yogurt; roll in chopped nuts. Place on waxed paper and freeze until hard. Store in the freezer in a covered container.

No-Cook Peanut Butter Gems

1/2 C. peanut butter	1/2 C. honey
1/2 C. wheat germ	1/2 C. sunflower seeds
1/2 C. nonfat instant milk powder	1/2 C. raisins

In a large bowl, combine all ingredients. Mix well and form into walnut-sized balls. Chill until firm and store in a covered container.

PICNIC AND TAILGATE PARTY IDEAS

--Before you leave on a picnic, stop to think about the essentials. If you picnic often, assemble your own checklist of items you don't want to be without once you reach your destination. Some items you'll want to include are napkins, large plastic garbage bags, can openers, bottle openers, washcloths, and waterproof vinyl tablecloths to put on the ground in case there are no tables. And, of course, remember paper plates, paper cups, plastic utensils, and serving spoons!

--Don't forget seasonings and condiments. Pack unbreakable containers filled with catsup, mustard, pickle relish, salt, and pepper.

--To keep your salads cold and crisp, carry the salad dressings in a separate container. Put the salad in a plastic or glass bowl with a tight-fitting lid or cover; place the salad bowl in a larger container filled halfway with crushed ice.

--Make sure you wash your hands before you handle any food at the picnic site. If you won't be where there are hand-washing facilities, carry wet washcloths in large sealed plastic bags: one bag should contain soapy washcloths, the other washcloths in clear water. As a last resort, carry foil-wrapped wipes.

--After you have cooked your food at home for the picnic, refrigerate it. Never let perishable food sit out at room temperature while you are waiting to leave on the picnic.

--To prevent spoilage, pack all perishables in containers with tight-fitting lids; place containers on crushed ice.

--To keep beverages cold, freeze half of the drink in ice cube trays. Pour remaining beverage over frozen cubes in a large thermos; beverage "ice" will keep drinks cold without diluting.

--If you don't have an ice chest or insulated container to pack cold foods in, use three thicknesses of brown paper grocery bags. Pack cold foods together in bags, double over tops, and transport in as cool a place as possible, out of direct sunlight.

--For a more carefree picnic, slice all rolls and butter them (or spread with mayonnaise or sandwich spread) before leaving home. Place halves back together, and pack in a plastic bag.

--To keep tossed salads from wilting, pack ingredients in separate containers and assemble salad at picnic site. Slice or cut tomatoes into wedges, then place in sealed plastic bag. Wash lettuce, wrap in paper towels, and place in sealed plastic bag. Wash and cut up other ingredients, and pack in plastic bags. Carry salad dressing in a nonbreakable container with a tightly screwed lid to prevent spills.

--Take a roll of paper towels to the picnic site so you can wipe off the table and clean up spills.

Cold Confetti-Style Meatloaf

1 T. vegetable oil

3/4 C. chopped carrot

1/4 C. chopped sweet
  red pepper

1/4 C. chopped green pepper

1/2 C. chopped onion

1/4 tsp. sage

1 1/4 lb. lean ground beef

1 egg, slightly beaten

1/3 C. bottled chili sauce

1 C. fresh bread crumbs

1/4 tsp. salt

Dash pepper

1/2 C. cheddar cheese,
  cut in cubes

In a medium skillet, heat oil over low heat; add carrot, red pepper, green pepper, onion, and sage. Cover and cook for 10 minutes, or until vegetables are tender but not browned. In a mixing bowl, combine beef, egg, chili sauce, bread crumbs, salt, and pepper; gently stir in vegetables and cheese. Line a lightly greased loaf pan with aluminum foil, leaving an overhang on the sides. Lightly grease the foil. Spoon the meat mixture into the prepared pan, packing lightly and smoothing the top. Bake at 375 degrees for 1 hour; cool on a wire rack for 10 minutes. Lift meatloaf from pan, allowing juices to drain back into the pan. Place the foil-covered loaf on a plate and refrigerate. When completely cooled, carefully peel off foil. Slice, place back in the shape of a loaf, and wrap in a clean piece of foil. Refrigerate overnight; pack in an insulated container to keep cold. Serves four.

Dilly Potato and Apple Salad

6 medium potatoes, boiled
until tender, peeled,
and cut into chunks

1 apple, pared, cored, and diced

1/2 C. chopped celery

2 hard-cooked eggs

1/3 C. chopped green onions

1/2 C. sour cream

1/2 C. mayonnaise

2 T. chopped dill

1/2 tsp. salt

1/4 tsp. pepper

In a large bowl, combine potatoes, apples, celery, eggs, and green onions; toss. In a small bowl, combine sour cream, mayonnaise, dill, salt, and pepper; mix until well blended. Pour dressing over potato-apple mixture and stir to coat well. Chill at least two hours. Pack in an insulated container.

Monterey Jack and Tomato Salad

1 1/2 C. Monterey Jack
cheese cubes

2 medium tomatoes, halved,
seeded and cut into wedges

1 pickled jalapeno peppers,
seeded and sliced
into thin slices

2 T. fresh parsley, chopped

2 T. vegetable oil

1/2 clove garlic, minced

Salt to taste

In a medium sized bowl, combine all ingredients; toss. Cover and refrigerate for at least two hours. Bring to room temperature before serving. Serves four.

Cheese-Stuffed Vegetables

3 oz. cream cheese, softened

2 oz. bleu cheese, softened

1 tsp. onion, finely chopped

1 tsp. fresh lemon juice

1 small cucumber, peeled
and trimmed

2 celery stalks, washed
and trimmed

2 oz. snow peas, washed and
trimmed, stem ends removed

In a small bowl, combine cream cheese, bleu cheese, onion, and lemon juice. Set aside. Cut cucumber into thick slices; scoop out some of seeds, creating a small cavity. Spoon filling into each. Cut open snow peas carefully on curved edge, being careful not to break. Spoon filling into each. Fill celery stalks with filling. Arrange vegetables in a shallow airtight container lined with damp paper towels; cover vegetables with more damp paper towels. Refrigerate until chilled, up to 24 hours. Pack in an insulated container. Serves four.

Beer Biscuits

3 C. biscuit mix

3 T. sugar

1 egg

1 12-oz. can beer
at room temperature

In a large bowl, mix all ingredients until moistened. Spoon into greased muffin tins, filling two-thirds full. Bake at 400 degrees for 18 minutes, or until golden.

Poppy Seed Bread

3 C. flour

2 1/2 C. sugar

1 1/2 tsp. baking powder

1 1/2 tsp. salt

2 1/2 T. poppy seeds

1 1/2 C. milk

1 1/4 C. vegetable oil

3 eggs

1 tsp. almond extract

1 1/2 tsp. vanilla

In a large bowl, mix all ingredients; beat until smooth. Bake in a greased and floured loaf pan at 350 degrees for 1 hour 15 minutes. Remove from pan while hot. Cool and slice.

Chocolate Buttermilk Cake

1 C. butter or margarine	2 eggs
4 T. cocoa	1/2 C. buttermilk or sour milk
1 C. water	1 tsp. baking soda
2 C. sugar	1 tsp. vanilla
2 C. flour	

In a large saucepan, melt butter. Stir in cocoa and water and bring to a boil. Sift together sugar and flour; add to hot mixture. Beat in eggs, milk, soda, and vanilla. Bake in a greased jelly roll pan (sheet pan) at 375 degrees for 15 minutes. Cake can also be baked in a greased 9 x 13 pan; bake at 375 for 35-40 minutes. Frost while hot with the following frosting:

Frosting

1/3 C. butter or margarine	1 tsp. vanilla
4 T. cocoa	1 lb. powdered sugar
4 T. canned evaporated milk	

In a small saucepan, combine all ingredients; cook until butter is melted and mixture is smooth. Pour onto hot cake.

Dad's Specialties

122B

SANDWICH RECIPES

Surprise Sandwiches

1 egg, slightly beaten
1/2 C. shredded cheddar cheese
3/4 C. chopped cooked ham

1 8-oz. can refrigerated
crescent rolls
2 tsp. sesame seeds

Set aside 1 teaspoon of beaten egg. Combine remaining egg with cheese and ham. Separate crescent roll dough into four rectangles; press perforated edges firmly to seal, flattening the dough slightly. Place 1/4 of the ham mixture along the long edge of each rectangle; roll up jelly-roll style, overlapping the ends of the roll slightly. Press ends together to seal. Brush with reserved egg and sprinkle with sesame seeds. Bake at 375 degrees for 15 minutes.

Crunchy Egg Salad Sandwich

2 T. mayonnaise
1/4 tsp. garlic salt
1/4 tsp. pepper
3/4 tsp. Dijon mustard
3 hard-cooked eggs, chopped
4 slices rye or
    pumpernickel bread

2 leaves lettuce
2/3 C. bean sprouts
16 raw pea pods, strings
    and ends removed
4 tsp. thinly sliced green onion

In a medium bowl, combine mayonnaise, garlic salt, pepper, Dijon mustard, and eggs; mix until well blended. On each of two slices of bread, layer 1 leaf lettuce, 1/3 C. bean sprouts, 8 pea pods, half the egg salad mixture, and 2 tsp. sliced green onions. Top with remaining slices of bread. Makes two sandwiches.

Carrot Salad Sandwiches

1/4 C. plain low-fat yogurt

1 tsp. honey

1/4 tsp. salt

1 C. shredded carrots

1/4 C. thinly sliced celery

1/4 C. raisins

4 slices whole wheat bread

2 leaves lettuce

2 slices Monterrey
  Jack cheese

2 T. roasted sunflower seeds

In a medium bowl, combine yogurt, honey, salt, carrots, celery, and raisins; mix until well blended. On each of two slices of bread, layer 1 leaf of lettuce, 1 slice of cheese, half the carrot mixture, and 1 T. sunflower seeds. Top with remaining slices of bread. Makes two sandwiches.

Cheesy Tuna Burgers

1 can water-packed tuna fish

1/2 C. shredded cheddar cheese

1 small onion, chopped

1 C. chopped celery

1/4 C. mayonnaise

6 hamburger buns

In a medium bowl, mix tuna, cheese, onion, celery, and mayonnaise. Spread an equal amount on each of six split buns. Bake at 350 degrees for 15 minutes, or until bubbly. Serves six.

Bavarian Beef Sandwiches

1 lb. lean ground beef

1/2 C. chopped onion

1/4 C. chopped green pepper

2 T. butter or margarine

1 10 3.4-oz. can beef gravy

2 C. shredded cabbage

6 hard rolls, split and toasted

1/4 C. shredded cheddar cheese

In a medium skillet, cook ground beef, onions, and green pepper in butter until beef is browned and vegetables are tender. Stir in gravy and cabbage; cook over medium heat for 10 minutes. Spoon 1/2 C. mixture on bottom half of each roll; sprinkle with cheese, and cover with top half of roll. Serves six.

Sloppy Joes

1 lb. ground beef

1 can condensed chicken
  gumbo soup

2 T. brown sugar

1/2 C. catsup

1 small onion, chopped

1 T. mustard

2 T. worcestershire sauce

2 T. flour

Salt and pepper to taste

In a medium skillet, cook ground beef until browned; drain fat. Stir in remaining ingredients and simmer for 10 minutes, or until thickened. Serve on split hamburger buns. Serves six.

Tangy Tuna Burgers

1 7-oz. can water-packed
  tuna, drained

1/2 C. fresh bread crumbs

1/2 C. chopped celery

2 T. minced onion

1/3 C. mayonnaise

2 T. bottled chili sauce

1 tsp. lemon juice

Lettuce leaves for garnish

Tomato slices for garnish

6 hamburger buns, split
  and toasted

In a medium bowl, combine tuna, bread crumbs, celery, and onion; stir until well mixed. Blend in mayonnaise, chili sauce, and lemon juice until evenly mixed. Form into patties; fry in a lightly oiled skillet over medium heat for about 5 minutes, turning once Serve on toasted bun with lettuce and tomato slices. Serves six.

Grilled Lasagna Sandwiches

8 slices bread

Softened butter or margarine

4 slices Mozzarella cheese

2 T. chopped onion

2 medium tomatoes, sliced

1/3 C. sour cream

2 tsp. oregano

Salt to taste

8 slices bacon, fried
crisp and drained

Spread both sides of each slice of bread with butter. For each sandwich, top a slice of bread with 1 slice cheese, a dollop of sour cream, onions, a sprinkle of oregano, several tomato slices, and a sprinkle of salt. Arrange two pieces of bacon on each, and top with the remaining slice of bread. Place each sandwich, cheese side down, in a skillet; cover and cook over medium heat until bread is golden and cheese is melted.

Chicken Salad Sandwiches

3/4 C. cooked chicken, diced

1/2 C. mayonnaise

2 T. chopped celery

2 T. chopped almonds

1 T. chopped fresh parsley

4 slices whole wheat bread

1/4 C. jellied cranberry sauce

In a medium bowl, combine chicken, mayonnaise, celery, almonds, and parsley. Set aside. Spread bread with cranberry sauce and top with chicken salad mixture. Makes two sandwiches.

Hot Chicken Sandwiches

2/3 C. mayonnaise

1 T. lemon juice

Dash tabasco sauce

2 C. cooked chicken, diced

3/4 C. sliced pitted ripe olives

1 C. shredded cheddar cheese

1/4 C. green onions, chopped

1/4 C. green pepper, chopped

1/2 C. celery, chopped

4 hamburger buns, split in half

In a medium bowl, combine mayonnaise, lemon juice, and tabasco sauce; stir until well blended. Stir in chicken, 1/2 C. sliced olives, 1/2 C. shredded cheese, green onions, green pepper, and celery. Spread buns with chicken mixture; top with reserved olive slices and cheese. Bake at 400 degrees for 10 minutes; place under broiler until cheese bubbles. Serves four.

Italian Soupburgers

1 lb. lean ground beef	1/3 C. water
1/4 C. chopped onion	1/3 C. catsup
1/8 tsp. oregano	6 hamburger buns,
1 can condensed	split and toasted
minestrone soup	12 slices Mozzarella cheese

In a skillet, cook ground beef, onion, and oregano until meat is browned and onion is tender. Stir in soup, water, and catsup; simmer for 10 minutes, stirring occasionally. Spread on toasted buns; top with cheese slices and broil until cheese is bubbly. Serves six.

Cheese and Veggie Sandwich

2 C. shredded Swiss cheese	1/2 C. mayonnaise
1 1/4 C. biscuit mix	1 hard-cooked egg, chopped
1 medium tomato, chopped	1/4 tsp. salt
1/2 cucumber, choppped	6 slices whole wheat bread

In a large bowl, combine cheese, biscuit mix, tomato, cucumber, mayonnaise, hard-cooked egg, and salt; stir until well mixed. Spread on slices of bread. Bake at 450 degrees for 10-12 minutes, or until cheese is bubbly. Serves six.

Monte Cristo Sandwiches

For each sandwich:

2 slices bread	Dash salt
Butter or margarine, softened	Dash pepper
1 thin slice cooked ham	1 T. cold water
1 thin slice Swiss cheese	1 T. vegetable oil
1 thin slice baked chicken	Vegetable oil for frying
1 thin slice cheddar cheese	Butter or margarine for frying
1 egg	

Spread both slices of bread with butter. On one slice, layer ham, Swiss cheese, chicken, and cheddar cheese. Cover with second slice of bread. Press sandwich firmly together, wrap in plastic wrap, and refrigerate until well chilled. In a small shallow bowl, combine egg, salt, pepper, cold water, and oil; whisk until well blended. Holding the sandwich firmly together, dip in egg mixture, first one side and then the other. Fry in a heavy skillet in mixture of oil and butter 1/4 inch deep. When browned on both sides, remove from skillet, drain on paper toweling, and bake at 350 degrees for 8-10 minutes. Slice in half and serve hot.

Backyard Hot Dogs

3 frankfurters, chopped

2 hard-cooked eggs, chopped

1/4 C. shredded cheddar cheese

2 tsp. chopped pickles

3 tsp. catsup

1 tsp. mustard

6 hot dog buns

In a medium bowl, combine frankfurters, hard-cooked eggs, cheese, pickles, catsup, and mustard; mix well. Spread on split hot dog buns. Wrap each in foil and bake at 350 degrees for 20 minutes. Serves six.

Beef Stroganoff Sandwiches

2/3 C. beer

1/3 C. vegetable oil

1 tsp. salt

1/4 tsp. pepper

1/4 tsp. garlic salt

2 lbs. 1-inch-thick steak

4 C. sliced onions

1/2 tsp. paprika

2 T. butter or margarine

1 C. sour cream

6 slices sourdough bread, toasted

In a small bowl, combine beer, oil, salt, pepper, and garlic salt; pour over steak, cover, and let stand for several hours at room temperature. Drain; broil steak until desired doneness. In a small skillet, saute onions and paprika in butter until tender, but not browned. Slice meat in thin slices on the diagonal. Arrange meat slices on toasted bread; top with onions and a dollop of sour cream. Serves six.

Roast Beef Sandwiches

1 lb. cooked roast beef,
 sliced thin

6 slices rye bread

1/4 C. sour cream

1 T. vinegar

3/4 tsp. Dijon mustard

3/4 tsp. sugar

1/4 tsp. salt

1 small Bermuda onion,
 thinly sliced

6 cherry tomatoes, thinly sliced

Arrange sliced beef on bread. In a small bowl, combine sour cream, vinegar, mustard, sugar, and salt; mix well. Spread sour cream mixture on beef. Top with onion and cherry tomato slices. Serves six.

Bleu Cheese Mushroom Burgers

2 lbs. lean ground beef

1 medium onion, chopped

1 T. bottled steak sauce

1/4 lb. bleu cheese, crumbled

1/2 lb. mushrooms,
 thickly sliced

In a large bowl, combine ground beef with onion, steak sauce, and salt and pepper to taste. Form into 12 thin patties. Top 6 patties with crumbled bleu cheese and mushroom slices. Top with remaining 6 patties and press edges together to seal. Grill, fry, or broil to desired doneness and serve on hamburger buns. Serves six.

Curried Meatball Pita Sandwiches

1 lb. lean ground beef

2 4-oz. cans diced green chiles

1 small onion, minced

1 egg

1/2 C. mashed potatoes

1 1/2 tsp. salt

1 tsp. curry powder

3 pita breads, split in half

1 medium cucumber,
 peeled and diced

1/2 C. red onion, diced

2 T. lime juice

2 T. chopped parsley

1/2 tsp. salt

In a medium bowl, combine ground beef, chiles, onion, egg, potatoes, salt, and curry; mix well and shape into 1-inch balls. Flatten slightly. Place in a shallow pan and bake at 350 degrees for

30 minutes, or until well browned. Drain on paper towels. In the meantime, in a medium bowl combine cucumber, red onion, lime juice, parsley, and salt; mix well. Stuff 4 meatballs into each split pita bread half and spoon cucumber relish in each one. Serves six.

Tangy Roast Beef Salad Sandwiches

1/2 C. chopped onion

1/4 C. chopped celery

1/2 C. sour cream

1/4 C. mayonnaise

2 T. lemon juice

1 T. fresh chopped parsley

1 T. horseradish

1 tsp. mustard

1 tsp. salt

1/4 tsp. pepper

1 lb. mushrooms, thinly sliced

1 lb. cooked roast beef,
    thinly sliced

6 pita breads

Shredded lettuce for garnish

In a medium bowl, combine onion, celery, sour cream, mayonnaise, lemon juice, parsley, horseradish, mustard, salt, and pepper; mix well. Set aside. In a large bowl, combine mushrooms and meat slices. Stuff pita breads with meat/mushroom mixture and serve with sour cream dressing and lettuce. Serves six.

Caesar Sandwich

2/3 C. mayonnaise

3 T. fresh lemon juice

1 tsp. minced garlic

1/4 tsp. pepper

12 slices 9-grain bread

1 small head Romaine lettuce,
    torn into bite-sized pieces

1/2 C. fresh Parmesan cheese,
    grated

6 hard-cooked eggs, sliced

In a large bowl, combine mayonnaise, lemon juice, garlic, and pepper; mix well. Spread 1 to 1 1/2 tsp. on 1 side of each slice of bread. Set aside. Add lettuce and cheese to remaining mayonnaise mixture and toss to mix well. Heap 1 C. lettuce mixture on each of 6 slices of bread; top with egg slices and remaining slices of bread. Serves six.

French Dip Sandwiches

1 1/2 lbs. cooked roast beef,
  sliced thinly
1 C. beef broth, heated

1 loaf French bread,
  split in half crosswise
  and warmed in oven

Layer thin slices of beef on half of French loaf; top with other half and slice into sandwich-sized portions. Serve with hot beef broth; dip sandwich into broth as it is eaten. Serves six.

Chili Burger

1 lb. lean ground beef
1/2 tsp. salt
1/4 tsp. pepper
1 tsp. chili powder
2 15-oz. cans chili beans

3 slices cheddar cheese,
  quartered
4 hamburger buns, split,
  toasted, and halved

In a medium bowl, combine ground beef, salt, pepper, and chili powder; mix well. Form into four patties. Broil to desired doneness. Place in individual serving dishes and top with 1/4 the beans; bake at 375 degrees until beans are bubbly hot. Top with three cheese quarters and broil until cheese melts. Serve with 4 bun halves. Serves four.

Deli Corned Beef Sandwiches

8 slices rye bread
Dijon mustard
1 lb. corned beef,
  trimmed and thinly sliced

4 slices pumpernickel bread
1 C. coleslaw

Spread rye bread with mustard; layer 4 slices with corned beef. Spread both sides pumpernickel with mustard and place on top of corned beef. Top with coleslaw and remaining rye bread. Serves four.

Open-Faced Waldorf Salad Sandwiches

2 apples, cored and diced
3/4 C. coarsely chopped walnuts
1/2 C. raisins
1/2 C. diced celery
2 T. cider vinegar

1/4 tsp. salt
4 thick slices whole-grain
    bread, toasted
4 T. cream cheese, softened

In a medium bowl, combine apples, walnuts, raisins, celery, vinegar, and salt; mix well. Spread 1 T. cream cheese on each slice of bread; top with a scoop of salad mixture. Serves four.

French Toast Sandwiches

1/4 C. apple butter
1/4 tsp. cinnamon
8 1/2-inch slices sausage

8 slices packaged frozen
    French toast

In a small bowl, combine apple butter and cinnamon; mix well and set aside. In a large skillet, cook sausage patties; drain on paper towels. Cook French toast slices according to package directions. Spread 1 T. apple butter on each of 4 French toast slices; top each with 2 sausage patties and second slice of toast. Serves four.

Breakfast Sandwiches

4 eggs, slightly beaten
2 T. milk
1/2 tsp. salt
1/4 tsp. pepper

1 T. butter or margarine
8 slices raisin bread, toasted
8 sliced bacon, cooked crisp

In a small bowl, beat eggs with milk, salt, and pepper. In a medium skillet, melt butter; add eggs, and scramble gently until done. Spoon 1/4 egg mixture on each of four slices of toast; top with 2 bacon slices and a second slice of toast. Serves four.

Spicy Chicken Salad Pitas

1/2 C. sour cream	3 C. cooked chicken, diced
3 T. mayonnaise	1 C. chopped tomato
1 T. lime juice	1/2 C. diced avocado
1 1/2 tsp. salad oil	3 T. chopped green onions
3/4 tsp. salt	1 C. shredded lettuce
1/2 tsp. ground red pepper	6 pita breads

In large bowl, combine sour cream, mayonnaise, lime juice, oil, salt, and red pepper; stir to mix well. Add chicken, tomato, avocado, and green onions; toss well. Split pitas one-third of the way; stuff with equal portions of shredded lettuce and chicken salad mixture. Serves six.

Broiled Ham and Cheese Sandwiches

2 T. Dijon mustard	12 oz. cooked ham, sliced
1 T. honey	4 slices rye bread, toasted
1 T. vegetable oil	4 slices Swiss cheese

In a small bowl, combine mustard and honey; set aside. In a large skillet, heat oil; add ham and cook over medium-low heat until ham is heated through. Spread honey mustard sauce on each slice of bread; layer with a slice of ham and a slice of cheese. Broil on a cookie sheet until cheese melts. Serves four.

Granny's Apple-Raisin Sandwiches

4 T. Dijon mustard	4 oz. bleu cheese, crumbled
2 T. honey	Watercress to garnish
1 medium sweet red pepper, sliced	8 slices raisin bread, toasted lightly
2 Granny Smith apples, cored and sliced thinly	

In a small bowl, combine mustard and honey; stir to mix well, and set aside. Spread honey-mustard sauce evenly on one side of each slice of bread. To make sandwiches, layer watercress, apple slices, red peppers, bleu cheese, apple slices, and red peppers; top with remaining slice of bread. Serves four.

Southwestern Beef Sandwiches

4 T. mayonnaise

3 T. prepared horseradish

8 slices black bread,
  lightly toasted

1 ripe avocado, peeled
  and sliced

12 oz. cooked roast beef,
  thinly sliced

1 small Bermuda onion,
  thinly sliced

Sprouts to garnish

In a small bowl, combine mayonnaise and horseradish; mix well and set aside. Spread mayonnaise-horseradish sauce evenly on one side of each slice of bread. To make sandwiches, layer avocado slices, roast beef, onion slices, sprouts, and top with remaining slice of bread. Serves four.

Harvest Sandwiches

1/2 C. plain low-fat yogurt

1/3 C. mayonnaise

2 T. chopped fresh parsley

3/4 tsp. curry powder

1/2 tsp. salt

2 C. carrots, shredded

1/4 C. raisins, chopped

2 C. red cabbage, shredded

2 T. walnuts, coarsely chopped

12 thin slices whole-grain bread

1 bunch watercress

4 tomato slices

In a small bowl, combine yogurt, mayonnaise, parsley, curry powder, and salt; mix until well blended. Set aside. In a medium bowl, combine carrots, raisins, and half the yogurt mixture; toss until well coated. In a separate bowl, combine cabbage, walnuts, and the remaining dressing; toss until well coated. On each of 4 slices of bread, layer equal amounts of watercress and carrot mixture; top with a second slice of bread, the cabbage mixture, and a slice of tomato. Top each with a remaining slice of bread. Serves four.

Bacon and Egg Salad Sandwiches

8 hard-cooked eggs, chopped

1/4 C. mayonnaise

1/2 tsp. dried dill weed

2 tsp. Dijon mustard

2 tsp. lemon juice

1/2 tsp. salt

1/4 tsp. pepper

Dash ground red pepper

8 thick slices
  pumpernickel bread

Lettuce to garnish

4 slices tomato

12 slices bacon, cooked crisp

In a bowl, combine eggs, mayonnaise, dill weed, mustard, lemon juice, salt, pepper, and red pepper; mix until well blended. Spread an equal amount of egg salad on 4 slices of bread; top with lettuce leaves, a slice of tomato, 3 slices of bacon, and the remaining slice of bread. Serves four.

Cucumber-Cottage Cheese Sandwiches

2 C. low-fat cottage cheese

1 cucumber, peeled, seeded,
  and chopped

1/4 C. green onions, chopped

Dash salt

8 slices sourdough bread

In a medium bowl, combine cottage cheese, cucumber, green onions, and salt; mix well and refrigerate until well chilled. Spoon onto sourdough bread and garnish with lettuce leaves if desired. Serves four.

Classic Club Sandwiches

24 slices white bread,
  toasted and buttered

8 slices cooked chicken

Mayonnaise

16 slices bacon, cooked crisp

16 slices tomato

Salt and pepper

Lettuce leaves to garnish

Arrange sliced chicken on 8 pieces of toast; spread chicken with mayonnaise and cover with another piece of toast. Spread with mayonnaise; arrange 2 slices bacon and 2 slices tomato on each. Sprinkle with salt and pepper, and top with lettuce and remaining piece of toast. Secure with wooden picks and cut each sandwich into four triangles. Serves six.

Pork-and-Bean Sandwiches

12 slices cracked wheat
   bread, buttered
6 slices cooked pork or ham

1 16-oz. can pork and beans
2 T. bottled chili sauce
2 tsp. mustard

Arrange sliced meat on 6 pieces of bread. In a medium bowl, combine pork and beans, chili sauce, and mustard; mash until well blended. Spread on sliced meat and top with remaining slices of bread. Serves six.

Hawaiian Ham Sandwiches

1 4 1/2-oz. can deviled ham
1/2 C. crushed pineapple,
   drained well

1/2 C. low-fat cottage cheese
3 T. mayonnaise
4 slices cracked wheat bread

In a medium bowl, combine deviled ham, pineapple, cottage cheese, and mayonnaise; mix until well blended. Spread on cracked wheat bread; garnish with lettuce if desired. Serves two.

Nutty Cream Cheese Sandwiches

1 C. cream cheese, softened
1/2 C. mayonnaise
1/2 C. walnuts, coarsely
   chopped

1/2 C. raisins, coarsely chopped
8 slices black or rye bread

In a medium bowl, combine cream cheese, mayonnaise, walnuts, and raisins; mix well. Spread on black or rye bread. Serves four.

Classic Tuna Sandwiches

1 7-oz. can water-packed tuna,
   drained and flaked
1 tsp. lemon juice

1 T. sweet pickle relish
1/4 C. mayonnaise
6 slices bread

In a medium bowl, combine tuna, lemon juice, pickle relish, and mayonnaise; spread evenly on 3 slices bread and top with remaining bread. Garnish with lettuce leaves if desired. Serves three.

Hot Chipped Beef Sandwiches

2 2 1/2-oz. jars dried beef, shredded

1 T. butter or margarine

1 tsp. minced onion

2 T. butter or margarine

3 T. flour

1/2 tsp. salt

1/4 tsp. pepper

Dash tabasco sauce

1 C. milk

Four thick slices bread, toasted and buttered

In a strainer, pour boiling water over shredded beef and let drain; set aside. In a small saucepan, saute onion in 1 T. butter until soft but not browned; set aside. In a medium saucepan, melt 2 T. butter; stir in flour, salt, pepper, and tabasco sauce until well blended. Pour in milk gradually, stirring with a whisk and cooking over medium-low heat until sauce is thick. Stir in onions and shredded beef. Pour over bread and serve open-faced. Serves four.

Grilled Ham and Cheese Sandwiches

12 slices bread, buttered on both sides

6 slices cooked ham

6 slices Swiss or American cheese

2 T. mustard

2 T. mayonnaise

Top half the buttered bread with a slice of ham and a slice of cheese; spread with mustard and mayonnaise, and top with the remaining slices of bread. Grill in a griddle over low heat for approximately 4-5 minutes, turning, until bread is golden brown and cheese is melted. Serves six.

Peanut Butter Surprise Sandwiches

1 C. peanut butter, creamy or chunky

2 bananas, mashed well

1/2 C. orange marmalade

8 slices bread

In a medium bowl, combine peanut butter, bananas, and orange marmalade; stir until well blended. Spread on bread. Serves four.

Classic Hero Sandwiches

1 loaf French bread,
  cut in half crosswise

4 T. mayonnaise

3 T. Dijon mustard

6 oz. cheddar cheese, sliced

1 medium green pepper,
  cut into rings

2 dill pickles, sliced

1 sweet red onion, sliced

6 oz. Swiss cheese, sliced

6 oz. ham, sliced

Lettuce to garnish

Spread half of bread loaf with mayonnaise, the other half with mustard. On half the bread loaf, layer ingredients in the order listed and top with other half of loaf. Cut into thick slices, secure with wooden picks, and serve. Serves six to eight.

Dessert Sandwich

2 eggs, lightly beaten

2/3 C. milk

1/4 tsp. salt

2 T. sugar

8 slices bread

1 C. strawberry preserves

Butter or margarine

1/2 C. powdered sugar

In a shallow bowl, combine eggs, milk, salt, and sugar; beat with a fork to mix until well blended. Spread four slices bread with strawberry preserves; top with remaining bread. On a griddle, melt butter or margarine; grill sandwiches over low heat for 4-5 minutes, turning, or until bread is golden brown. Sprinkle with powdered sugar and serve warm. Serves four.

Dad's Specialties

BARBECUE RECIPES

Barbecued Chicken

1/3 C. brown sugar	3 T. vegetable oil
1/3 C. soy sauce	1/2 tsp. dry mustard
1/4 C. water	3 lbs. chicken breasts

In a small saucepan over low heat, stir together brown sugar, soy sauce, water, oil, and dry mustard until sugar is dissolved. Let mixture cool. Place chicken in a bowl; pour cooled sugar mixture over chicken, cover, and marinate at room temperature for two hours or overnight in the refrigerator. Turn chicken two to three times during marinating. Barbecue on grill, basting with marinade, until done, approximately 10 minutes on each side.

Barbecued Pork Chops

1/2 C. catsup	1/2 tsp. nutmeg
1 C. water	1 tsp. salt
1/3 C. vinegar	1 tsp. celery seed
1 whole bay leaf	4 pork chops

Combine catsup, water, vinegar, and spices. Place pork chops in a shallow dish; pour sauce over chops, and marinate for 1-2 hours at room temperature (or covered in the refrigerator overnight). Barbecue chops on grill, basting with marinade, until done.

Japanese Kebabs

1 boneless, skinless chicken breast, cut in cubes	1/4 C. pineapple juice
	3 T. soy sauce
1/2 lb. cooked ham, cut in cubes	1 T. vegetable oil
2 fresh zucchini, cut in cubes	1 tsp. cornstarch
1 C. pineapple chunks, drained	

Alternate ham cubes, chicken cubes, zucchini cubes, and pineapple chunks on skewers. Combine pineapple juice (reserved from canned pineapple chunks), soy sauce, oil, and cornstarch in a jar; screw on the jar lid and shake until all ingredients are combined well. Place skewers in a shallow pan; pour the pineapple juice mixture over the skewers. Rotate skewers until all food is coated with mixture. Broil over grill for five minutes on each side, basting with the pineapple juice mixture. Makes four kebabs.

Barbecued Short Ribs

4 lbs. beef short ribs	2 cloves garlic, minced
3/4 C. soy sauce	2 T. sesame seeds
1/4 C. water	2 T. brown sugar
3 green onions, sliced thin	1/4 tsp. ginger

"Butterfly" the ribs by cutting the meat lengthwise down to the rib, then spreading the meat out so it can be laid flat on the barbecue grill. Spread the ribs in a shallow dish. Combine soy sauce, water, green onions, garlic, sesame seeds, brown sugar, and ginger in a jar; screw on lid and shake until all ingredients are combined well. Pour over ribs and let marinate for two hours at room temperature. Grill for five minutes on each side, basting with marinade. At five minutes, ribs will be brown and crusty on the outside but still slightly pink on the inside.

Dad's Shish Kebabs

1/2 lb. lean beef, cut in cubes	8 cherry tomatoes
2 boneless skinless chicken breasts, cut in cubes	8 mushroom caps
	3 T. vegetable oil
1/2 lb. pork, cut in cubes	3 T. lemon juice
1 medium onion, cut in chunks	dash salt
2 green peppers, cut in cubes	dash pepper

Alternate beef, onion, chicken, peppers, pork, tomatoes, and mushrooms on skewers. Brush with oil and lemon juice; sprinkle with salt and pepper to taste. Grill for 20 minutes, turning skewers often. Makes 4 kebabs.

Fruited Pork Chops

8 thinly sliced pork chops

1/2 C. apricot jam

1 T. soy sauce

1 T. water

1 T. dry onion flakes

1/2 tsp. garlic salt

1/2 tsp. Tabasco sauce

In a large bowl, combine all ingredients except pork chops; mix well. Place pork chops in a shallow pan; pour sauce over pork chops until they are evenly covered, and refrigerate for at least one hour. Grill over hot coals for 30 minutes, turning often and basting with sauce. Heat remaining sauce, and serve with pork chops. Serves four. If desired, you can substitute other fruit jam (such as apple, peach, or pineapple preserves) for apricot.

Sweet and Sour Halibut Kebabs

6 T. margarine, melted

1/4 C. red wine vinegar

1/4 C. catsup

3 T. brown sugar, packed firmly

1/2 tsp. salt

1/4 tsp. pepper

1/8 tsp. garlic salt

1/2 C. unsweetened
   pineapple juice

2 tsp. cornstarch

3/4 lb. 1-inch thick halibut steak

18 chunks green pepper

18 large mushrooms

18 cherry tomatoes

In a small saucepan, combine melted margarine, vinegar, catsup, brown sugar, and spices. Heat to boiling, stirring occasionally. In a small bowl, stir pineapple juice into cornstarch until smooth; gradually stir into hot mixture, and bring to a boil again, stirring frequently. Boil, stirring frequently, two minutes, or until thick. Cover; chill until sauce is completely cooled. Cut halibut steaks into 1-1/2-inch squares; marinate in cooled sauce at room temperature for at least one hour. Drain, reserving sauce. Thread six skewers with alternating fish, green peppers, mushrooms, and cherry tomatoes; brush kebabs generously with sauce. Grill over medium coals for 10 minutes, turning and basting frequently with sauce. Serve immediately with remaining sauce.

Tips on Using Barbecues

Preparing meats. Before you put your meat on the barbecue, trim off all excess fat to prevent a flare-up. To keep steaks, pork chops, or ham slices from curling as they cook, "score" the edges (make shallow cuts about 1/4 inch apart) with a sharp knife.

Steaks and chops should be at least one inch thick; thinner cuts will get too done before they are browned. In general, you should grill tender cuts of meat only. Less tender cuts can be barbecued if you marinate or pound them first.

For the average appetite, allow 1/4 to 1/2 lb. of boneless meat per person, and 3/4 to 1 pound of bone-in meat per person.

Cooking meats. If you're cooking meat that might stick to the grill (such as lean meats and fish), brush the grill with a little vegetable oil before you start the barbecue. Remember that cooking time will always vary with the cut, thickness, and shape of the meat, the temperature it was when you placed it over the coals, the position of the meat on the grill, weather conditions, and desired degree of doneness. Use the time listed in recipes as a general guide, but allow for variations.

When barbecuing, season the meat after you turn it. Salting raw meat draws the juices out of it. And use tongs instead of a fork to turn your meat--piercing the meat with a fork lets delicious juices escape.

To test for doneness, use a sharp knife to make a small slit near the bone; check the color of the meat.

Basting. To baste meats with barbecue sauce, use a thick, wide brush. A new paint brush is ideal!

Some sauces can be used throughout the cooking time, but others should be used during only the last 15 to 30 minutes. Sauces that contain a lot of tomato sauce or sugar tend to burn easily, and should be used only during the last 15 minutes.

Kebab tips. For kebabs, use sturdy skewers that are long enough to fit completely across the grill. If you use bamboo skewers, soak them in water for 30 minutes before threading food on them to keep them from burning.

To keep foods from sticking to the skewers, lightly oil the skewers before threading on the food.When threading foods on a skewer, leave a small gap between all pieces of food to allow for complete cooking. You should leave at least four inches between the food and the skewer handle to allow for proper heat penetration.

Use a whole water chestnut, a chunk of raw potato, or a chunk of raw carrot on the end of the skewer to keep food from slipping off as it cooks.

142

Mushroom-Stuffed Chicken

2 T. margarine
1/2 C. mushrooms,
   chopped fine
1/3 C. green onion, chopped
1/4 C. tomato sauce
1 1/2 C. cooked rice

1 3-lb. broiler fryer chicken,
   cut into quarters
2 C. barbecue sauce (use
   bottled, or prepare one of
   the sauces listed in this
   chapter)

In a large frying pan, melt margarine; stir in mushrooms and green onions, and saute over low heat until vegetables are still slightly crisp. Stir in tomato sauce and rice, and heat through. Loosen the skin on each chicken quarter, forming a pocket between the chicken and the skin; spoon one-fourth of the rice mixture into each pocket and secure with toothpicks or skewers. Grill chicken on greased grill, skin-side up, five inches from low coals, for 20 minutes. Turn chicken, brush with barbecue sauce, and grill for an additional 40 minutes, basting with barbecue sauce every 10 minutes. Serves four.

Spicy Vegetarian Kebabs

Small white boiling onions
Cauliflowerets
Whole mushrooms

Large zucchini chunks
Cherry tomatoes
Barbecue sauce

Alternate vegetables as desired on skewers; grill over medium coals for 15 minutes, turning and basting frequently with barbecue sauce. Serve immediately.

How Hot Are Those Coals?

Want to figure out how hot your coals are?

It's easy--and all you need is your hand!

Here's how to do it: hold your hand, palm side down, above the coals at the height your food will be cooking. Then count seconds, saying "one one thousand, two one thousand, three one thousand," and so on.

If you have to move your hand after two seconds, the coals are hot. If you need to move your hand after three seconds, the coals are medium-hot; four seconds, medium; five seconds, medium-low; six seconds, low.

Stew on the Barbecue

1 lb. lean ground beef

1 egg, beaten

1/4 C. dry bread crumbs

1/2 tsp. dry mustard

1 tsp. worcestershire sauce

3/4 lb. fully cooked
cocktail frankfurters

3/4 lb. small new red potatoes,
boiled in skins and cut
into chunks

1/2 lb. small white boiling
onions, sliced and separated
into rings

1/2 lb. carrots, shredded
coarsely

1 10-oz. pkg. frozen corn,
thawed

1/4 lb. fresh mushrooms, sliced

1 15-oz. can tomato sauce

1 14-oz. can beef broth

1/2 tsp. sugar

1/2 tsp. basil

1/2 tsp. oregano

In a bowl, combine ground beef, egg, bread crumbs, dry mustard, and worcestershire sauce. Shape into marble-sized meatballs; arrange on a cookie sheet; bake in a 500-degree oven for 5 minutes, or until browned. Cover and refrigerate. In a large saucepan, combine tomato sauce, beef broth, sugar, basil, and oregano; simmer for 10 minutes. Fill four foil loaf pans about half full with stew ingredients (meatballs, frankfurters, potatoes, onions, carrots, corn, and mushrooms). Pour in enough sauce to cover. Cover pans with foil and grill 5 inches above medium coals for 30 minutes. Garnish with sour cream or grated parmesan cheese if desired. Serves four.

Shrimp Kebabs

18 large shrimp,
peeled and deveined

12 strips bacon

18 cherry tomatoes

18 large mushrooms

1 large zucchini, halved and
cut into 12 chunks

1/4 C. honey

4 tsp. orange juice

Thread three shrimp on each of six skewers, alternating with two strips of bacon, three cherry tomatoes, three mushrooms, and two chunks of zucchini. Spiral-wrap the bacon around the vegetables and shrimp as you thread them on the skewers. In a small bowl, combine honey and orange juice; brush generously over kebabs. Grill 6 inches from coals for 10 minutes or until the shrimp is bright pink and bacon is golden crisp, turning and basting frequently with honey mixture. Serve kebabs over rice if desired.

Lemon Chicken

1/4 C. lemon juice	1/2 tsp. paprika
1 tsp. grated lemon peel	1/4 tsp. onion salt
1 tsp. vegetable oil	1/4 tsp. pepper
1/2 tsp. salt	1 3-lb. broiler fryer,
1/2 tsp. ginger	cut into pieces

In a shallow baking dish, combine all ingredients except chicken; mix thoroughly. Add chicken pieces, turning to coat well. Cover and refrigerate for at least three hours. Grill chicken over medium coals for 45 minutes, turning and basting frequently. Serves eight.

Basic Barbecue Equipment

When you're starting out, collect the basic equipment for barbecuing--it makes outdoor cooking safer and easier. A basic checklist includes the following:
- **Tongs, preferably those that open and close like scissors;** you can use tongs to spread coals, turn meats, and grasp hard-to-grip foods
- **Metal spatula, preferably one with a long handle;** use it to turn meats instead of piercing them with a fork
- **Basting brush;** a new 1 1/2 inch wide paintbrush works well
- **Skewers;** the best ones are sturdy 16-inch skewers with large, easy-to-grip handles. Avoid skewers that are attached to each other; you should be able to turn skewers individually. Metal skewers distribute heat most evenly; if you use bamboo skewers, they have to be soaked in water first so they won't burn
- **Small grill basket for cooking** small foods (like vegetables) or foods that crumble when cooked (like fish); baskets come in many shapes and sizes, and most have hinged lids that enable you to turn them over during cooking

145

Barbecued Stuffed Steaks

6 New York steaks

1 6-oz. pkg. long grain
and wild rice mix,
prepared according to
package instructions

1 egg, beaten

1/4 C. green onions,
sliced thinly

Barbecue sauce

Using a sharp knife, cut a pocket in each steak. Combine rice, egg, and green onions; stuff about 1/2 C. rice mixture into the pocket of each steak. Grill over hot coals, basting frequently with barbecue sauce; cook 6 minutes on each side for medium-rare steak, longer for more well-done steak. Serves six.

Teriyaki Chicken

1/4 C. soy sauce

1/4 C. sugar

2 T. catsup

1/4 tsp. ginger

6 chicken breasts,
skinned and deboned

In a large bowl, combine soy sauce, sugar, catsup, and ginger; add chicken, turning to coat well. Cover and refrigerate for at least two hours. Grill 12 inches above medium coals 15-20 minutes on each side, or until done, basting frequently with marinade.

Island Teriyaki Steak

1/2 C. soy sauce

1/4 C. brown sugar

1 tsp. ginger

1/4 tsp. cracked pepper

1 1/2 lbs. sirloin steak, cut
into 1-inch-wide strips

1 15-oz. can pineapple chunks

4 whole water chestnuts

In a deep bowl, combine soy sauce, brown sugar, ginger, and pepper; mix well. Add steak strips, and stir to coat steak well. Cover and marinate for two hours at room temperature or overnight in the refrigerator. Lace steak accordion-style on four skewers, alternating with pineapple chunks; place a water chestnut on the end of each skewer to hold meat in place. Grill over medium coals for 15 minutes, turning and basting frequently with marinade. Serves four.

Fruited Chicken Bundles

4 chicken breasts, skinned
 and boned

1/2 C. raisins

1/4 C. sliced water chestnuts

1/3 C. dried apricots,
 snipped into fine pieces

1/4 C. unsweetened flaked
 coconut

2 T. butter or margarine,
 softened

2 T. light corn syrup

6 T. butter or margarine,
 melted

Place each chicken breast between two pieces of plastic wrap; pound until approximately 1/4 inch thick. Set aside. In a small bowl, combine raisins, water chestnuts, apricots, coconut, softened butter, and corn syrup. Place 1/4 C. raisin mixture on the end of each chicken breast; roll chicken breasts up and secure with wooden picks. Grill over medium coals for 45 minutes, turning and basting occasionally with melted butter. Garnish with slices of orange. Serves four.

Beef Burgandy Kebabs

1 lb. sirloin steak,
  cut into cubes

8 mushroom caps

1/2 C. Burgundy wine

1 tsp. worcestershire sauce

1 clove garlic

1/2 C. vegetable oil

2 T. catsup

1 T. cider vinegar

1/2 tsp. marjoram

12 pearl onions

2 summer squashes,
  cut into thick slices

2 medium zucchini,
cut into thick slices

1 green pepper, cut into slices

1 red pepper, cut into slices

10 cherry tomatoes

In a mixing bowl, combine wine, worcestershire sauce, garlic, oil, catsup, vinegar, and marjoram; mix well. Place steak and mushrooms in a large bowl; pour sauce over. Cover and refrigerate for at least two hours. Drop onions into boiling water for two minutes, squash and peppers for one minute. Drain meat and mushrooms, reserving marinade; toss vegetables in marinade. Drain and reserve marinade. Thread meat and vegetables, alternating, on five skewers; grill 5 inches above medium coals for 15 minutes, turning and basting frequently with marinade. Serves five. Can be served over rice if desired.

Lime-Glazed Beef and Chicken Kebabs

1 T. lime peel, finely shredded

1/2 C. lime juice

4 T. vegetable oil

1/4 tsp. salt

2 chicken breasts, skinned and
  boned and cut into chunks

1/2 lb. sirloin steak,
  cut into chunks

1 red sweet red pepper,
  cut into squares

1 small summer squash,
  cut into thick slices

1 medium onion,
  cut into wedges

2 T. honey

1 tsp. sesame seeds

In a large bowl, combine lime peel, lime juice, oil, and salt; mix well. Add chicken and beef chunks; cover and refrigerate for three to four hours, turning once each hour to distribute marinade. Thread chicken and steak on four skewers, alternating with pepper, squash, and onion. Grill over medium-hot coals for 6 minutes. Turn kebabs; brush with a mixture of 1/4 C. marinade, honey, and sesame seeds. Grill 6 more minutes. Brush with mixture again before serving. Serves four.

Armenian Lamb Kebabs

2 1/2 T. lemon juice	2 tsp. salt
1 1/2 T. lime juice	1 tsp. ground coriander
1/4 C. vegetable oil	1 tsp. ginger
2 T. grated onion	1 1/2 lbs. lamb, cut into cubes
1 clove garlic, crushed	8 pearl onions
1 tsp. crushed red pepper flakes	8 cherry tomatoes

In a large glass bowl, combine lemon juice, lime juice, oil, onion, garlic, red pepper flakes, salt, coriander, and ginger; mix well. Stir in lamb cubes. Cover and marinade at room temperature for two hours. Peel onions; cook in boiling water for three minutes; rinse under cold running water and pat dry. Thread lamb on four skewers, alternating with onions and tomatoes; brush with marinade. Grill over hot coals for six minutes, turning once and brushing with marinade. Serves four.

Tips on Using Gas Barbecues

Using a gas barbecue? Remember these guidelines:

Preheat your grill on the high setting with the lid open for ten to fifteen minutes before you start cooking. Once the grill is preheated, turn the control to the desired setting.

When you leave the grill cover open or closed while you cook is a matter of personal preference. With the lid closed, foods cook faster and have a more "smoked" flavor.

Remember that the heat pattern on a gas grill will change with the wind direction and the grill location. For most even cooking, place the grill in a sheltered area.

If you experience a "flare-up" on a gas grill, use a spray gun filled with water to put out the flames. The finer the mist, the better. Douse only the actual flames; if you sprinkle the water over a wide cooking area, you'll lower the temperature of the coals too much, and your food will steam instead of grilling.

Grilled Salmon

4 salmon steaks,
  cut 1 inch thick
  (thawed if frozen)

1/4 C. vegetable oil

1/4 C. white wine

1 tsp. shredded lime peel

2 T. lime juice

1/4 tsp. pepper

2 cloves garlic, minced

Place salmon steaks in a shallow dish. In a small bowl, combine oil, wine, lime peel, lime juice, garlic, and pepper; mix well. Pour mixture over salmon; turn salmon to coat well with marinade. Cover and refrigerate for at least six hours. Drain salmon, reserving marinade; use paper towels to pat excess moisture from salmon. Grill over medium-hot coals for 7 minutes, brushing occasionally with marinade; turn and grill for another 8 minutes. When done, salmon should flake easily when tested with a fork. Serves four.

Barbecued Meatballs

1 lb. lean ground beef

1/4 C. green onions, minced

1/4 C. chopped onion

3 T. soy sauce

2 T. sesame seeds

1 T. sugar

1 T. vegetable oil

Combine all ingredients in a large bowl; mix well. Shape into one-inch balls; cover and refrigerate at least one hour. Thread meatballs on skewers, leaving space between each. Grill 6 minutes per side over medium-hot coals. Garnish with pineapple chunks, papaya chunks, or kiwi fruit slices. Serves four or makes 20 appetizers.

Barbecued Turkey Breast

1 1/2 lbs. boneless turkey
  breast, cut 1 inch thick

1 C. white wine

1/2 C. soy sauce

1/2 C. vegetable oil

1 1/2 T. lemon juice

2 garlic cloves, crushed

In a medium bowl, combine wine, soy sauce, oil, lemon juice, and garlic; mix well. Arrange turkey slices in a shallow dish; pour marinade over turkey. Cover and marinate in refrigerator at least six hours. Drain turkey, reserving marinade. Grill over hot coals 30 minutes, turning frequently and brushing with marinade. Serves four.

BARBECUED VEGETABLES

Creamy Corn and Peppers

4 ears fresh corn	1/8 tsp. salt
1 sweet red pepper, seeded and finely chopped	dash pepper
	dash Tabasco sauce
1/2 C. heavy cream	

Using a sharp knife, cut kernals from each ear of corn. In a large bowl, combine corn with all other ingredients; mix well. Divide corn mixture evenly onto six 9-inch-square pieces of foil; fold foil over and seal tightly so steam cannot escape. Grill over medium-hot coals for 15 minutes. Serves six.

Buttered Mushrooms

1 lb. mushrooms, stems removed	1/2 tsp. salt
	1/2 tsp. pepper
1/4 C. butter, melted	

Cut mushrooms into thick slices; divide evenly on four 9-inch square pieces of foil. In a small bowl, combine butter, salt, and pepper; drizzle over mushrooms. Fold foil over and seal tightly so steam cannot escape. Grill over medium-hot coals for 15 minutes. Serves four.

Grilled Asparagus

1 lb. asparagus spears

Wash asparagus and snap off, discarding woody ends. In a saucepan, cook asparagus in boiling water for 3 minutes. Drain and rinse under cool running water. Grill over medium-hot coals for 3 minutes or until tender, turning once. Serve immediately with butter. Serves four.

Grilled Corn on the Cob

4 fresh ears of corn

Peel back husks enough so you can remove cornsilk; return husks to original position. In a large pan, cover corn with water and soak for 30 minutes. Drain. Grill over medium-hot coals for 25 minutes, turning frequently. Serves four. (If corn is mature, you should cook for an additional 10 minutes.)

Grilled Peppers

1 sweet red pepper, quartered and seeded
1 green pepper, quartered and seeded
1 sweet yellow pepper, quartered and seeded
1 T. vegetable oil

Brush the skin side of each pepper quarter with oil. Grill over medium-hot coals for 10 minutes, or until peppers are tender and slightly charred. Serves four.

Grilled Potatoes

4 large baking potatoes
1/4 C. butter, melted

Scrub potatoes; cut in half lengthwise. With a sharp knife, make slashes through flesh only (without cutting skin) 1/4 inch apart in a grid pattern. Place potato, cut side up, on a flat surface; squeeze gently so that the flesh spreads slightly. Brush each half with melted butter so that butter drips into "grids." Grill over medium-hot coals for 35 minutes, turning over once. Serves four.

Spicy Zucchini

4 small zucchini,
   cut into lengthwise slices
3 cloves garlic, crushed
1/2 C. vegetable oil

1 T. basil
pinch salt
dash freshly ground
   black pepper

Place zucchini in shallow dish. In a small bowl, mash garlic with 2 T. of oil until smooth. Whisk in remaining oil, basil, salt, and pepper. Pour over zucchini and marinate for 30 minutes. Drain. Grill over hot coals for 5 minutes on each side. Serves four.

Cheesy Broccoli

1 1/2 lb. broccoli

1/3 C. vegetable oil

2 1/2 T. lemon juice

1/4 tsp. salt

1/8 tsp. black pepper

3/4 C. freshly grated
Parmesan cheese

Peel broccoli stalks and trim to 3-1/2-inch pieces. Cut each stalk in half vertically, cutting through flowerets. Place broccoli in shallow dish. In a bowl, combine oil, lemon juice, salt, and pepper; pour over broccoli and toss to coat. Cover and marinate at room temperature for 30 minutes. Drain. Put Parmesan cheese in a plastic bag; put broccoli, one piece at a time, in the bag and shake to coat with cheese. Grill over medium coals for 10 minutes on each side. Serves four to six.

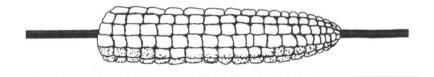

How to Start a Fire in Your Barbecue

To start your fire, follow these easy steps:

1. Stack your coals in the center of the grill in a pyramid shape.

2. Douse the coals with liquid starter; *never* use gasoline or kerosene to start the fire. Wait two to three minutes to allow the starter to penetrate the coals.

3. Light the coals in several places on the pyramid.

4. Wait 40 to 45 minutes until the coals are ashen gray around the edges and red hot in the centers.

5. Using a long-handled fork or tongs, spread the coals in a tight, even layer over the bottom of the barbecue. Your food should be completely underlined with coals.

6. For special flavor, soak aromatic wood chips in water for 30 minutes and scatter them over the hot coals. Start cooking your food when the chips begin to smoke. Use chips sparingly--they add strong flavor! For variation, try hickory, mesquite, cherry, apple, or alder chips.

Cheese Dip on a Grill

1/2 lb. cheddar cheese,
  shredded

1/2 lb. Monterey Jack cheese,
  shredded

1/2 C. butter or margarine

4 oz. salsa

1 small loaf French bread,
  cut into bite-sized cubes

In a cast-iron skillet, combine cheeses and butter. Place on grill over medium-hot coals; whip constantly with a wire whisk until cheeses and butter are melted and smooth. Stir in salsa. Keep skillet at the edge of the grill, stirring occasionally. To serve, dip bread cubes into the cheese mixture.

BARBECUE SAUCE RECIPES

Easy Barbecue Sauce

1/4 C. sugar

1 T. flour

1 tsp. salt

1 tsp. ginger

1/2 C. catsup

3 T. soy sauce

1 tsp. worcestershire sauce

1 T. white vinegar

In a large bowl, combine sugar, flour, salt, and ginger. Mix well. Add catsup, soy sauce, worcestershire sauce, and vinegar; mix until well blended. Use on any meats on outdoor grill. Makes enough to barbecue 3 lbs. meat.

Stove-Top Barbecue Sauce

1 1/2 C. catsup

1/2 C. worcestershire sauce

1/2 C. onion, chopped

2 tsp. celery salt

1/2 tsp. pepper

4 C. tomato juice

1/2 C. vinegar

1/2 C. brown sugar

2 tsp. dry mustard

2 tsp. ground cloves

1 tsp. paprika

2 tsp. salt

Combine all ingredients in a large kettle; simmer over medium-low heat for 25 to 30 minutes, or until thick. Keep refrigerated and use as needed for grilled meats.

Orange Barbecue Sauce

1/3 C. chopped onion

3 T. butter or margarine

1/3 C. honey

3 T. fresh-squeezed
   lemon juice

3 T. soy sauce

1 T. fresh-grated orange peel

1 tsp. salt

3/4 C. orange juice

1 1/2 T. cornstarch

In a small saucepan, saute onion in butter until tender. Add honey, lemon juice, soy sauce, orange peel, and salt. In a small bowl, blend orange juice into cornstarch; gradually stir orange juice mixture into hot mixture. Heat, stirring constantly, until sauce is thickened. Makes about 1 1/2 cups; is delicious on grilled chicken or pork.

Tangy Barbecue Sauce

1 C. catsup

4 T. brown sugar

1/2 C. white vinegar

4 T. worcestershire sauce

2 tsp. celery seed

1 tsp. chili powder

1 tsp. seasoned salt

In a mixing bowl, combine all ingredients in the order listed, mixing with a wire whisk until well blended. Especially good on grilled spare ribs!

Barbecue Clean-up Tips

To make clean-up easier, use these easy tips:
- **Before you start cooking, brush a little vegetable oil on the grill;** foods won't stick, and clean-up will be a breeze!
- If you are using skillets or pans on the grill, coat the bottom of each with a thin layer of bar soap. It'll be simple to clean off the soot after barbecuing.
- To clean a dirty grill, let it cool.

Use a stiff wire brush to scrape off all particles--you don't even need water!
- If you've got a stubborn mess on your hands, let your grill cool. Put it in an extra-strong garbage bag, sprinkle dishwashing powder over it, and pour in enough steaming hot water to cover the grill. Tie the bag closed, place it on a flat surface, and let it sit for an hour or two. You should be able to easily scrub off soot and burned-on food.

Smoky Barbecue Sauce

1 can tomato soup

1/4 C. sugar

1 T. vinegar

dash pepper

1/4 tsp. cloves

1 1/2 tsp. liquid smoke

1/2 soup can water

1 T. worcestershire sauce

1 tsp. salt

1/4 tsp. cayenne pepper

1/4 tsp. allspice

In a mixing bowl, combine all ingredients in order listed, mixing with a wire whisk until well blended. Let stand for at least one hour before using. Makes 2 cups.

Sweet and Sour Barbecue Sauce

1 8-oz. can crushed pineapple

1 C. catsup

1 C. unsweetened
   pineapple juice

1/2 C. brown sugar, packed

1/2 C. vinegar

Put undrained pineapple in a blender; cover and blend until finely chopped. In a saucepan, stir together pineapple, catsup, pineapple juice, brown sugar, and vinegar; bring to a boil, stirring constantly. Reduce heat and simmer, uncovered, until sauce thickens. Makes about 3 cups--especially good on beef or hamburgers!

Veggie Barbecue Sauce

1/2 C. finely chopped onion

1/2 C. finely chopped
   green pepper

1/2 C. finely chopped celery

3/4 C. finely chopped
   mushrooms

4 cloves garlic, minced

1 T. vegetable oil

1 1/2 C. tomato juice

1/2 C. bottled hickory smoke
   flavored barbecue sauce

1 1/2 C. bottled barbecue sauce

In a large saucepan, cook the vegetables in the garlic and oil until tender, but not browned. Stir in tomato juice and bottled barbecue sauces. Heat to boiling, stirring constantly; reduce heat and simmer, stirring occasionally, for 1 hour. Uncover and simmer, stirring occasionally, for another hour, or until sauce is thickened. Makes 3 cups sauce.

Three-Alarm Barbecue Sauce

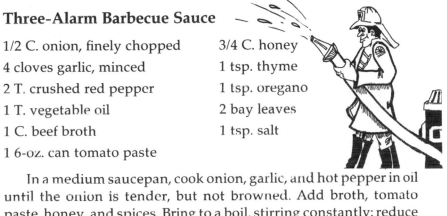

1/2 C. onion, finely chopped	3/4 C. honey
4 cloves garlic, minced	1 tsp. thyme
2 T. crushed red pepper	1 tsp. oregano
1 T. vegetable oil	2 bay leaves
1 C. beef broth	1 tsp. salt
1 6-oz. can tomato paste	

In a medium saucepan, cook onion, garlic, and hot pepper in oil until the onion is tender, but not browned. Add broth, tomato paste, honey, and spices. Bring to a boil, stirring constantly; reduce heat and simmer uncovered, stirring occasionally, for 30 minutes. Strain through a sieve or fine strainer and discard any onion and garlic solids. Makes 1 1/2 cups.

BARBECUED HAMBURGER RECIPES

Guacamole Burgers

1 8-oz. pkg. avocado dip	1 tsp. worcestershire sauce
1 T. fresh lemon juice	1/4 tsp. garlic salt
1 T. green onion, chopped	1 1/2 tsp. salt
2 lbs. lean ground beef	1 C. cheddar cheese, grated
1 egg, slightly beaten	1 C. chopped tomato

In a mixing bowl, combine dip mix, lemon juice, and green onion; stir until well blended. Set aside. In a large mixing bowl, combine ground beef, egg, worcestershire sauce, garlic salt, and salt. Shape into 16 patties. Place 2 T. cheese in the center of each of 8 patties. Top with remaining 8 patties, pressing edges to seal. Grill over medium-hot coals for 12 minutes on one side; turn over, and top each patty with 2 T. guacamole sauce. Grill for another 12 minutes. Top each with chopped tomato. Serves eight.

Pizza Burgers

1 1/2 lb. lean ground beef	1/3 C. chopped olives
1 tsp. salt	1/4 C. prepared pizza sauce
1/4 tsp. pepper	1 1/2 T. basil
1 C. shredded mozzarella cheese	

In a bowl, combine all ingredients; form into four patties. Grill over hot coals for 3 minutes on first side, 8 minutes on other side (longer for well-done burgers). Top burgers with additional pizza sauce, slices olives, and strips of mozzarella cheese.

Tex-Mex Burgers

1 1/2 lbs. lean ground beef	1/2 C. crushed tortilla chips
1 tsp. salt	2 T. canned green chilis, drained and chopped
1/4 tsp. pepper	
1/2 C. canned refried beans	2 T. prepared taco sauce
1/2 C. shredded cheddar cheese	

In a bowl, combine all ingredients; form into four patties. Grill over hot coals for 4 minutes on first side, 8 minutes on other side (longer for well-done burgers). Top burgers with additional heated refried beans, taco sauce, shredded cheese, sliced seeded green chilis, and whole tortilla chips, as desired.

Need A Barbecue? Try A Wheelbarrow!

If you don't have a barbecue, don't despair--an old wheelbarrow will do the trick!

Here's how to convert an old wheelbarrow into a low-cost, versatile, portable barbecue:

Fill the wheelbarrow with six inches of dirt, sand, or gravel. Then simply stack bricks up along the sides of the wheelbarrow, and place your barbecue grill across the bricks. Vary the heat by stacking fewer or more bricks. Scatter your coals over the dirt or sand, and there you have it!

One must: make sure you cover your "barbecue" when it's not in use to keep out cats and rain. If the sand gets wet, you'll need to change it--leaving wet sand in the wheelbarrow will rust out the bottom!

Cheese and Onion Burgers

1 1/2 lbs. lean ground beef	1 tsp. thyme
1 tsp. salt	4 slices Brie cheese
1/4 tsp. pepper	4 T. Dijon mustard
2/3 C. coarsely chopped onion, sauteed until tender	

In a bowl, combine ground beef, salt, pepper, onions, and thyme; mix well and form into four patties. Grill over hot coals for 4 minutes on first side, 8 minutes on other side (longer for welldone burgers). Top each burger with a slice of Brie and a tablespoon of Dijon mustard.

Oriental Burgers

1 1/2 lbs. lean ground beef	1/4 C. water chestnuts, drained and diced
1 tsp. salt	
1/4 tsp. pepper	2 T. prepared teriyaki sauce
3/4 C. canned pineapple chunks, drained and diced	1 tsp. ginger

In a mixing bowl, combine all ingredients. Form into four patties. Grill over hot coals 4 minutes on first side, 8 minutes on other side (longer for well-done burgers). Top each burger with additional pineapple chunks and water chestnuts.

Pickle Burgers

1 1/2 lbs. lean ground beef	1 C. crushed pretzels
1 tsp. salt	1 T. prepared mustard
1/4 tsp. pepper	1 small red onion, sliced
1/2 C. bread and butter pickle slices, diced	

In a mixing bowl, combine ground beef, salt, pepper, pickles, pretzels, and mustard; form into four patties. Grill over hot coals 4 minutes on first side, 8 minutes on other side (longer for well-done burgers). Top burgers with red onion slices and additional pickle slices.

159

Creole-Style Burgers

1 1/2 lbs. lean ground beef
1 tsp. salt
1/4 tsp. pepper
1/2 C. finely chopped
    yellow bell pepper
1/2 C. finely chopped tomato

2 T. finely chopped
    green onion
2 T. catsup
1 tsp. minced garlic
1 tsp. oregano

In a mixing bowl, combine all ingredients; mix well and form into four patties. Grill over hot coals 4 minutes on first side and 8 minutes on other side (longer for well-done burgers). Top burgers with more chopped tomato, more chopped bell pepper, and barbecue sauce.

BARBECUED HOT DOG RECIPES

Stuffed Hot Dogs

4 hot dogs
4 thick slices American cheese

4 slivers sweet pickle
4 slices bacon

With a sharp knife, split hot dogs almost through. Stuff one slice of cheese and one sliver of pickle into each weiner. Wrap one slice bacon loosely around each weiner and secure with wooden picks. Place the weiners cut-side down on grill; grill over medium-low coals 6 minutes on each side.

Rodeo Hot Dogs

1 loaf French bread
1 tsp. prepared mustard
1 T. butter or margarine,
    softened

6 frankfurters
6 slices American cheese
6 tomato slices
2 T. catsup

Cut loaf of bread into thirds horizontally. On bottom layer of bread, spread mustard and butter. Cut frankfurters in half lengthwise and place on bread. Top with middle layer of bread. Arrange cheese and tomato slices on middle layer. Spread top layer

160

of bread with catsup, and put on the top layer. Wrap the loaf in foil, sealing edges. Grill over medium-low coals for 30 minutes. Serves six.

Fresh Salsa Hot Dog Topping

2 medium tomatoes,
   seeded and chopped

1/3 C. medium taco sauce

1/4 C. minced onion

2 T. chopped fresh parsley

2 1/2 C. shredded lettuce

In a medium bowl, combine tomatoes, taco sauce, onions, and parsley. Top each grilled hot dog with salsa and 1/4 C. shredded lettuce. Makes enough topping for eight franks.

Italian Two-Pepper Topping

1 green pepper, cubed

1 sweet red or yellow pepper,
   cubed

1 clove garlic, minced

1/2 tsp. oregano

1 tsp. vegetable oil

4 slices Mozzarella cheese,
   cut into fourths

In a small frying pan, stir-fry peppers, garlic, and oregano in oil for 3 to 5 minutes. Top each grilled hot dog with two slices of cheese and a spoonful of pepper topping. Makes enough topping for eight franks.

Chicago-Style Hot Dog Topper

1 small cucumber,
   cut into 8 wedges

4 tsp. mustard

1/2 C. sweet pickle relish

8 slices tomato,
   each cut in half

Top each grilled frankfurter with mustard and pickle relish. Arrange a cucumber wedge on one side and 2 tomato slices on the other side. Makes enough topping for eight franks.

Dad's Specialties

DUTCH OVEN RECIPES

Steak and Mushrooms

2 C. sliced mushrooms

4 steaks

Salt to taste

Pepper to taste

In small Dutch oven over medium coals, brown mushrooms in small amount of bacon drippings; remove from oven and set aside. Brown steaks on both sides; side aside. Place two steaks in bottom of oven; cover with a layer of mushrooms; place other two steaks on top of mushrooms; top with remaining mushrooms. Season with salt and pepper. Cover, place on low fire with coals on top of oven lid, and bake for 20-30 minutes. Serves four.

Dutch Oven Burger and Rice

1/3 lb. bacon,
   cut in small pieces

1 C. chopped onion

4 stalks celery, chopped

1 lb. lean ground beef

1 C. uncooked long-grain rice

1 quart stewed tomatoes
   with juice

1 C. water

1-2 tsp. salt

Broccoli spears, carrots,
   green beans, and mushrooms
   as desired

In Dutch oven, combine the bacon, onion, celery, and ground beef; cook over hot coals until ground beef is browned and bacon is crisp. Drain grease. Stir in rice, tomatoes, water, and salt. Add any vegetables desired. Cover and cook over hot coals with coals on lid for 30 minutes, stirring occasionally; add another cup of water and cook for an additional 20 minutes. Serves six.

Pork Chops and Scalloped Potatoes

4 large pork chops

4 large potatoes, sliced thin

2 large onions, sliced thin

1 can cream of mushroom soup

1 C. grated cheddar cheese

Trim pork chops to remove bones and excess fat; in medium Dutch oven, brown chops on both sides in vegetable oil or bacon drippings. Remove from oven. Layer half the potatoes in the bottom of the oven, then half the onions, then two chops, then half the cream of mushroom soup. Repeat the layers. Sprinkle grated cheddar cheese on top, and cover. Place oven on coals and arrange coals on lid. Cook 1-2 hours, until potatoes are tender. Serves four.

Chickaree Chicken

1 C. flour

1 T. salt

1 T. coarsely ground
   black pepper

4 skinless, boneless
   chicken breasts

1 T. butter or margarine

In a paper sack, combine flour, salt, and pepper; shake to mix. Drop chicken pieces in the paper bag, one at a time, and shake to coat completely with flour. Melt butter in medium Dutch oven; brown chicken in butter, turning to brown both sides. Cover oven and place coals on top of lid. Cook over medium-low heat for 1 hour, or until chicken is tender. Remove chicken from oven, stir 2-3 T. of flour mixture into the drippings, and whisk in enough milk to make a thickened gravy. Serve with hot biscuits if desired. Serves four.

Wilderness Beef Stew

2 lbs. stew meat,
   excess fat trimmed off

2 large potatoes, cut in cubes

4 carrots, cut in thick slices

4 stalks celery, sliced

1 can whole-kernel corn,
   drained

1 pkg. dry onion soup mix

2 C. hot water

In medium Dutch oven, brown stew meat on all sides in vegetable oil or bacon drippings. Add vegetables. Sprinkle onion soup mix over the meat and vegetables. Pour in hot water, cover, and place coals on top of lid. Cook over medium-low heat for 2-3 hours, or until meat and vegetables are tender. Serves six.

Clam Chowder

2 6-oz. cans minced clams,
    drained; reserve juice

3/4 C. chopped onion

3/4 C. diced celery

1 1/2 C. diced potatoes

1/3 C. butter or margarine

1/3 C. flour

2 C. half & half or light cream

3/4 tsp. salt

Dash of pepper

1 T. red wine vinegar

1 1/2 tsp. chopped parsley

Place onion, celery, and potatoes in a 12-inch Dutch oven; cover with juice from canned clams. (If vegetables aren't covered, add enough water to cover.) Simmer until potatoes are tender. In a second oven, melt butter; stir in flour and cook for 2 minutes. Add cream and whisk until smooth and thick. Stir in vegetables, clams, and seasonings. Heat through. Serves six.

Fish Roll-ups

3 carrots, cut in strips

6 broccoli spears, trimmed

6 filets of white fish

3 T. butter or margarine, melted

In a 14-inch Dutch oven, steam carrots and broccoli until crisp and tender. Wrap a fish filet around one broccoli spear and several carrot strips; secure by tying with string. Cook fish, turning as needed, until done. Fish should flake easily with a fork. Baste with melted butter and serve. Serves six.

It Takes More Than Just a Dutch Oven!

Want to try your hand at Dutch oven cooking?

Then a Dutch oven is just the beginning of what you'll need!

Dutch ovens come in a variety of sizes and materials; the most versatile are 12- and 14-inch ovens in cast iron. Lighter materials, such as aluminum, can disintegrate if you leave them in a campfire too long.

With Dutch oven in hand, you're ready to get started. Go over this basic checklist to make sure you have the rest of what you'll need:

--A small shovel

--Long-handled metal tongs

--Commercial charcoal briquettes; you can also make your own charcoal from campfire coals (hardwood are best)

--Heavy-duty aluminum foil

--A pair of heavy oven mitts

Dutch Oven Sloppy Joes

3 lbs. lean ground beef
1 medium onion, chopped
3 3/4 C. water
3 6-oz. cans tomato paste

3 pkgs. dry Sloppy Joe
  seasoning mix
4 C. biscuit mix
1 1/3 C. water

In a 12-inch Dutch oven, cook ground beef and onion until beef is browned and onion is transparent. Add tomato paste, 3 3/4 cups water, and seasoning mix; stir to combine. Cover and bring to a simmer; simmer 10 minutes. In a large bowl, combine biscuit mix and 1 1/3 cups water to make a soft dough. Drop by spoonfuls onto simmering sloppy joe mixture. Cover and bake until golden brown, or until an inserted knife comes out clean, with coals on lid of oven. Serves six.

Beanhole Beans

3 C. dry beans (pinto,
  Navy, great northern,
  or red kidney)

4 hamhocks
2 medium onions, chopped
1 C. grated cheddar cheese

This "Seasoning" Doesn't Come From a Salt Shaker

Before you use your Dutch oven for the first time, you need to "season" it--and you can't do it with a salt shaker!

First, wash your oven thoroughly with hot soapy water; it will remove residual oils from manufacturing if your oven is new, and will remove any cooking residue if your oven is used.

Next, "bake" your Dutch oven in a preheated 350-degree oven for approximately 30 minutes to dry out any moisture in the pores. Let cool. Rub the inside with shortening, being careful to completely cover the entire surface. Return to a 350-

degree oven for another 30 minutes to complete the seasoning.

Finally, wipe any excess shortening or oils from the oven, and you're ready to go!

In a large Dutch oven, cover beans with water; soak overnight. Drain. Place hamhocks in bottom of oven; add onions, beans, cheese, and enough water to cover all ingredients. Place a lid on the oven and place oven in a pit; cover lid with coals, hot rocks, and dirt. Cook for 3-4 hours, or until beans are tender. Serves six to eight.

Cheesy Green Beans

2 cans French-cut
  green beans, drained
1 can cream of mushroom soup

1/2 C. shredded cheddar cheese
1 T. bottled pimentoes, chopped

Place beans in bottom of small Dutch oven; add remaining ingredients and stir well. Cook until mixture is heated. Serves six.

Candied Yams

6 medium yams
1/4 C. butter or margarine
1 1/2 c. brown sugar, packed

In medium Dutch oven, cook yams until fork-tender, but still firm. Peel and slice into 1/2-inch slices. Melt butter in oven; brown yams on both sides. Sprinkle with brown sugar, and dot with additional butter. Cover and bake for 30 minutes. Serves six to eight.

Dutch Oven Baked Beans

1/4 lb. bacon
1/2 lb. lean ground beef
1 small onion, chopped
1 small green pepper, chopped
1/4 C. brown sugar, packed

1/4 C. catsup
8 oz. homestyle chili sauce
1 T. prepared mustard
1/4 lb. cooked ham, cut in cubes
1 31-oz. can pork and beans

In 12-inch Dutch oven, brown bacon and ground beef; add onion and green pepper, and cook until tender. Drain off fat. Add brown sugar, catsup, chili sauce, and mustard. Simmer for 15 minutes. Add beans and ham; cover and simmer for 2 hours with coals on lid. Serves six.

Twice-Baked Potatoes

2 medium baking potatoes

1/2 head broccoli, cut
   in bite-sized pieces

8 mushrooms, sliced

1 T. minced onion

1/4 C. butter or margarine

1/2 C. cream

1/2 tsp. salt

1/4 tsp. pepper

1/2 C. colby cheese, grated

Dash paprika

Scrub potatoes, oil skins lightly, and place on rack in 12-inch Dutch oven. Cover and bake over high heat, with coals on lid, for 1 hour or until potatoes are tender. Remove from oven and let cool. Melt butter in oven; saute onions until clear. Add mushrooms and cook until tender. Remove from oven and set aside. Steam broccoli for 8-10 minutes, or until tender. Remove from oven and rinse with cold water. Split baked potatoes in half. Carefully remove flesh; place in bowl with butter, cream, salt, and pepper; whip until fluffy. Layer whipped potatoes, mushroom mixture, and broccoli in each potato shell; top with cheese and sprinkle with paprika. Return to hot oven for 10-15 minutes, or until heated through and cheese is melted. Serves four.

It's the Pits!

The most carefree way to cook in a Dutch oven is in a pit. With a little preparation, you can virtually forget your food for hours on end!

Here's how it's done:

In a well-drained area, dig a pit that is about six inches deeper than your oven with its lid on and about one foot bigger around than your oven. Line the bottom and sides of the pit with dry flat stones; if you can get it, dry lava rock is ideal.

When you're ready to start cooking, lay a fire in the bottom of the pit with plenty of dry firewood; toss enough extra rocks to cover the lid of your oven. Light the fire. Once it has burned down to the coals, remove the coals and the extra stones from the pit.

Now comes the easy part: lower your oven into the pit, cover the lid with the hot stones from the fire, rake the hot coals on top of the pit, and cover the whole thing with the dirt you removed when you dug the pit.

Take off for four or five hours, and enjoy yourself! While you're gone, the hot rocks do the cooking for you. . .all you have to do is eat!

Campfire Potatoes and Onions

4-6 strips of bacon

4 large potatoes, sliced thin

2 large onions, sliced thin

Salt to taste

Pepper to taste

Line bottom of a 12-inch Dutch oven with bacon strips; fry until bacon is crisp. Layer potato and onion slices in oven; salt and pepper to taste. Cover and cook for approximately 30 minutes with coals on lid; turn oven often to avoid hot spots. Serves six.

Dutch Oven Vegetable Delight

2 C. small red potatoes

2 C. carrots, cut lengthwise

2 C. cauliflower, separated
   into flowerets

2 C. broccoli flowerets

2 C. white pearl onions

2 C. mushrooms, sliced

1 tsp. seasoned salt

Salt and pepper to taste

2 C. shredded cheddar cheese

Combine vegetables and seasonings in a Dutch oven; cover and steam over low coals for about 40 minutes. Sprinkle with cheese; cover and cook until cheese is melted, 1-2 minutes. Serves eight.

Dinner Rolls

1 C. lukewarm water

1/4 C. butter or margarine,
   melted

1/4 C. sugar

1 tsp. salt

1 egg

1 T. yeast or 1 yeast cake,
   dissolved in 1/4 C.
   lukewarm water

2 3/4 C. flour

In a large bowl, combine all ingredients. Beat well, form into a large ball, cover, and let raise for 1 hour. Knead for 10 minutes and shape into desired rolls. Spray the bottom of a 12-inch Dutch oven with vegetable spray; cover bottom of oven with rolls. Cover and bake for approximately 12 minutes, or until tops and bottoms of rolls are browned. If bottoms brown first, remove Dutch oven from fire and keep lid on to complete cooking. Serves six.

Sourdough Biscuits

1 1/4 C. warm water	1 T. sugar
1 T. active dry yeast	1 C. sourdough starter batter
1 tsp. salt	4 C. flour
1 T. shortening	

Dissolve yeast in warm water. Add salt, shortening, sugar, sourdough start, and 2 C. of the flour. Beat until smooth. Add enough of the remaining flour to make a soft dough; blend well and knead lightly until well mixed. Cover and allow to double in bulk, approximately 1 hour. Punch down. Pinch off golf-ballsized pieces and roll into balls. Place side-by-side in greased cake pans that will fit in the bottom of your Dutch oven. Cover and again allow to double in bulk. Place three pennies in the bottom of the oven, and put the cake pan on the pennies; cover with the oven lid and cover the lid with hot coals. Bake the biscuits until golden brown on the top and the bottom, checking every few minutes. Be careful: biscuits burn easily!

Potato Rolls

3/4 C. warm water	3/4 tsp. salt
1/3 C. sugar	1/3 C. shortening, softened
1 T. active dry yeast	1 egg
1/3 C. instant potato flakes	3 1/2 to 4 C. flour
1/3 C. hot water	

Mix 1 1/2 C. warm water and sugar in a large bowl; sprinkle yeast into water, and set aside to soften. Mix instant potatoes in hot water; set aside to cool. When yeast has dissolved completely, add salt, shortening, eggs, and cooled potatoes. Mix well. Add 2 C. flour and beat until smooth. Cover with a towel and let rest for 10 minutes. Mix in enough of the remaining flour to form a soft, easy-to-handle dough. Turn onto a lightly floured surface and knead until smooth and elastic. Place in a greased bowl, turn once so dough is greased, cover with a damp towel, and let double in bulk (1 1/2 to 2 hours). Shape into rolls and place in greased cake pans; cover and let double in bulk. Place on baking rack in 12-inch Dutch oven; cover and bake for 12-15 minutes with coals on lid. Serve with whipped honey butter. Makes two dozen rolls.

Quick and Easy Peach Cobbler

2 large cans sliced peaches
1 1/2 dry yellow cake mixes
Cinnamon to taste

Completely line a 12-inch Dutch oven with foil. Put the peaches in the bottom of the oven; sprinkle the dry cake mix over the peaches. Sprinkle with cinnamon to taste. Cover and bake for 35-45 minutes. Serve with ice cream or top with milk or cream if desired.

Whipped Honey Butter

1/4 C. butter or
   margarine, softened
1/4 C. honey

1 egg yolk
1/2 tsp. vanilla

In a small bowl, combine all ingredients. Beat until butter is light and fluffy. Serve on warm rolls or bread. Makes 1/2 cup.

How Many Coals Should You Use?

You want to cook--but not scorch--what's in the Dutch oven. So how many coals will get the job done?

That depends!

The cooking that takes place on the bottom of the oven is direct heat that transfers to the food. It gets the hottest the most quickly, and it's where most scorches occur. A general rule of thumb is to use one coal per diameter inch--in other words, you'd put 12 coals underneath a 12-inch Dutch oven.

The lid is a different story: that heat is radiant, so the food can tolerate more heat from the top. Remember, though, that the lid of your oven is concave--heat rays are focused toward the center of the oven. For even browning, put most of the coals on the lid around the outside rim; put only six or eight in the center. After about ten minutes, lift the lid and check to make sure the food is cooking evenly.

Fruited Baked Apples

4 apples

2 oranges, peeled, seeded, and separated into segments

4 T. brown sugar

Slice the top fourth off each apple; hollow out the core and seeds, being careful not to puncture the bottom of the apple. Fill each apple with orange segments; sprinkle with brown sugar. Replace the top on each apple and place the apples directly in the coals. Cook until soft. Let cool slightly before serving. Serves four.

Pudding Cake

1 yellow or chocolate pudding-type cake mix

3-4 chocolate candy bars

Spray the bottom and sides of a 12-inch Dutch oven with vegetable spray. Sprinkle a few teaspoons of dry cake mix in the bottom of the oven and shake back and forth to coat the bottom evenly. Mix the cake according to package directions and pour into the oven, checking to make sure the oven is level. Cover and bake with coals on lid until cake pulls away from the sides of the oven and is springy to the touch. Remove from heat. Place chocolate bars on cake; when warm, spread over cake. Serve warm.

Fruit Cobbler

1/4 C. butter or margarine	2 C. biscuit mix
1 C. brown sugar, firmly packed	1/4 C. brown sugar, firmly packed
3 cans sliced peaches, drained (reserve juice)	

In 14-inch Dutch oven, melt butter; stir in 1 C. brown sugar. Cover with peach slices. Bring peach mixture to a boil. In a large bowl, mix biscuit mix and 1/4 C. brown sugar; stir in enough peach juice to make a batter. Pour batter over simmering peaches in oven; cover and bake 10 minutes. Remove lid, sprinkle top of cobbler with additional brown sugar, replace lid, and cook an additional 10 minutes. Serve warm with cream.

Pineapple Upside-Down Cake

3 cans pineapple chunks,
  drained (reserve juice)
1/4 C. butter or margarine
1 C. brown sugar, firmly packed

1 lemon cake mix
1/2 C. brown sugar,
  firmly packed

Completely line a 14-inch Dutch oven with foil, shiny side up. Spray foil with vegetable spray. Put butter in oven until melted; stir in 1 C. brown sugar and pineapple chunks. Bring to a boil. In a large bowl, combine dry cake mix, 1/2 C. brown sugar, and enough reserved pineapple juice to make a batter. Pour batter over boiling pineapple chunks. Cover with lid and bake until cake is browned and pulls away from sides. Invert cake and remove foil; serve warm.

Dutch Oven Fudge

1/2 C. butter or margarine
1 can evaporated milk
5 C. sugar
2 C. chocolate chips

1 C. chopped nuts
1 heaping C. marshmallow
  creme

Melt butter in bottom of 12-inch Dutch oven, turning oven as butter melts so entire inside of oven is coated. Add milk and sugar; cook and stir until thickened (the mixture should make a sucking noise when you stir it). Remove from heat; pour into a large bowl. Quickly stir in chocolate chips, nuts, and marshmallow creme. Beat until the mixture is stiff; scrape bowl and pour mixture into greased or foil-lined cookie sheet. Spread quickly. When cool, cut into pieces.

Lemon Poppy Seed Cake

1 pkg. lemon or
  yellow cake mix
1 pkg. instant lemon pudding
4 eggs

1/2 C. vegetable oil
1 C. water
1/2 C. poppy seeds

Combine all ingredients in a large bowl; mix for five minutes. Bake in a covered greased or foil-lined oven for 40 minutes, or until cake pulls away from sides of oven. Serve warm.

Dad's Specialties

174B

CHILI RECIPES

Home-Style Chili

3 C. kidney beans
6 C. water
1 1/2 lbs. ground beef
1 large onion, chopped
4 tsp. salt
1 C. chopped celery
1 tsp. pepper

4 tsp. chili powder
1 #2 1/2 can tomatoes,
  pureed in blender
2 cans tomato sauce
1/2 C. catsup
1 tsp. celery salt

Wash beans; cover with water and soak overnight. In a skillet, cook meat and onions until meat is browned and onions are tender. Add to beans in a heavy kettle. Stir in remaining ingredients except celery. Bring to a boil, reduce heat, and simmer for 4 to 6 hours, stirring occasionally. Add more water if necessary to keep chili from scorching. Add celery and simmer 30 minutes more. Serves twelve. Leftovers can be frozen!

Freeze-Ahead Chili Mix

5 lbs. lean ground beef

3 onions, chopped

1 quart tomatoes

1/2 C. flour

1/2 C. quick-cooking oatmeal

2 T. chili powder

2 T. paprika

1 T. oregano

4 T. sugar

4 T. salt

1 1/2 tsp. garlic powder

In a skillet, cook ground beef and onions until beef is lightly browned and onions are tender. Add tomatoes and cook mixture slowly until well done. Combine flour, oatmeal, and seasonings; mix well. Add flour-oatmeal mixture to meat mixture. Press mixture into loaf pans; cover with foil, seal tightly, and freeze. When frozen solid, remove from pans, wrap in waxed paper, and wrap in foil; seal and label. When ready to make chili, thaw one block of mix. Add equal amount of beans, and simmer until heated. Use a heavy pan to prevent scorching, or heat in a double-boiler.

Vegetable-Beef Chili

1 T. vegetable oil

1 lb. lean ground beef

1 C. chopped onions

1 clove garlic, minced

1 1/2 tsp. cumin

1 1/2 tsp. oregano

1 1/2 tsp. seeded, chopped hot chile pepper

1 1/2 C. water

2 C. mushrooms, sliced

2 medium tomatoes, chopped

1/2 C. chopped green pepper

1/2 C. chopped sweet red pepper

1/2 C. diced zucchini

1/4 C. diced celery

1/4 C. coarsley shredded carrot

1 T. chili pepper, or to taste

1 16-oz. can red kidney beans, drained

In large kettle, heat oil. Add beef, onions, and garlic; cook until beef is browned and onions are tender. Add cumin, oregano, chile pepper, and water; bring to a boil. Add all remaining ingredients except beans; bring to a boil, reduce heat, and simmer for 1 hour. Add the beans, and heat through. Serves four.

Pork Chili

2 T. vegetable oil

4 strips bacon, diced

2 lbs. stewing pork,
cut into cubes

1/2 C. flour

1 C. chopped onion

3 cloves garlic, minced

3 T. chili powder

1-3 jalapeno peppers, stemmed,
seeded, and chopped

2 C. chicken broth

1/4 tsp. salt

2 15-oz. cans pinto beans,
drained and rinsed

Heat oil in kettle; add bacon, cook until crisp, and remove with a slotted spoon. Drain on paper towels and set aside. Put flour in a paper bag; add pork cubes, and shake to coat well. Remove pork and shake off any excess flour. Saute pork in bacon drippings until evenly browned. Reduce heat to medium. Stir in cooked bacon, onion, and garlic; cook about 8 minutes, or until onion is transparent and garlic is soft. Add chili powder, jalapeno peppers, and chicken broth. Heat to boiling, reduce heat, and simmer uncovered for 2 hours or until pork is tender and sauce is thick. (If sauce gets too thick during cooking, add water to thin slightly.) Stir in salt. To serve, heat beans; ladle meat and sauce over beans. Serves six.

Chicken Chili

2 lbs. skinless, boneless
chicken breasts, cut
into cubes

1/4 C. vegetable oil

1 c. chopped onion

3 cloves garlic, minced

1 sweet red pepper,
seeded and diced

1 4-oz. can mild green chilis,
drained and chopped

1 16-oz. can whole tomatoes
with liquid, chopped

1 1/2 T. tomato paste

3 T. chili powder

1 tsp. oregano

1 C. chicken broth

2 T. cornmeal

1/4 tsp. salt

In a large kettle, saute chicken in oil, stirring frequently, until chicken is white and firm to the touch. Reduce heat to medium; add onion and garlic, cooking until onion is transparent and garlic is soft. Add all remaining ingredients except salt; stir well to combine. Bring to boiling; reduce heat and simmer, uncovered, for 30 minutes or until chicken is tender, stirring occasionally. Stir in salt. Serves six.

Vegetarian Chili

1/2 C. dried red kidney beans

1/2 C. dried pinto beans

8 C. cold water

1 1/2 C. chopped onion

3 cloves garlic, minced

1/2 C. diced carrot

1/2 C. diced celery

1/3 C. vegetable oil

1 C. dried lentils, washed

4 T. chili powder

1 T. oregano

2 tsp. coriander

2 T. paprika

1 16-oz. can whole tomatoes
   with liquid, chopped

1 sweet red pepper,
   seeded and chopped

2 C. sliced mushrooms

1/4 C. soy sauce

1/4 tsp. salt

Wash red kidney beans and pinto beans, discarding any stones or misshapen beans. Place beans in a large bowl, cover with 5 C. of the cold water, and soak overnight. Rinse and drain. Set aside. In a large kettle, saute onions, garlic, carrots, and celery in oil until onion is transparent. Add drained beans, lentils, chili powder, oregano, coriander, paprika, tomatoes, and the other 3 C. water; stir to combine well. Bring to a boil, reduce heat, and simmer uncovered, stirring occasionally, for 1 1/2 hours. Add the sweet red pepper, mushrooms, and soy sauce; simmer another 2 hours, adding more water if necessary, until beans are tender. Stir in salt. Serves six.

Midwestern-Style Chili

1/2 lb. lean ground beef

1 medium onion, chopped

1 small green pepper, chopped

1 clove garlic, minced

1 28-oz. can whole tomatoes
   with liquid, chopped

1 8-oz. can tomato sauce

2 T. chili powder

1/2 tsp. salt

1 15-oz. can red kidney beans
   or red beans, drained

In a large kettle, brown ground beef with onion, green pepper, and garlic. Add remaining ingredients except beans; bring to a boil, reduce heat, and simmer covered, stirring occasionally, for 30 minutes. Add beans; continue simmering for 15 minutes. Serves six.

Sweet Dixie Chili

1/2 lb. ground sausage

1 medium onion, chopped

1 medium green pepper, chopped

1 C. chopped celery

1 16-oz. can tomato juice

1 16-oz. can whole tomatoes with juice, chopped

1 T. chili powder

1 T. brown sugar, firmly packed

1 bay leaf

1 15-oz. can red beans, drained

In large kettle, brown sausage with onion, green pepper, and celery; drain. Add remaining ingredients except beans. Bring to a boil; reduce heat, cover, and simmer 45 minutes, stirring occasionally. Add beans and continue simmering for 15 minutes. Serves six.

Add Zest to Canned Chili

If you don't have time to cook it from scratch, canned chili can be a good alternative--if you take a minute to dress it up!

The next time you open a can, try making some of these improvements:

--Water too-thick chili down with tomato juice, beer, or red wine

--Add chopped fresh or canned tomatoes with liquid

--Saute chopped onions, chopped green pepper, and minced garlic in a little vegetable oil; stir into the canned chili

--Stir in tomato sauce, and top with shredded cheese and avocado chunks

How to Put Out The Fire

Wondering what to serve with chili?

You can calm the fire of spicy chili with bread--so use your imagination! A popular accompaniment is sweet cornbread; you can also try home-style biscuits or moist soda bread. Cool gelatin salad helps take the gas out of beans. And remember an icy drink!

Cincinnati Parlor Chili

1 lb. ground beef

1 medium onion, chopped

1 clove garlic, minced

2 8-oz. cans tomato sauce

1 C. water

1/2 oz. unsweetened chocolate

1 T. red wine vinegar

1 T. chili powder

1 tsp. allspice

1/2 tsp. cinnamon

1/2 tsp. salt

1 15-oz. can red beans, drained

Hot cooked spaghetti

Shredded cheddar cheese

Chopped onions

How Hot? . . . A Guide to Fresh Chiles

What kind of chile should you chop up and toss in the kettle with your simmering chili?

The answer depends on how hot you want that brew!

As a rule, the smaller the fresh chile, the hotter it is. The hottest chiles also are the ones that are the most narrow with the most pointed or rounded ends. Chiles that are broader at the top with blunt ends are more mild.

No matter what you might have heard, color doesn't determine hotness: red chiles have simply been ripened by the sun. And even though you should discard the seeds, they aren't the hottest part-- the spice comes from capsaicin, found in the veins. To make a chile milder, scrape out the membranes. Always discard the tops.

If chiles are plump and firm and blemish-free when you buy them, you can usually store them in a plastic bag in the refrigerator for about two weeks. Red chiles will not store as long as green chiles will.

When you're ready to simmer up some chili, look for these varieties:

Serrano. Watch out--these are some of the hottest! They are bright green, very thin, and very long. You can also find them canned in the ethnic section of the grocery store.

Jalapeno. Jalapeno are also extremely hot. They're dark green, thin, and two to three inches long. Most stores also have them canned or pickled.

California. These are mild; they are medium green, broad at the top, and blunt on the ends. When canned, they're usually called simply "green chiles." You can usually find them either whole or chopped in the can.

Poblano. Another mild chile, these look like a green pepper. You can't find them canned, but some stores have them in dried form.

A word of warning: fresh chiles, especially the hot varieties, can be very irritating to your skin. Wash your hands immediately after chopping chiles; avoid prolonged contact with juices. If your skin is sensitive, wear rubber gloves.

In a large kettle, brown ground beef, onion, and garlic; drain. Add tomato sauce, water, chocolate, vinegar, and seasonings. Bring to a boil; reduce heat, cover, and simmer for 45 minutes, stirring occasionally. Add beans, and continue simmering for 15 minutes. Serve chili ladled over spaghetti; top with cheese and onions. Serves four.

San Francisco Vegetarian Chili

1 medium onion, chopped	1 C. red wine, water, or beef broth
1 medium green pepper, chopped	1 T. chili powder
2 C. sliced mushrooms	1 tsp. cumin
1 clove garlic, minced	1 tsp. oregano
2 16-oz. cans stewed tomatoes with liquid, chopped	1/4 tsp. red pepper sauce
	1 medium zucchini, chopped
1 8-oz. can tomato sauce	1 15-oz. can red beans, drained

In large kettle, saute onion, green pepper, mushrooms, and garlic in a little vegetable oil until tender. Add remaining ingredients except zucchini and beans. Bring to a boil, reduce heat, and simmer covered for 45 minutes, stirring occasionally. Stir in zucchini and beans and continue simmering for 15 minutes until zucchini is crisp-tender. If desired, garnish each serving with sour cream, sliced avocado, and shredded Monterey Jack cheese. Serves six.

The Best Chili Toppers

Once you've ladled up a steaming bowl of chili, top it with one or more of the following:
- --Spanish onion, sliced and separated into rings or finely chopped
- --Sliced chile peppers, either hot or mild
- --Dollops of sour cream
- --Shredded cheese; use cheddar, Monterey Jack, or a combination of the two
- --Shredded raw carrot
- --Shredded raw celery
- --Sliced or cubed avocado, sprinkled with fresh lime juice
- --Slivers of sweet or dill pickle
- --Raisins
- --Coarsely chopped almonds

Dad's Specialties

MEXICAN, TEX-MEX, AND PIZZA SPECIALTIES

Two-Way Enchiladas

Enchilada Sauce

2 T. butter
1/3 C. chopped onion
1/3 C. chopped green pepper
1 15-oz. can tomato sauce
3/4 C. condensed chicken
    bouillon
1/3 C. sliced pitted ripe olives

2 T. hot salsa
1 tsp. chili powder
1 tsp. cumin
1 tsp. sugar
1/4 tsp. salt
1/8 tsp. pepper

Bean Filling

2 T. butter
1/2 C. chopped onion
1/2 C. chopped green pepper
1 8-oz. pkg. cream cheese

3 T. milk
2 C. canned garbanzo beans,
    drained
1/4 tsp. salt

Beef Filling

1 lb. lean ground beef
1/2 C. chopped onion
1/2 C. chopped green pepper

1 8-oz. pkg. cream cheese
3 T. milk
1/4 tsp. salt

Tortillas

1 14-oz. pkg. large corn tortillas
3/4 C. shredded colby cheese
3/4 C. chredded Monterey Jack cheese

For sauce, melt butter in large saucepan; saute onion and green pepper in butter until tender-crisp, about 3 minutes. Stir in remaining sauce ingredients. Simmer, uncovered, 15 minutes, stirring occasionally. Set aside, and prepare bean or beef filling (directions below). Preheat oven to 350 degrees. Wrap tortillas in foil; heat in oven for 10 minutes to soften. Dip each tortilla in sauce. Spoon 1/4 C. filling over each tortilla and roll up; place seam side down in a rectangular baking dish. Spoon remaining sauce over tortillas. Cover baking dish with foil; bake 25 minutes. Remove foil; sprinkle enchiladas with cheeses. Return to oven just long enough to melt cheeses (about 3 minutes). Serve hot.

Bean filling: Melt butter in small skillet; saute onion and green pepper in butter until tender-crisp. Beat cream cheese and milk until smooth; stir in sauteed vegetables, beans, and salt.

Beef filling: Cook ground beef, onions, and green peppers in a skillet until the meat is brown and crumbly. Drain well. In a mixing bowl, beat cream cheese and milk until smooth. Stir in meat mixture and salt.

When Eating Mexican, Speak the Language!

Ready to bite into a crisp Mexican something-or-the-other, but you're not sure you have the lingo down?

It's easy, once you know a few terms!

Tex-Mex food--a version of Mexican food made popular in the border states of California, Texas, and New Mexico--commonly features the following:

Burrito: a large flour tortilla that is filled with a mixture of beans, meat, and/or vegetables, and folded.

Chimichanga: a large flour tortilla that is filled with a bean and/or meat mixture, folded like a burrito, and then deepfat fried until crispy.

Cilantro: a leafy herb that looks like parsley.

Flauta: two corn tortillas that are overlapped, filled with a meat or bean mixture, rolled, and deep-fat fried until crispy.

Guacamole: a mixture made of mashed ripe avocado, seasoned with various other foods (most often tomatoes, garlic, or onion).

Salsa: a spicy sauce made of tomatoes, chiles, onions, and various other ingredients.

Tortilla: a round, flat bread, made of either flour or corn.

Tostada: a flat, fried corn or flour tortilla topped with a variety of toppings, most commonly cooked shredded beef or chicken, refried beans, lettuce, onions, tomatoes, sour cream, cheese, and salsa.

Tortilla Skyscrapers

1 pkg. flour tortillas

1 can refried beans

1 lb. lean ground beef
(optional)

1 green pepper, chopped

1/2 lb. shredded cheddar cheese

1/2 lb. shredded Monterey
Jack cheese

1 can chopped olives

4 green onions, sliced thin

2 tomatoes, chopped

1 small head lettuce, shredded

1 C. sour cream

Salsa

In a skillet, fry tortillas in oil until crisp; drain on paper towels. Line 2 cookie sheets with foil. Place 2 tortillas on each. On each tortilla, build the following layers: first layer, ground beef, beans, salsa; second layer, tortilla; third layer, cheddar cheese and green pepper; fourth layer, tortilla; fifth layer, Monterey Jack cheese, olives, and onions. Bake at 350 degrees until cheese melts, about 10-15 minutes. Top as desired with lettuce, chopped tomato, salsa, and sour cream.

Saltado

1 lb. round steak,
cut in thin wedges

1/4 tsp. salt

1/4 tsp. pepper

1/4 T. cumin

2 T. vegetable oil

1 medium onion, cut in wedges

1 medium tomato, cut in wedges

Season meat with spices. Cook meat in hot oil until browned; add onions and cook for 2 minutes more. Add tomatoes, and cook for 2-3 minutes. *Do not overcook.* Serve over rice; serves four.

Beef and Cheese Enchiladas

1 15-oz. can tomato sauce

1 4-oz. can chopped green
chiles, undrained

1 T. chili powder
(more if desired)

3 C. shredded sharp
cheddar cheese

1 C. shredded cooked beef

12 tortillas

Vegetable oil

1/4 C. sliced green onions

1/4 C. sliced radishes

In a bowl, combine tomato sauce, chilis, and chili powder; mix well. Combine 1 C. tomato sauce mixture, 2 C. cheese, and meet. Dip tortillas in hot oil; drain. Place 1/4 C. cheese mixture on each tortilla; roll up tightly. Place, seam-side down, in a rectangular baking dish. Top with remaining tomato sauce mixture; cover. Bake at 350 degrees for 40 minutes. Sprinkle with remaining cheese and continue baking until cheese is melted. Top with green onion and radish slices. Serves six.

Layered Mexican Dip

1 16-oz. can refried beans

Sour cream

1/4 C. salsa

1 8-oz. jar pasteurized
   processed cheese spread

2 T. green onions, sliced

Tortilla chips

In a bowl, combine beans, 1/4 C. sour cream, and salsa; mix well. Set aside. In another bowl, combine 1/4 C. sour cream, cheese spread, and green onions; mix well. In a shallow pan or pie plate, layer alternating layers of the bean mixture and the processed cheese spread mixture. Top with additional sour cream and a layer of tortilla chips. Serve as a dip with tortilla chips. Makes 3 cups.

Layered Taco Salad

1 lb. lean ground beef

1 envelope taco seasoning mix

1 C. hot water

1 24-oz. carton small-curd
   cottage cheese

1 envelope low-calorie
   ranch salad dressing mix

1/2 small head lettuce,
   finely chopped

2 fresh tomatoes, seeded
   and chopped

1 4-oz. can mild green chiles,
   drained and chopped

2 C. shredded cheddar cheese

Taco shells

In a skillet, cook ground beef until browned; stir in taco seasoning mix and water, and simmer for 5-10 minutes, or until thickened, stirring frequently. Spread in a 9 x 13 pan, and set aside.

In a medium bowl, blend dry ranch dressing mix and cottage cheese; spoon on top of ground beef mixture. Add layers of lettuce, tomatoes, green chiles, and cheese. Serve with taco shells.

Chicken Enchiladas

2 C. chopped, cooked chicken

1 4-oz. can diced green chiles

2 T. butter or margarine

1/8 C. flour

1/4 tsp. salt

1 1/4 C. chicken broth

3/4 tsp. chicken bouillon
    granules

1/2 C. sour cream

3/4 C. grated cheddar,
    mozzarella, or
    Monterey Jack cheese

6 12-inch flour or corn tortillas

In a bowl, combine chicken and chiles; set aside. In a saucepan, melt butter; stir in flour and salt and cook for 2 minutes. Stir in chicken broth all at once; cook until thickened and bubbly, stirring constantly with a wire whisk. Add bouillon granules and cook 2 additional minutes. Remove from heat; stir in sour cream and cheese. Stir 1/2 C. sauce into chicken-chile mixture. Dip each tortilla into remaining sauce; fill each with 1/4 C. chicken mixture, roll up tightly, and place seam-side down in a rectangular baking dish. Pour remaining sauce over the top. Sprinkle with cheese. Bake at 350 degrees for 20 minutes, or until bubbly. Serves six.

Cheese Enchiladas

12 flour tortillas

4 C. grated cheddar cheese

1 C. green onion tops, chopped

2 T. margarine

1 large onion, chopped

1 green pepper, chopped

1/2 T. chili powder

2 T. flour

2 8-oz. cans tomato sauce

2 C. water

In a skillet, melt margarine; cook onions and pepper in margarine until tender-crisp. Add flour, salt, and chili powder; stir until combined well. Add tomato sauce and water; cook until thickened, stirring frequently. In a mixing bowl, combine cheese and green onion tops. Set aside. Dip each tortilla in sauce; fill each with cheese mixture, roll up tightly, and place seamside down in a 9 x 13 baking dish. Make only a single layer. Pour remaining sauce over tortillas and sprinkle with cheese and onions. Bake, covered, at 375 degrees for 25 minutes or until bubbly. Serves six.

Mexican Marinated Salad

1 head lettuce,
   torn into pieces
1 green bell pepper, chopped
1 red bell pepper, chopped
3 tomatoes, chopped
1 red onion, sliced
1 bunch fresh coriander
   (cilantro), chopped

1 clove garlic, crushed
1/2 C. red wine vinegar
1/2 C. vegetable oil
1/2 tsp. pepper
1/2 tsp. paprika
1/4 tsp. salt
1/2 C. black olives

In a large shallow dish, arrange lettuce, green pepper, red pepper, tomatoes, and onion slices, broken into rings. Sprinkle with coriander and toss lightly to mix. In a small bowl, combine garlic, red wine vinegar, oil, pepper, paprika, and salt; mix thoroughly. Pour vinegar mixture over vegetables; toss lightly, cover, and refrigerate for at least one hour before serving. Sprinkle with black olives and serve.

Santa Fe Bean Salad

1 1/2 C. cooked pinto beans
1 1/2 C. cooked small
   kidney beans
1 C. cooked whole-kernel corn
1/4 C. chopped green
   bell pepper
1/4 C. chopped red bell pepper
3 green onions, sliced

1/4 C. fresh cilantro
2 ripe tomatoes, chopped
1/4 C. vegetable oil
2 T. wine vinegar
1 clove garlic, mashed
Dash chili powder
Dash cumin

In a large serving bowl, combine pinto beans, kidney beans, corn, green pepper, red pepper, green onions, cilantro, and tomatoes; chill. In a small bowl, combine oil, wine vinegar, garlic, chili powder, and cumin; chill. Just before serving, toss pinto bean mixture and dressing. Serves four.

Beef and Bean Tostados

Vegetable oil

8 6-inch corn tortillas

1 lb. lean ground beef

1 medium onion, chopped

1 clove garlic, minced

1 15-oz. can tomato sauce

2 tsp. chili powder

1 tsp. oregano

1 tsp. salt

1/4 tsp. cumin

1/4 tsp. crushed red peppers

1 15-oz. can refried beans

2 C. shredded Monterey Jack cheese

4 C. shredded lettuce

3 medium tomatoes, sliced

1 avocado, sliced

Dairy sour cream

1 8-oz. jar hot chili salsa

Heat 1/4 inch of oil in skillet; fry one tortilla at a time until slightly brown and crisp (about 30 seconds on each side). Drain on paper towels. Keep warm in 200-degree oven no longer than 15-20 minutes. Cook beef, onion, and garlic until beef is browned; drain. Stir in tomato sauce, chili powder, oregano, salt, cumin, and red peppers. Heat to boiling; reduce heat. Simmer uncovered for 15 minutes. Place 1/3 C. heated refried beans on each tortilla; spread with 1/3 C. meat mixture. Sprinkle each tostada with cheese and lettuce. Arrange tomato and avocado slices on top. Top with sour cream and serve with chili salsa. Serves six to eight.

Flour Tortillas

2 C. flour

1 tsp. baking powder

1 tsp. salt

1/4 tsp. sugar

2 T. shortening

3/4 C. warm water

Combine flour, baking powder, salt, and sugar; cut in shortening with a pastry blender, two knives, or fingers. Make a well in the center of the mixture; pour in half the water. Add the rest of the water, a few drops at a time, and work with hands until you have a firm dough. Knead 15 or 20 times, then allow to rest for 10 minutes. Form dough into egg-sized balls; roll each ball with a rolling pin until about 6 inches in diameter and 1/8 inch thick. To cook tortillas, heat a griddle or skillet (preferably cast iron). Cook each tortilla until it has light brown flecks on each side. Keep warm and dry until served.

Whole Wheat Tortillas

3 C. whole wheat flour

1 C. white flour

2 tsp. salt

2 tsp. baking powder

1/4 C. shortening

1 1/2 C. hot water

Sift dry ingredients together. Cut in shortening until mixture is crumbly; stir in water gradually, using only enough to make a pliable but not sticky dough. Knead dough on floured board for 5 minutes. Form egg-sized balls and let dough rest for 15 minutes. With a rolling pin, roll each ball until at least 6 inches in diameter. Cook on a hot griddle, about 1 minute on each side. Don't overcook-- tortillas will be tough.

Mexican Quiche

1 9-inch unbaked pie shell

4 eggs, slightly beaten

1 T. butter or margarine

1/2 C. diced onion

1 4-oz. can green chiles,
    drained and chopped

2 C. coarsely grated sharp
    cheddar cheese

1 C. sour cream

1/2 C. milk

1/2 tsp. salt

1/4 tsp. pepper

Heat oven to 425 degrees; bake pie shell for 15 minutes. Brush bottom of baked crust with a little of the beaten egg and bake 2 additional minutes. In a skillet, melt butter; stir in onion and green chiles, cooking until tender. Sprinkle into pie shell; top with grated cheese. Pour remaining eggs into mixing bowl; beat in sour cream, milk, salt, and pepper. Pour mixture into pie shell. Place in oven preheated to 425 degrees; reduce heat to 350 and bake for 30 minutes, or until knife inserted in center comes out clean. Serves six.

Sopaipillas

4 C. white flour

1 T. baking powder

1 tsp. salt

1 T. sugar

2 T. shortening

3/4 C. warm water

Vegetable oil for deep frying

Sift dry ingredients together; cut in shortening until the mixture looks crumbly. Add enough water to make a firm, smooth dough. Knead dough briefly. Cover and let rest 15 minutes. While heating oil in a frying pan, roll dough out to 1/4-inch thickness. Cut into 3-inch squares and fry in hot oil until golden on both sides, turning frequently. Drain on paper towels. Serve hot dusted with powdered sugar or with honey butter.

Mexican Bread Pudding

1 C. brown sugar, firmly packed

1 1/2 C. water

2 T. butter or margarine

1 tsp. ground cinnamon

1 tsp. grated orange peel

5 C. 1/2-inch cubes toasted French bread

1/2 C. chopped almonds or walnuts

1/2 C. raisins

1 tart apple, chopped

1 C. shredded Monterey Jack cheese

Heat brown sugar, water, margarine, cinnamon, and orange peel to boiling; reduce heat and simmer, uncovered, 5 minutes. Layer half the bread cubes, nuts, raisins, apple, and cheese in ungreased casserole dish; repeat layers. Pour hot brown sugar syrup over the top. Bake uncovered at 350 degrees for 30 minutes or until syrup is absorbed. Serves six.

Beef Fajitas

1/4 C. freshly squeezed lime juice

1 1/2 lbs. steak, trimmed

2 large cloves garlic, sliced

1/4 tsp. crushed red peppers

2 C. salsa

1 C. sour cream

8 flour tortillas

Lime slices for garnish

Pour lime juice into a shallow dish; with the tip of a sharp knife, lightly score both sides of the steak in a diamond pattern, and place steak in dish. Sprinkle with sliced garlic and crushed red peppers. Turn steak over several times until well coated and let marinate at room temperature, turning several times, for 30 minutes. Heat tortillas in a warm (200-degree) oven; set aside, keeping warm. Remove meat from marinade, reserving marinade. Broil steak 5 inches from heat source for 4 to 5 minutes on each side, basting with marinade. Cut steak into thin slices. Place 3-4 slices of steak on each warmed tortilla; top with 1/4 C. salsa and 2 T. sour cream. Fold tortillas in half and garnish with lime slices. Serves four.

Easy Guacamole

2 ripe avocados

1 small tomato, diced

1 clove garlic, crushed

1 T. lemon juice

1/2 tsp. chili powder

1/2 tsp. salt

Peel avocados; remove pit, cut in half, and mash in a bowl with a fork. Stir in tomatoes, garlic, lemon juice, chili powder, and salt until blended. Cover tightly; refrigerate until chilled (will keep for up to 24 hours). Makes 1 1/2 cups.

Home-Baked Tortilla Chips

8 6-inch corn tortillas

Vegetable oil for frying

1/4 tsp. salt

Using scissors, cut each tortilla into 6-8 pie-shaped wedges. Pour oil into a skillet until it is about 1 inch deep; heat. Fry tortilla wedges, turning once, until crisp and golden, about 1 minute. Drain well on paper towels and sprinkle with salt. Store tightly covered in a cool place. Makes 48-64 chips.

If desired, you can sprinkle chips with a dash of chili powder or seasoned salt.

Home-Style Refried Beans

2 T. vegetable oil

1 15-oz. can pinto beans
with liquid

1/2 tsp. salt

Dash pepper

In a heavy skillet over high heat, heat oil. Pour in beans and liquid a little at a time, mashing with the back of a spoon or a potato masher until in a coarse paste. Reduce heat and cook until beans are desired consistency, adding more water as needed. Season with salt and pepper. Makes 2 cups.

Seasoned Refried Beans

2 T. vegetable oil

1 15-oz. can pinto beans
with liquid

1/2 C. finely chopped onion

1 clove garlic, minced

1 bay leaf

1 green chili, finely chopped

1/4 C. tomato sauce

1/2 tsp. salt

In a heavy skillet over high heat, heat oil. Pour in beans and liquid a little at a time, mashing with the back of a spoon or a potato masher until in a coarse paste. Reduce heat; stir in onion, garlic, bay leaf, chili, and tomato sauce. Simmer for 15 minutes or until onion is tender, adding more water until beans are of a desired consistency. Remove bay leaf. Season with salt. Makes 2 1/2 cups.

South-of-the-Border Cornbread

2 T. vegetable oil

2 C. whole-kernel corn, chopped

3 eggs

1 C. sour cream

1 C. yellow cornmeal

1 C. green chiles, chopped

1 tsp. baking soda

1 tsp. salt

2 c. shredded Monterey
Jack cheese

Combine all ingredients but oil; mix thoroughly. Heat oil in a large skillet; pour bread batter into skillet and bake for 45 minutes or until firm. Cut in small squares and serve warm with soups, stews, or other main dishes. Serves four.

Chunky Salsa

1 13-oz. can green tomatoes, drained and chopped fine

1 small onion, chopped fine

1 clove garlic, minced

3 canned jalapeno peppers, chopped fine

4 sprigs parsley, chopped

1/4 tsp. salt

In a medium bowl, mix all ingredients. Cover and refrigerate at least 24 hours before serving; flavor gets better the longer you wait. Makes 2 cups.

Spicy Avocado Salsa

1 medium avocado, peeled, pitted, and diced

1 large fresh tomato, diced

2 T. onion, finely chopped

1 clove garlic, minced

1 T. fresh parsley, chopped

1 T. lemon juice

1/4 tsp. hot red pepper sauce

In a medium bowl, combine all ingredients. Stir until well mixed; cover tightly and refrigerate until well chilled. Makes 2 cups.

Huevos Rancheros

1/4 C. oil

4 6-inch corn tortillas

8 eggs

1 C. salsa

1 small avocado, peeled, pitted, and sliced

1 jalapeno chili, sliced

Pour 2 T. oil into heavy skillet; heat. Fry tortillas one at a time, turning once, for 30 seconds. Drain well on paper towels. Place one tortilla on each of four plates; keep warm. Heat remaining 2 T. oil in same skillet; fry each egg. Place 2 eggs on each tortilla; top with 1/4 C. salsa and garnish with avocado slices and chiles. Serve immediately. Serves four.

Bean Burritos

6 flour tortillas, warmed

1 15-oz. can pinto beans, drained

1 tsp. vegetable oil

Dash salt

1 clove garlic, minced

2 green onions, finely chopped

3/4 C. shredded Monterey Jack cheese

1/2 small head lettuce, shredded

In a large skillet, heat oil; add beans gradually, mashing with the back of a spoon or a potato masher until a coarse meal. Stir in salt and garlic. Spoon a little of the bean mixture down the center of each tortilla; top with green onions and cheese. Roll up tightly. Heat tortillas in a 300-degree oven for about 5 minutes, or until cheese is melted. To serve, surround with shredded lettuce and spoon salsa or taco sauce over top. Serves four.

Spicy Tamale Pie

4 C. water

1 1/2 C. yellow cornmeal

1 1/2 tsp. salt

1 1/2 lbs. lean ground beef

1/2 lb. sweet Italian sausage

2 T. onion, finely chopped

1/4 C. chopped celery

1/4 C. chopped green pepper

1/2 C. whole-kernel corn

1/2 C. shredded cheddar cheese

1/2 C. pitted black olives

1/2 C. chicken broth

1 15-oz. can whole tomatoes, undrained

2 tsp. chili powder

1/2 tsp. cumin

1/2 C. shredded Monterey Jack cheese

In a large kettle, heat 2 1/2 C. of the water to boiling. In a medium bowl, mix remaining 1 1/2 C. water and cornmeal. Pour slowly into boiling water, stirring constantly; cook until thickened; cover. Line a baking dish with 3/4 of the cornmeal mush; spread evenly with a wet spoon. In a large skillet, brown the ground beef, sausage, and onion; stir in celery, green pepper, corn, cheddar cheese, olives, chicken broth, tomatoes, chili powder, and cumin. Simmer until thickened, about 15 minutes. Spoon beef mixture into mush-lined dish; top with remaining corn mush. Bake at 325 degrees for 2 hours. Sprinkle with shredded Monterey Jack cheese and return to oven until cheese is melted, about 5 minutes. Serves six.

Chilies Rellenos

3 4-oz. cans whole green chilies

8 oz. Monterey Jack cheese,
  cut into long narrow strips

Vegetable oil for frying

1 C. flour

1 tsp. baking powder

1/2 tsp. salt

3/4 C. yellow or white cornmeal

2 eggs

1 C. milk

Rinse chilies and pat dry with a paper towel. Slit just below the stem and carefully remove the seeds. Gently stuff a strip of cheese into each chili, taking care not to split the chilies. Sift flour, baking powder, and salt into a medium bowl; stir in cornmeal until well blended. In a small bowl, beat eggs; stir in milk. Pour egg mixture into flour mixture, stirring until well blended; add more milk if necessary to make a smooth batter. Heat oil in a large skillet. Dip stuffed chilies into batter and fry until golden. Drain on paper towels. Serves six.

Chicken Enchilada Pie

4 boneless chicken breasts,
  cooked and shredded

2 C. sour cream

2 cans cream of chicken soup

1 small can diced green chiles

1 small onion, diced and
  sauteed until transparent

12 6-inch corn tortillas,
  torn into bite-sized pieces

1 1/2 C. shredded cheddar
  cheese

In blender, combine sour cream, cream of chicken soup, chiles, and onions; blend until smooth. Spread 1/4 of sauce in the bottom of a 9 x 13 pan; top with 1/2 the torn tortillas. Repeat layers, ending with a layer of sauce. Sprinkle with cheese. Bake at 350 degrees for 30 minutes. Serves six.

Taco Shells

1 C. flour

1 C. fine cornmeal

1 tsp. salt

In a mixing bowl, combine ingredients and mix well. Pour in

enough water to make a stiff dough. Roll out on floured surface to 1/4-inch thickness. Cut with the lid of a saucepan. Fry each round in hot oil, turning once, using tongs to form into a U-shape while frying. Makes 6 to 8 shells.

Mexican Haystacks

1 bag tortilla chips	2 small tomatoes, chopped
1 lb. lean ground beef, browned and drained	1 C. ripe pitted olives, sliced
	2 C. shredded cheddar cheese
1 15-oz. can chili beans, warmed	1/2 C. sour cream
1 medium onion, chopped	1/2 C. salsa
1/2 small head lettuce, shredded	

For each serving of Mexican haystacks, place small mound of tortilla chips on a plate. Spoon meat over chips. Top with beans and other toppings. Spoon sour cream and salsa on top.

Mexican Filled Sandwiches

1/2 C. vegetable oil	2 cans ripe pitted olives, chopped
1 lb. cheddar cheese or Monterey Jack cheese, shredded	2 T. vinegar
	3 green onions, chopped
3 green chiles, chopped	1 8-oz. can tomato sauce
4 hard-cooked eggs, chopped	2 dozen French rolls

In a mixing bowl, combine oil, cheese, chiles, eggs, olives, vinegar, onions, and tomato sauce; mix well. Without breaking the rolls completely in half, hollow out; stuff with mixture. Wrap in foil. Heat in 350-degree oven for 30 minutes. Serve immediately.

Mexican Salad

3 hard-cooked eggs	1/4 onion, chopped
1 sweet pickle, diced	2 C. cooked whole-kernel wheat
2 stalks celery, diced	1 C. mayonnaise
6 radishes, sliced	1 large carrot, shredded
1 C. cooked ham or beef, shredded or cubed	1/4 C. green pepper, chopped

Mix all ingredients in a large bowl until combined; cover and refrigerate. To serve, dollop onto a lettuce leaf and top with a slice of tomato. Serves six.

Rolled Beef Tacos

1 lb. lean ground beef, browned and drained

1 tsp. pepper

1 tsp. salt

1 T. chili powder

2 tsp. cumin

12 6-inch corn tortillas

1/4 C. butter or margarine

Vegetable oil for frying

In a bowl, combine beef, pepper, salt, chili powder, and cumin; mix well. Set aside. In a skillet, melt butter; saute tortillas just until soft. Remove to a plate. Place a small amount of meat mixture on each tortilla and roll each into a cigar shape. Fry in oil until crisp. Drain on a paper towel. Keep warm in a 250-degree oven until ready to serve. If desired, garnish with sour cream, guacamole sauce, or salsa. Serves six.

Mexican Corn Bake

1 15-oz. can cream-style corn

1/4 C. yellow cornmeal

2 eggs

2 C. grated cheddar cheese

1/3 C. vegetable oil

1/2 tsp. garlic salt

1 can green chiles, diced

In a bowl, combine corn, cornmeal, eggs, cheese, and oil; mix well. Spread half the mixture in a lightly greased baking dish. Sprinkle with diced chiles, then cheese. Spread remaining corn mixture on top. Bake at 350 degrees for 30 minutes, or until lightly browned.

Nachos

1 bag nacho cheese-flavored tortilla chips

1 15-oz. can refried beans

2 C. shredded cheddar cheese

1 C. guacamole

1/2 C. sour cream

1/2 C. salsa

Dump tortilla chips on a cookie sheet, pizza pan, or other shallow pan. Spoon refried beans over chips. Sprinkle with cheese. Place under broiler just until cheese melts, about 3-4 minutes. Remove from oven and top with guacamole, sour cream, and salsa. If desired, garnish with ripe pitted olives, sliced.

Quick and Easy Thick-Crust Pizza

1 loaf frozen bread dough, thawed but not raised

1 bottle prepared pizza sauce

1 medium onion, chopped

1/2 green pepper, diced

1/2 C. ripe pitted olives, sliced

1/2 C. mushrooms, sliced

2 C. shredded mozzarella cheese

Spread bread dough on the bottom of a greased cookie sheet or pizza pan. Let raise for 20 minutes. Spread pizza sauce over dough; sprinkle on onion, green pepper, olives, and mushrooms. Top with shredded cheese. Bake at 350 degrees for 20 minutes or until edges of crust are browned.

Pizza Rolls

1 8-oz. can tomato sauce

1 lb. mozzarella cheese, shredded

1 6-oz. can sliced mushrooms

1 can chopped ripe olives

1/4 C. vegetable oil

1 loaf French bread, cut in half horizontally

In a bowl, mix tomato sauce, cheese, mushrooms, olives, and oil. Spread on French bread. Broil until cheese is melted, about 5 minutes. Serve immediately.

Home-Style Pizza Sauce

1 8-oz. can tomato paste

2 12-oz. cans tomato sauce

2 medium onions, chopped fine

1 C. water

2 T. vegetable oil

2 tsp. salt

3 tsp. oregano

3 cloves

Combine all ingredients in a large saucepan; bring to a boil, reduce heat, and simmer, stirring frequently, for 20 minutes or until thickened. Remove cloves. Use to top pizza. Makes 4-5 cups.

Deep-Dish Pizza

1 1-lb. loaf frozen white bread
dough, partially thawed

Vegetable oil

1 15 1/2-oz. jar pizza sauce
or 2 C. home-style sauce

8 oz. mozzarella cheese,
thinly sliced

1 large green bell pepper,
cut in thin strips

1 medium red bell pepper,
cut in thin strips

1/4 C. grated parmesan cheese

2 tsp. oregano

4 oz. sliced pepperoni

Grease two 9-inch deep-dish pie plates. Cut the loaf of bread dough in half; put half the dough in each plate. Brush surface of dough lightly with oil, cover, and let thaw completely. Pat out dough to cover the bottom and sides of pan; cover again and let double in bulk. Cover each with half the pizza sauce and half the remaining ingredients, in order, except pepperoni. Bake in 425-degree oven for 10 minutes. Top with pepperoni and bake for 15 additional minutes or until edges of crust are golden. Serve immediately. If you want to freeze one of the pizzas, reheat it in foil in 350-degree oven for 20 minutes; remove foil and bake for an additional 20 minutes or until heated through.

South-of-the-Border Mini Pizzas

3/4 C. salsa

1 6-oz. can tomato paste

6 English muffins,
 split and toasted

1 C. shredded cheddar cheese

1 C. shredded mozzarella cheese

1/2 C. pitted ripe olives, sliced

1/4 C. green chili peppers,
 chopped

1 C. sour cream

Combine salsa and tomato paste until well mixed; spread on English muffins. Sprinkle with cheeses; top with olives and chilis. Bake on a cookie sheet in a 350-degree oven for 10 minutes, or until cheeses and sauce are bubbly. Top with sour cream and serve immediately. Serves four.

Multigrain Pizza

1 C. whole wheat flour

1 C. white, oat, rice,
 or soy flour

1/4 C. cornmeal

1 tsp. baking powder

2/3 C. milk

1/4 C. vegetable oil

8 slices bacon

1/2 lb. lean ground beef

2 8-oz. bottles pizza sauce

1/2 green bell pepper,
 cut into thin rings

1/2 red bell pepper,
 cut into thin rings

1 C. fresh mushrooms, sliced

1/4 C. pitted ripe olives, sliced

2 C. shredded mozzarella cheese

1 C. shredded cheddar cheese

1/4 C. grated parmesan cheese

In a bowl, combine flours, cornmeal, and baking powder; pour in milk and oil and mix well. Oil your hands lightly and press the dough into a greased pizza pan. Press up edges to hold filling. Bake at 425 for 12 to 15 minutes or until golden. In a skillet, fry bacon until crisp; remove, drain on paper towels, and crumble. In skillet, cook beef until browned and crumbly; drain. Spread pizza sauce over crust; spoon meat over sauce; sprinkle bacon over meat; and top with remaining ingredients. Return to oven and bake for 10-15 minutes. Serves four.

Pizza Popover

1 lb. lean ground beef

1 large onion, chopped

1 6-oz. can tomato paste

1 tsp. oregano

1 C. mushrooms, fresh or
canned, sliced

2 C. shredded mozzarella cheese

2 eggs

1 C. milk

1 C. flour

1 tsp. vegetable oil

Grated parmesan cheese

In skillet, cook ground beef and onion until meat is browned and onion is tender; drain. Stir in tomato paste, oregano, 3/4 cup water, and 1/2 tsp. salt; mix well and spoon into 9 x 13 baking pan. Top with mushrooms and sprinkle with cheese. In a mixing bowl, beat together eggs, milk, flour, and oil until smooth; pour over meat mixture. Bake at 350 degrees for 40 minutes or until golden. Sprinkle with parmesan cheese. Cut into wedges and serve immediately. Serves six.

Easy Deep-Dish Pizza

1 lb. lean ground beef

1 small onion, chopped

1 8-oz. can tomato sauce

1/2 tsp. oregano

1/2 tsp. salt

Dash garlic salt

1 can refrigerated biscuits

1 small can mushrooms, sliced

2 C. shredded cheddar cheese

In skillet, cook ground beef and onions until beef is browned and onions are tender. Drain. Stir in tomato sauce, oregano, salt, and garlic salt; simmer for 10 minutes. Separate biscuits and press over the bottom and sides of a greased deep pie plate. Spoon meat mixture into crust; top with mushrooms and sprinkle with cheese. Bake at 350 degrees for 15-20 minutes, or until crust is golden. Serves four.

Pizza Burgers

1 1/2 lb. lean ground beef

1/3 C. grated parmesan cheese

1/4 C. finely chopped onion

1/4 C. chopped ripe pitted olives

1 tsp. salt

1 tsp. oregano

1 6-oz. can tomato paste

8 slices mozzarella cheese

8 cherry tomatoes, cut in half

8 slices French bread, toasted

In a mixing bowl, combine ground beef, parmesan cheese, onion, olives, salt, oregano, and tomato paste; mix well and form into eight oval patties. Broil 10 minutes on first side and 5 minutes on other side. During last 2 minutes, place a slice of mozzarella cheese on each patty. Garnish with cherry tomatoes and serve on French bread. Serves four.

Tangy Mini Pizzas

1 4 1/2-oz. can deviled ham

1 8-oz. can tomato sauce

1/2 tsp. oregano

1 T. minced onion

2 tsp. grated parmesan cheese

8 English muffins, split in half

16 strips cheddar cheese

In a bowl, combine deviled ham, tomato sauce, oregano, onion, and parmesan cheese; cover and refrigerate overnight. When ready to serve, spread mixture on English muffins; place two strips of cheddar cheese in a criss-cross pattern on each. Cook under the broiler until the cheese melts and the tomato mixture bubbles, about 10 minutes. Serves six.

Simple Pizza Crust

1 C. flour

1 T. baking powder

1/2 C. milk

1/4 tsp. salt

2 T. vegetable oil

In a bowl, mix flour, baking powder, and salt; pour in milk and oil and mix well. Knead five times and shape into a ball. Press out on an ungreased cookie sheet and bake at 450 degrees for 9 minutes. Makes enough crust for two pizzas.

Dad's Specialties

FISH RECIPES

Savory Baked Fish

1/4 C. butter or margarine, melted

1 T. lemon juice

1/4 tsp. pepper

1/4 tsp. paprika

1/4 tsp. basil

1/8 tsp. garlic salt

1 lb. white fish filets

1/4 C. dry bread crumbs

In a deep bowl, combine butter, lemon juice, pepper, paprika, basil, and garlic salt. Dredge fish pieces in the butter mixture and roll in bread crumbs. Arrange fish in a single layer in a lightly greased shallow baking dish. Spoon remaining butter mixture over fish. Bake uncovered at 475 degrees for 15 minutes or until fish barely flakes with a fork. Serves four.

Salmon Supper Casserole

1 7 3/4-oz. can boneless, skinless salmon with liquid

3 C. cooked egg noodles

1 1/2 C. grated cheddar cheese

1 C. frozen peas, thawed

1/4 C. sliced green onions

2 T. fresh parsley, chopped

1 can cream of celery soup

1/2 C. sour cream

1 T. lemon juice

1/2 tsp. dry mustard

1/2 tsp. salt

Pepper to taste

Grated parmesan cheese

Flake salmon with a fork. In a large mixing bowl, combine salmon with all other ingredients except parmesan cheese. Spoon into a buttered casserole dish. Sprinkle with parmesan cheese. Bake at 375 degrees for 35 minutes or until bubbly. Garnish with lemon slices. Serves six.

South-of-the-Border Salmon Loaf

1 15 1/2-oz. can boneless,
    skinless salmon with liquid

1 1/2 C. cooked rice

1 8 3/4-oz. can cream-style corn

1/3 C. chopped green pepper

2 T. chopped green onions

3 T. diced green chiles

1 1/2 C. grated Monterey
    Jack cheese

1 egg, beaten

1/4 tsp. seasoned salt

3-4 drops Tabasco sauce

Flake salmon with a fork. In a large mixing bowl, combine salmon with all other ingredients. Spoon into a greased loaf pan. Bake at 350 degrees for 1 hour. Remove from pan and let stand 5 minutes before serving. Serves six.

Baked Fish with Orange Sauce

1 lb. white fish filets

1 tsp. salt

1/4 tsp. pepper

1/4 tsp. ginger

1/2 C. orange juice

3 T. fresh lemon juice

1 green onion, thinly sliced

1 tomato, peeled, seeded,
    and chopped

3 T. chopped green pepper

2 T. butter or margarine, melted

3 oranges, peeled, seeded,
    and thinly sliced

Rinse fish and pat dry with paper towels; place in a shallow bowl. Sprinkle with 3/4 tsp. salt, pepper, and ginger. Mix orange and lemon juices, pour over fish, and marinate for 30 minutes.

How to "Eyeball" a Perfectly Cooked Fish

Worried about cooking a fish just right?

No need to fret--you can simply "eyeball" it!

Flake a little of the fish off with a fork at the end of the cooking time. If it flakes, still looks juicy, and is opaque at its thickest part, it's perfectly done!

Fish that flakes *too* easily is overcooked--and it will be dry. Fish that is too moist and still looks translucent isn't done enough.

For a foolproof rule of thumb, measure the fish at its thickest part before you start cooking it--then simply cook it 10 minutes for each inch of thickness. Add an extra 2 minutes per inch if you're cooking the fish in sauce. If the fish is frozen when you start cooking it, double the time.

Drain, reserving marinade. Place fish in a single layer in a lightly greased shallow baking pan. Top fish with green onion, tomato, and green pepper; sprinkle with remaining 1/4 tsp. salt and drizzle with melted butter. Bake at 350 degrees for 15 minutes. Pour reserved marinade over fish and top with orange slices; bake for 15 additional minutes, or until fish flakes easily with a fork. Serves four.

Seafood Gumbo

1/4 C. flour	3/4 tsp. salt
1/4 C. vegetable oil	1/4 tsp. red pepper hot sauce
1/2 C. chopped onion	1/2 lb. crab meat
1/2 C. chopped celery	1/2 lb. shelled shrimp
1/4 C. chopped green pepper	2 T. fresh parsley, chopped
1 clove garlic, minced	Hot cooked rice
4 C. water	

In a kettle, blend flour and oil; cook over medium heat, stirring constantly, until the mixture is a dark reddish color, about 15 minutes. Add onions, celery, green pepper, and garlic; cook and stir until vegetables are lightly browned, about 8 minutes. Add water, salt, and red pepper sauce. Bring to a boil; reduce heat, cover, and simmer for 1 hour. Stir in crab meat and shrimp; simmer for an additional 20 minutes. Stir in parsley and season to taste with salt and pepper. Serve over mounds of hot cooked rice. Serves four to six.

Fish: Is It Fat or Lean?

"Fat" fish isn't like "fat" beef: you can't see visible marbles of fat running through it. Instead, "fat" refers to the amount of fatty acids in fish flesh. And you don't have to worry about this kind of fat, either: research has shown that the omega-3 fatty acids found in fish help lower blood cholesterol and may help prevent heart disease.

What's the difference, then? Fatty fish have more calories and are usually stronger in flavor. Lean fish generally need to be cooked with butter, margarine, wine, broth, or sauce so they do not get too dry during baking or broiling.

Popular fatty fishes include tuna, swordfish, butterfish, salmon, smelt, mackerel, bluefish, and bass.

The most popular lean fishes are halibut, red snapper, sole, cod, catfish, haddock, flounder, orange roughy, pike, perch, shark, and monkfish.

Lemony Halibut

4 halibut filets

1/2 tsp. salt

Fresh-ground black pepper
   to taste

3 T. green onions, thinly sliced

2 T. fresh grated lemon peel

3 T. butter or margarine

Lemon wedges for garnish

Rinse fish and pat dry with paper towels. Season with salt and pepper; arrange in a single layer in a lightly greased baking dish. Sprinkle fish with green onions and lemon peel; dot with butter. Bake, basting with pan juice, about 15 minutes, or until fish flakes with a fork. To serve, spoon baking juices over top and garnish with lemon wedges. Serves four.

New England Fish Chowder

2 lbs. white fish filets

2 C. water

2 T. butter or margarine

2 medium onions, sliced

4 large potatoes, diced

1 c. celery, chopped

1 bay leaf, crumbled

1 quart milk

2 T. butter or margarine

1 tsp. salt

Freshly ground black pepper
   to taste

In a kettle, simmer fish in water for 15 minutes; drain, reserving broth. Set aside. Melt butter; saute onions until transparent. Add fish, potatoes, celery, bay leaf, salt, and pepper. Pour in fish broth and enough water to cover fish and vegetables. Simmer for 30 minutes. Add milk and butter and simmer 5 additional minutes. Serves six.

Tuna Coney Islanders

1 C. sharp cheddar cheese,
   cubed

3 hard-cooked eggs, chopped

1 7-oz. can tuna, drained

2 T. chopped onion

2 T. chopped sweet pickle

1/2 C. mayonnaise

6 hot dog buns

In a mixing bowl, combine all ingredients except buns; mix

lightly. Split buns and fill with tuna mixture. Wrap each bun in foil and bake in 250-degree oven for 30 minutes. Serve hot. Serves six.

Hot Crab Sandwiches

1 C. cooked crab meat

1/2 C. mayonnaise

2 T. chopped green pepper

2 T. chopped onion

1/2 C. shredded cheddar cheese

3 hard-cooked eggs, chopped

4 whole-grain hamburger buns

In a bowl, combine all ingredients except buns; mix well. Pull a little out of the center of each hamburger bun and fill with crab mixture. Wrap each bun in foil and bake at 300 degrees for 20 minutes. Serve hot. Serves four.

If You Don't Catch the Fish Yourself...

...you can still end up with a great "catch"!

Here's how:

If you're buying frozen fish, make sure packages are tightly wrapped and free of ice crystals. Squeeze the package--it should be firm and solid. Steer clear if you feel air pockets. The fish itself should have a clear color, should have only mild fresh odor, and should be free of ice crystals. Store frozen fish in the freezer in its original package; fat fish can be frozen for three months, lean fish for six. *Never* refreeze fish once it has even partially thawed. Thaw fish in its original wrapper in the refrigerator.

When buying fresh fish, look for fish that is moist, glossy, and firm-textured. The flesh should be white or light pink to red; if the fish is still whole, make sure the eyes are clear and the gills are red. Fish should have only a mild, fresh odor; stay away from fish that smells "fishy". Keep fresh fish wrapped loosely in foil or waxed paper in the refrigerator no longer than one day.

209

Jambalayah

1/2 C. chopped celery
1/2 C. chopped onion
1/2 C. chopped green pepper
3 T. butter or margarine
1/4 C. catsup
1 can condensed tomato soup

1 T. worcestershire sauce
1/4 tsp. salt
2 C. cooked, peeled shrimp
 with tails removed
Hot cooked rice

In a kettle, saute celery, onion, and green pepper in butter until tender. Add soup, catsup, worcestershire sauce, and salt; simmer, covered, for 10 minutes, stirring occasionally. Add shrimp and simmer for 5 additional minutes. Serve over hot rice. Serves four.

Salmon Chowder

1/2 C. chopped green pepper
1/2 C. chopped onion
1 15-oz. can boneless,
 skinless salmon, drained
1 C. chicken broth

1 15-oz. can whole tomatoes
1 15-oz. whole-kernel corn,
 drained
1 can okra, drained
Dash garlic salt

In a kettle, green pepper, onion, and salmon in chicken broth until vegetables are tender. Stir in tomatoes, corn, okra, and garlic salt. Simmer for 15 additional minutes. Serves four to six.

Salmon Steaks Teriyaki

4 salmon steaks
1/4 C. vegetable oil
2 T. soy sauce
1/4 C. lemon juice

1/2 tsp. dry mustard
1/2 tsp. ginger
1/8 tsp. garlic salt

Place the salmon steaks in a shallow pan. In a small bowl, combine oil, lemon juice, soy sauce, dry mustard, ginger, and garlic salt; mix well. Pour over steaks and marinate at room temperature for 1 hour, turning once. Drain, reserving marinade. Place steaks on a broiler pan and broil 3 inches from heat for 5 minutes; turn and brush with marinade, broiling for 5 additional minutes. Serves four.

Halibut Casserole

3 1/2 lbs. halibut filets

1 onion, sliced

2 C. water

1 tsp. salt

1/4 C. butter or margarine

1/2 C. flour

5 C. milk

1/4 C. chopped green pepper

1 C. shredded cheddar cheese

1/2 can pimentoes

1/2 C. buttered bread crumbs

In a kettle, combine halibut, onion slices, water, and salt; steam for 30 minutes. Drain, discarding onion slices. Set aside. In kettle, melt butter; stir in flour and cook for 2 minutes. Pour in milk and stir with a wire whisk, stirring continually until sauce is thickened. Stir in green pepper, cheese, and pimentoes. Flake halibut with a fork and stir into sauce. Pour into a lightly greased casserole dish; top with bread crumbs. Bake at 300 degrees for 1 hour. Serves six.

Easy Seafood Bisque

1 can cream of shrimp soup

1 can medium shrimp, drained and rinsed

1 pkg. frozen baby lima beans, cooked according to package directions

1 soup can milk

1 6-oz. can crab meat, drained and flaked

Hot cooked rice

Combine all ingredients except rice in a small kettle; simmer for 30 minutes. Serve over hot rice. Serves four.

Creamy Onion-Halibut Bake

4 halibut steaks

1/3 C. bottled creamy onion dressing

1 C. dry bread crumbs

1 tsp. parsley, chopped

2 T. fresh grated parmesan cheese

1/4 tsp. paprika

In a bowl, combine bread crumbs, parsley, cheese, and paprika. Rinse fish steaks and pat dry with a paper towel. Dip each steak in onion dressing, then in bread crumb mixture. Bake uncovered in a buttered shallow dish at 500 degrees for 15 minutes. Serves four.

Golden Shrimp Bake

6 slices white bread

1 lb. cheddar cheese, cubed

1 lb. small shrimp, cooked and peeled with tails removed

1 8-oz. can water chestnuts, drained and sliced

1/2 C. thinly sliced green onions

4 eggs

1 1/2 C. milk

1/2 tsp. dry mustard

1/2 tsp. paprika

Cut crusts from bread; cut bread in 1-inch cubes. Arrange half the bread cubes in a well-buttered casserole dish. Sprinkle with half the cheese cubes, water chestnuts, and onions. Top with shrimp. Arrange remaining bread cubes over shrimp, and top with remaining cheese cubes, water chestnuts, and onions. In a bowl, beat together the eggs, milk, and dry mustard; pour over bread, and sprinkle with paprika. Cover and chill overnight. Bake uncovered at 350 degrees for 1 hour. Let cool for 10 minutes before serving. Serves six.

Shrimp Roll-Ups

2 lb. white fish filets, cut in strips

1/4 lb. small cooked shrimp, shells and tails removed

1 C. sharp cheddar cheese, shredded

1 can golden cream of mushroom soup

2 T. white wine

Dash nutmeg

Is It Live, or Is It. . . ?

If you're talking fresh shellfish, it had better be live!

When buying lobster or crab, make sure the fish is lively-it should be moving its head and snapping its claws. If you're buying live clams or oysters, shells should be tightly closed. Make sure you cook live shellfish the same day you buy it, and use the meat immediately.

If you're buying frozen or partially frozen shellfish, look for fish that is free of ice crystals in a tightly wrapped package that is also free of ice crystals. You can keep frozen shellfish in the freezer for about three months; cooked crab or lobster meat should be kept frozen for only one month.

If shrimp or prawns are offered on ice, make sure they are firm to the touch, dry, and a slight blue-green color. They should not have an odor or be blemished.

Place a small mound of shrimp on each filet strip; roll filets around shrimp, and secure with wooden picks. Place fish rolls in a shallow baking dish. In a mixing bowl, combine soup and wine; mix well. Pour over fish; sprinkle with cheese and nutmeg. Bake at 350 degrees for 25 minutes. Serves four.

Halibut in Batter

1 C. milk

1 tsp. baking powder

1 egg

1 C. flour

1 tsp. salt

1 T. butter or margarine, melted

2 lbs. halibut or other white
   fish filets, cut into
   bite-sized pieces

Vegetable oil for frying

In a large mixing bowl, combine milk, baking powder, egg, flour, salt, and melted butter; beat with a whisk until well mixed. The batter should be thick enough to coat a spoon. Heat vegetable oil, several inches thick, in a large skillet; dip fish pieces in batter and fry in hot oil until golden brown and crisp. Drain on paper towels. Serves four.

Fish-Potato Bake

1 lb. white fish filets,
   cut in serving-portion sizes

1 can cream of shrimp soup

1/2 C. sour cream

2 T. chopped green onions

1 T. horseradish

1/4 tsp. paprika

3 drops Tabasco sauce

1 1-lb. pkg. frozen potato rounds

Rinse fish filets and pat dry with a paper towel; arrange in a shallow baking dish. In a mixing bowl, combine soup, sour cream, green onions, horseradish, paprika, and Tabasco sauce; mix well. Spoon sauce over fish filets, making sure all fish is completely covered. Top with frozen potatoes. Bake at 400 for 35 minutes, or until fish flakes easily with a fork. Serves four.

Mushroom-Fish Casserole

2 lbs. white fish filets

3 T. butter or margarine

3/4 C. white wine

2 tsp. onion, minced

1 C. fresh mushrooms, sliced

3/4 C. heavy cream

1 C. flour

1/2 tsp. salt

1/4 tsp. pepper

1/2 C. fresh parmesan cheese, grated

Lemon juice to taste

Rinse fish filets and pat dry with a paper towel. In a large skillet, saute fish filets in butter; place filets in a casserole dish. Pour wine over fish; bake at 350 degrees for 15 minutes. When fish has finished baking, pour off wine into a mixing bowl. In the same skillet, saute onions and mushrooms in butter, adding more butter if necessary. With flour in a deep bowl, dredge sauteed onions and mushrooms in flour. Add the cream, salt, pepper, and the wine that was poured off the fish; simmer for 5 minutes. Pour the sauce over the fish. Bake at 350 degrees for 10-15 minutes. Sprinkle with parmesan cheese and lemon juice to taste. Serves four.

Crunchy Seafood Casserole

1/2 lb. shrimp, cooked, with shells and tails removed

1 6 1/2-oz. can crab meat, drained

1 medium green pepper, chopped

1 medium onion, chopped

1 C. celery, chopped

1 tsp. worcestershire sauce

1/2 tsp. salt

1/4 tsp. pepper

1 C. mayonnaise

1 small can Chinese noodles

1/4 C. sliced almonds

Combine all ingredients except noodles and almonds; mix well. Spoon into a casserole dish. Top with noodles; sprinkle with almonds. Bake at 375 degrees for 20 minutes. Serves six.

Halibut-Broccoli Pie

1 9-inch unbaked pie shell

1 C. cheddar cheese, grated

1 1/2 C. cooked halibut, flaked

1 10-oz. pkg. frozen broccoli

1 C. celery, diced

2 T. green onions, sliced

3 hard-cooked eggs, sliced

2 tsp. lemon juice

1 C. mayonnaise

2 sprigs parsley

Sprinkle the cheese over the pie shell; bake at 400 degrees for 8-9 minutes, or until golden. In a saucepan, cook the broccoli according to package directions, adding celery and green onions. Drain. Combine flaked halibut, broccoli, celery, green onions, hard-cooked eggs, lemon juice, and mayonnaise; mix well. Pour into cooked pie shell. Bake at 375 degrees for 20 minutes, or until bubbly. Serves six.

Crab Mornay

1 6-oz. can crab, drained,
  reserving liquid

1/4 C. celery, chopped

1/4 C. green onions, chopped

1 clove garlic, minced

2 T. butter or margarine

4 tsp. flour

1/4 tsp. salt

Dash cayenne pepper

1 C. milk

1/2 C. Swiss cheese, shredded

1 T. fresh chives, snipped

Broccoli spears, cooked
  and drained

Flake crab and set aside. In a skillet, saute celery, green onions, and garlic in butter until tender. Blend in flour, salt, and cayenne; cook, stirring, until thickened. Combine milk and enough reserved crab liquid to equal 1 1/3 cups. Add to mixture in skillet, stirring constantly until mixture thickens and bubbles. Add cheese, and stir until melted. Fold in crab and chives; warm through. Pour over cooked broccoli spears. Serves four.

Lemon Baked Fish

1 lb. white fish filets
1/4 C. butter or margarine
3 T. lemon juice
1/4 C. onion, diced

1 1/2 tsp. worcestershire sauce
1/4 tsp. salt
1 T. dried parsley flakes

Rinse fish filets and pat dry with a paper towel; arrange in a shallow baking dish. In a small skillet, melt butter; add lemon juice and onions, sauteeing until onions are transparent. Stir in worcestershire sauce, salt, and parsley flakes. Pour sauce over fish. Bake at 350 degrees for 20 minutes, or until fish flakes easily with a fork. Serves four.

Salmon Rice Patties

2/3 C. instant rice
3/4 C. boiling water
2 C. salmon, drained and flaked
1/2 C. mayonnaise
1 T. lemon juice

1 tsp. minced onion
3/4 tsp. salt
1/4 tsp. pepper
1/2 C. cornflakes, finely crushed

In a saucepan, add rice to boiling water; mix enough to moisten, cover, and let stand for 15 minutes. Stir in salmon, mayonnaise, lemon juice, onion, salt, and pepper; mix well. Let stand for 10 minutes. Shape into 8 patties; role in crushed cornflakes. Refrigerate for at least 2 hours. Arrange patties on ungreased cooking sheet; bake at 450 degrees for 15 minutes, or until golden brown. Serves eight.

Crabs in a Shell

1 pkg. large pasta shells,
    cooked, drained, and cooled
1 6-oz. can crab meat, drained
2 T. green onions, chopped

1/2 C. celery, chopped
Dash of cayenne pepper
1 C. mayonnaise

In a mixing bowl, combine all ingredients except shells; mix well. Stuff macaroni shells with mixture. Chill for at least 2 hours; serve as appetizers.

Shrimp Cocktail

1 46-oz. can tomato juice

2 cans shrimp, drained and
  broken in tiny pieces

1 small bottle catsup

4 T. horseradish

1 C. celery, finely chopped

1/2 tsp. salt

3 T. worcestershire sauce

3 T. sugar

1/2 tsp. garlic salt

Juice of 1/2 lemon

Combine all ingredients; mix well. Chill overnight. Serve as appetizer.

Hot Shrimp Dip

1 C. sour cream

8 oz. cream cheese

1 can cream of shrimp soup

1 tsp. horseradish

1 can shrimp, drained
  and broken

Combine all ingredients in a small saucepan; heat over low heat. Keep warm; serve with squares of French or rye bread.

Dilled Shrimp Dip

2 C. sour cream

1 C. mayonnaise

2 T. dried parsley flakes

2 T. onion flakes

1 T. dill weed

1 T. seasoned salt

Combine all ingredients and mix thoroughly. If dip is too thick, thin with dill pickle juice. Can be used as a sauce or a dip.

Cucumber Sauce for Fish

1 cucumber, peeled and seeded

1 C. sour cream

1 C. mayonnaise

1 tsp. dill seed

Sprinkle halved cucumber with salt; wrap in plastic wrap and refrigerate for several hours, or until dried. Chop cucumber into fine pieces. Add sour cream, mayonnaise, and dill seed, and mix well. Delicious as a sauce for fish, especially salmon.

Spicy Lime Juice Marinade

1/3 C. fresh lime juice

3 T. vegetable oil

1 medium jalapeno pepper, seeded and minced

Combine all ingredients until well mixed. Can be used with both fatty and lean fish: marinate fish for 15 minutes, and baste with marinade during cooking. Makes 1/2 cup.

Yogurt Marinade

1 tsp. coriander

1/2 tsp. cumin

1/4 tsp. turmeric

1/2 tsp. ground red pepper

1/8 tsp. ginger

1/8 tsp. black pepper

1 C. plain, low-fat yogurt

In a nonstick skillet over medium heat, combine spices; cook for 2 minutes, stirring constantly. Cool for 2 minutes. Stir spices into yogurt until well blended. Can be used for fatty fish that will be baked or broiled: marinate fish for 60 minutes, and baste with marinade during cooking. Makes 1 cup.

How To Marinate Fish

Marinades are simple to make and can add a zesty flavor to fish. Best of all, marinades are easy to use. Here's how:

If the marinade has any perishable ingredients in it, make sure you store it in the refrigerator --but bring it up to room temperature before you begin marinating the fish in it.

For the easiest marinade ever, dump the marinade and the fish in a double-thickness plastic bag; then seal the bag and put it in a bowl (in case of leaks). Then simply flip the plastic bag over two or three times during marinating to evenly distribute the marinade!

If the fish is delicate, marinate for no longer than 15 minutes. Generally, the longer you marinate, the stronger the flavor: if you're using a mild-flavored marinade, steep fish for up to an hour in it. If the marinade has a strong flavor, marinate for no longer than 15-20 minutes.

To keep fish moist and enhance flavor, remember to baste the fish with the marinade while you are baking, broiling, or grilling.

Oriental Marinade

1/3 C. vegetable oil

1/3 C. soy sauce

1/4 C. green onions, thinly sliced

1 T. ginger

1 1/2 T. wine vinegar

1 garlic clove, minced

1 tsp. jalapeno pepper,
seeded and minced

Mix all ingredients until well blended. Can be used for fatty or lean fish: marinate for 15 minutes, baste with marinade during cooking. Makes 1 cup.

Dad's Specialties

220B

POPCORN RECIPES

Easy Popcorn Balls

1 C. unpopped corn, popped

2 C. brown sugar,
firmly packed

1/2 C. butter or margarine

1/2 C. light corn syrup

Pop corn; keep warm in low oven. In heavy saucepan, combine remaining ingredients. Cook, stirring constantly, until mixture boils and sugar is completely dissolved. Pour mixture over popped corn and stir to coat evenly. Shape into popcorn balls. Makes about 2 dozen balls.

Marshmallow Popcorn

3/4 C. light corn syrup

1/4 C. butter or margarine

2 T. water

1 lb. powdered sugar

1 C. miniature marshmallows
or 10 regular-sized
marshmallows

5 quarts popped corn

In a heavy saucepan, combine corn syrup, butter, water, powdered sugar, and marshmallows. Stir over low heat until mixture begins to boil. Pour over popped corn and shape into balls. Makes about 30 balls.

Fruit-Flavored Popcorn Balls

1 6-oz. pkg. fruit-
flavored gelatin

1 C. sugar

1 C. light corn syrup

1 T. butter or margarine

6 quarts popped corn

In a heavy saucepan, combine gelatin, sugar, corn syrup, and butter. Bring to a boil, stirring, and boil for 1 minute. Pour over popped corn and shape into balls.

Apple Corn

4 quarts popped corn

1/2 C. butter or margarine

1 C. dried apples, chopped

1/2 C. brown sugar

1/2 tsp. cinnamon

1/4 tsp. ginger

1/4 tsp. nutmeg

Pinch ground cloves

Keep popped corn warm in a 250-degree oven. In a heavy saucepan, melt butter; add apples, sugar, and spices and cook over low heat for about 5 minutes. Pour over popped corn and toss to coat evenly.

Cotton Candy Popcorn

2 C. sugar

1/4 C. butter or margarine

1/2 C. water

1 tsp. salt

1 tsp. vanilla

1-2 drops red food coloring

6 quarts popped corn

In a medium saucepan, mix sugar, butter, water, and salt; bring to a boil and cook for 4 minutes. Remove from heat, stir in food coloring and vanilla, and pour over popped corn.

Candied Popcorn

5 quarts popped corn

1 1/2 C. pecans

1/2 C. almond halves

1 1/3 C. sugar

1 C. butter or margarine

1 tsp. vanilla

1/2 C. light corn syrup

In a large bowl combine popped corn, pecans, and almonds; spread evenly on two cookie sheets. In a heavy saucepan, combine sugar, butter, vanilla, and corn syrup. Cook, stirring occasionally, until the mixture is caramel-colored and forms a soft ball when a small amount is dropped into cold water. Pour hot syrup over popcorn on cookie sheets. Butter fingers well and work fast to mix so that popcorn is coated. Can be formed into balls or served in bowls.

Caramel Corn Bars

2 C. brown sugar, firmly packed
1/2 C. butter or margarine
1 C. light corn syrup

1 can sweetened
    condensed milk
5 quarts popped corn

In a heavy saucepan, combine brown sugar, butter, and corn syrup; cook, stirring frequently, until a small amount forms a soft ball when dropped into cold water. Stir in sweetened condensed milk and cook over low heat, stirring frequently, until mixture is smooth. Pour over popped corn and stir until corn is evenly coated. Press into a lightly buttered 9 x 13 pan and let cool. Cut into bars.

Hints for Better Popcorn

If you're brewing up one of the recipes in this section, follow these guidelines for the best results:

--Don't use shortening to grease a pan or cookie sheet that you will pour popcorn into. Shortening has a flavor, and the popcorn will pick it up.

--If you're making candied popcorn of any kind, do it on a dry, cool day. If there's too much humidity in the air, your popcorn will turn out sticky.

--Before you start your recipe, sift through your popped corn. Sort out and discard any shells, skins, burned corn, and unpopped kernels of corn.

--If you're cooking ingredients to pour over popcorn, use a heavy saucepan; you'll be less likely to scorch your syrup. If you grease the inside of the saucepan lightly with butter or margarine before you begin, you'll be less likely to have a boilover.

--If you want to, you can substitute margarine for butter, but it's best for popcorn treats that will be served hot. When margarine cools, it tends to separate, leaving a greasy feel, so butter is best for popcorn treats that will be served cool.

Betty's Candied Corn

3/4 C. light corn syrup

4 T. butter or margarine

2 T. water

1 C. miniature marshmallows

1 lb. sifted powdered sugar

1/4 tsp. food coloring

10 quarts popped corn

In a large pan over low heat, combine corn syrup, butter, and water. Add marshmallows, stirring until melted. Stir in powdered sugar and food coloring; cook, stirring constantly, until sugar has dissolved and mixture is bubbling. Pour slowly over popped corn and stir to coat evenly. Mound on a serving platter; break off pieces, and enjoy!

Easiest-Ever Caramel Corn

1 1/2 C. brown sugar,
   firmly packed

1 1/2 C. butter or margarine

3/4 C. granulated sugar

3/4 C. light corn syrup

1 T. vanilla

2 C. unpopped popcorn,
   popped

In a heavy saucepan, combine brown sugar, butter, granulated sugar, corn syrup, and vanilla; bring to a boil, stirring constantly, and boil for 1 minute. Pour over popped corn, stirring to coat evenly. Form into balls.

South-of-the-Border Popcorn

1 C. shredded Monterey
   Jack cheese

1/4 C. butter or margarine,
   melted

1 tsp. taco seasoning mix

2 quarts popped corn

In a small saucepan, melt butter; add cheese and stir until smooth. Stir in taco seasoning mix, stirring to combine well. Pour over popped corn and stir to coat evenly.

Popcorn Snack Mix

3 quarts popped corn

2 C. bite-sized crispy
   corn square cereal

2 C. pecan halves

1/2 C. honey

1/3 C. vegetable oil

1 tsp. grated lemon rind

In a large shallow baking pan, combine popcorn, cereal, and pecans; stir to mix. In a small saucepan, stir together honey, vegetable oil, and lemon rind; bring to a boil, stirring constantly, and boil for 1 minute. Pour over popcorn mixture, stirring to coat evenly. Bake at 300 degrees for 30 minutes, stirring occasionally. Cool, stirring occasionally. Store in a tightly covered container. Makes 16 cups.

Red Hawaiian Popcorn

1/2 C. butter or margarine

1 C. tropical fruit
   punch concentrate

1 C. light corn syrup

1/2 C. sugar

1/2 tsp. salt

1/2 tsp. vanilla

1/4 tsp. almond extract

1 tsp. baking soda

6 quarts popped popcorn

1 C. raisins

In a large kettle, melt butter; blend in punch concentrate, corn syrup, sugar, and salt. Bring to a boil, stirring frequently. Boil for 10 minutes; remove from heat and blend in vanilla, almond extract, and baking soda. Pour over popcorn; stir to coat evenly. Spread on two cookie sheets; bake at 300 degrees for 15 minutes, stirring occasionally. Loosen from pans, sprinkle with raisins, and cool. Store in an airtight container.

How to Buy and Store Popcorn

What should you look for when buying popcorn?

The moisture inside the kernels is what makes the popcorn pop, and corn that has been dried out usually will pop very little (or not at all).

So look for popcorn sealed in airtight containers, and make sure the container hasn't been punctured or opened.

Once you open your container at home, keep your popcorn in a sealed airtight container between uses. A jar with a tightly screwed lid is ideal!

Maple Walnut Popcorn

1/4 C. thick maple syrup

1/2 C. walnuts, broken into coarse pieces

2 quarts popped corn

Pour maple syrup over popped corn and stir to coat evenly; add walnuts and mix well. Store in a tightly covered container.

Cheddar Cheese Popcorn

4 quarts popped corn

3 T. butter or margarine, melted

1/2 tsp. salt

1 1/2 C. shredded sharp cheddar cheese

Lightly grease a large roasting pan; fill with popcorn. Gradually pour in melted butter, tossing to coat evenly. Stir in salt. Sprinkle with cheese. Bake at 425 for 2-5 minutes, stirring several times to distribute the cheese and break up the popcorn. Serve immediately.

Barbecued Popcorn Mixup

2 tsp. onion powder

1 1/2 tsp. chili powder

1 1/2 tsp. lemon pepper

1 tsp. garlic powder

1/2 tsp. dry mustard

1/4 tsp. paprika

1/4 tsp. salt

4 quarts popped corn

3 C. tiny fish-shaped cheese crackers

3 C. thin pretzel sticks

1/4 C. butter or margarine, melted

In a small bowl, mix onion powder, chili powder, lemon pepper, garlic powder, dry mustard, paprika, and salt. In a large bowl or roasting pan, mix popcorn, crackers, and pretzels. Gradually pour in butter, stirring to coat evenly. Sprinkle with spice mixture and mix well. Serve immediately.

Chocolate Peanut Popcorn Squares

2 T. butter or margarine

1 10 1/2-oz. pkg. miniature
  marshmallows

1/2 C. milk chocolate,
  butterscotch, or
  peanut butter chips

1 C. peanuts

4 quarts popped corn

1/2 C. milk chocolate chips

2 tsp. butter or margarine

In a medium saucepan, melt butter; stir in marshmallows and chips until both are coated with melted butter. Cook, stirring frequently, until mixture is smooth. Carefully fold in peanuts and popcorn until evenly coated; with buttered hands, press mixture into a buttered 9 x 13 pan. In a small saucepan, combine chocolate chips and 2 tsp. butter and cook over low heat until melted; drizzle over popcorn mixture. Cool and cut into squares.

Honey Popcorn

1 1/2 C. sugar

1/2 C. honey

1/2 C. milk

1 T. butter or margarine

8 quarts popped corn

In a small bowl, combine sugar, honey, and milk; stir well to blend and let stand for 20 minutes. In a saucepan, bring the honey mixture to a boil; stir in butter and boil, stirring constantly, until the mixture forms "strings" when it is dropped from a spoon. Pour over popped corn and stir to coat evenly. Spread corn on waxed paper to cool and store in a tightly covered container.

A Sprinkle of This, a Dash of That...

...makes popcorn more fun to eat!

In addition to the recipes you'll find in this section, don't be afraid to experiment. Once your popcorn has popped, drizzle it with melted butter. Then sprinkle on the spices of your choice: curry powder, chili powder, taco seasoning mix, seasoned salt, oregano, onion salt, lemon pepper, cinnamon, nutmeg, or allspice are ideas to start with. Or try sprinkling your cooked, buttered popcorn with grated parmesan cheese, shredded cheddar cheese, or shredded mozarella cheese for a great change of pace.

Baked Caramel Corn

1 C. butter or margarine,
cut in chunks

2 C. brown sugar,
firmly packed

1/2 C. light corn syrup

1 tsp. salt

2 C. peanuts

1/2 tsp. baking soda

1 tsp. vanilla

6 quarts popped corn

In a heavy saucepan, mix butter, brown sugar, corn syrup, salt, and peanuts; bring to a vigorous boil, stirring constantly. Cook for 2 minutes over medium heat. Remove from heat and add baking soda and vanilla. Pour syrup over popped corn, stirring to coat evenly. Bake at 250 degrees for 1 hour, stirring every 15 minutes to distribute coating. Let cool; break into chunks.

Peanut Butter Popcorn

1 C. sugar

1/2 C. honey

1/2 C. light corn syrup

1 C. peanut butter

1 tsp. vanilla

4 quarts popped corn

1-2 C. peanuts

In a medium saucepan, combine sugar, honey, and light corn syrup. Bring to a boil, and boil for 2 minutes, stirring constantly. Remove from heat, add peanut butter and vanilla, and stir until blended. Pour over popped corn, add peanuts, and stir until corn is evenly coated.

That Popcorn is 80,000 Years Old...

...and it's a native American! The native Americans knew a good thing when they saw it: they had grown and eaten popcorn for centuries before the European explorers ever landed on our shores. In fact, popcorn was served at the first Thanksgiving feast when the Indians entertained their American colonist friends.

It all started with a wild grass grown in Mexico more than 80,000 years ago. Early poppers simply speared a cob of corn on a stick, held it over the fire, and watched the fireworks begin. Later, they mixed popcorn kernels with heated sand in clay pots. The colonists didn't want any to get away, so they bent sheets of iron into cylinders with lids--and they loved it so much that they served it with sugar and cream, much like we eat cold cereal today.

Snacker's Delight Popcorn

2 quarts popped corn	1 C. raisins
1 C. peanuts	1 C. sunflower seeds
1 C. cashews	1 C. shredded coconut

Combine all ingredients and serve to evenly mix. Store in a tightly covered container.

Sugar and Spice Popcorn

3 T. butter or margarine	1/4 tsp. nutmeg
2 T. sugar	2 quarts popped corn
1/2 tsp. cinnamon	

In a small saucepan, melt butter over low heat; stir in sugar and spices and cook until sugar is dissolved. Drizzle over popcorn, stirring to evenly coat.

Pumpkin Pie Popcorn

4 T. melted butter or margarine	8 C. popped corn
2 tsp. honey	1 tsp. pumpkin pie spice

Stir together melted butter and honey; drizzle over popcorn, and toss to mix. Sprinkle with pumpkin pie spice, and toss again. Serve immediately.

If You Don't Have a Popcorn Popper...

...you can still make delicious popcorn at home!

Here's how:

Simply pour enough oil into a pot to cover the bottom. Then pour in enough popcorn kernels to cover the bottom in a single layer. Cover the pot and shake it gently over a medium-hot burner on the stove, shaking gently so all the popcorn gets coated with oil. As soon as you hear the last few pops, remove the pot from the stove.

Use only vegetable oil, such as corn oil, or special popcorn oil you can find commercially bottled. Never use butter or margarine to pop corn--it burns and smokes when it's heated high enough to make corn pop.

Dad's Specialties

230B

IF I HAD A HAMMER. . . CHAPTER 6
HOME MAINTENANCE AND REPAIR MADE EASY

Believe it or not, keeping a home in great shape takes more than a hammer and a pocketful of nails! Good home maintenance and repair starts before you even move in--when you're first surveying your potential house and neighborhood--and encompasses things you've probably never before considered.

Luckily, you can do it all--with a little know-how and some basic tools!

LOOKING THINGS OVER: SPOTTING PROBLEMS BEFORE YOU BUY

If you want fewer and easier home repairs down the road, it's worth spending some time before you ever pay a dollar down on a house, townhouse, or condominium. What it boils down to is this: you want a "healthy" house! Check the house, inside and out, for the following signs of good repair:

- Doors that open and close easily, without rubbing or sticking.
- Unbroken windows that open and close easily.
- Fireplaces with dampers that open and shut freely, with unobstructed flues, and with brickwork or stonework that is not damaged.
- Bathrooms with sinks and tubs that fill quickly and drain rapidly without gurgling.
- Bathroom fixtures that are free of rough spots, cracks, stains, chips, spots, or other damage.
- Kitchen appliances that are in good working order.
- A chimney that is constructed of solid, undamaged brick and tight flashing. A good chimney should be two feet above the roof, unobstructed by trees, and equipped with a flue liner.
- Foundation walls that are free of large cracks.
- Windows with square exterior frames that have been painted, with sills free of termite or weather damage. A solid unbroken line of putty should surround the window panels. The best windows

are double- or triple-glazed storm windows set in metal frames.
- Snug-fitting outside doors of solid wood or metal with slightly raised sills and cracks between siding and frame filled with solid caulking.
- Exterior siding that is free of damage and nail pops and that is equipped with flashing wherever siding joins another exterior surface.
- Garage doors that open and close smoothly.
- Rain gutters that have closed joints and downspouts that point away from the house.
- Plenty of outdoor lighting with outdoor grounded electrical outlets for convenience.
- Exterior concrete sidewalks, driveways, and patios that are slightly sloped to facilitate water drainage.
- A dry basement.
- Plenty of ventilation and insulation in the crawl space and attic space.

Inevitably, a few problems will crop up that no one could have foreseen, but there are tell-tale signs that warn of most major problems (and even a few minor ones). **The following should serve as red flags,** alerting you to potential problems with a house:
- An uneven floor (put a marble in the center; if it rolls, the floor isn't level)
- A floor that creaks
- Worn, cracked, split, or stained flooring
- Large cracks in the interior walls or numerous cracks in the interior walls
- Water stains on ceilings and walls (usually indicative of a leaky roof)
- Leaky faucets or drains in kitchen or bathrooms
- Mold, mildew, or standing water under the sinks in the kitchen or bathrooms (usually indicative of leaky pipes)
- Conspicuous sections of new copper, brass, iron, steel, or plastic pipes (usually a signal that more will have to be replaced soon)
- A noisy furnace
- A sagging or leaning roof
- The ability to see sunlight through the roof in the attic
- Worn, loose, or missing roof shingles; slate shingles that are discolored, chipped, or broken; asphalt shingles that are "shiny"
- Wide or long cracks in the foundation

- A significant amount of missing or cracked mortar in exterior masonry
- Wood siding that has split, cracked, or splintered; metal siding that is discolored, dented, or worn; mildew or signs of obvious decay near joints or the lower edge of siding
- Sagging, rusting, or splitting rain gutters and downspouts
- Signs of termite, carpenter ant, or carpenter bee infestation (look for a white powdery substance, sawdust, or mud termite tubes on the foundation, windowsills that are near the ground, under the porch, and on the stoops)
- Large vertical wall cracks and bulging walls in the basement
- Sagging, decaying, or broken floor beams and joists
- Large floor cracks in the basement or garage
- Signs of water damage in the basement (peeling paint, mildew, rust stains, or water marks)
- Cracking, crumbling, or broken exterior concrete (sidewalks, driveway, and patio)
- Large trees within twenty feet of the house

CHOOSING A GOOD NEIGHBORHOOD

If the house you're considering checks out, or even passes with flying colors, you need to look beyond: what is the neighborhood like? If you've succeeded in finding a healthy house, you'll want it to be situated in a "healthy" neighborhood, too!

The type of neighborhood a house is located in won't really impact repairs, but it can definitely affect value. Make sure the neighborhood is zoned residential; you want to make sure that no one can set up a business or an industrial plant nearby. The homes surrounding you should be of comparable or better quality; look for well-kept homes and yards.

You'll also want to choose a neighborhood that is close to good schools, shopping, churches, hospitals, dentists, day-care centers, cultural attractions, and other community services. You'll want easy access to public transportation and a well-controlled flow of traffic to avoid bottlenecks and the noise and pollution that goes along with them.

You'll probably want to steer clear of a house located in a neighborhood close to an airport, railroad tracks, major highways, industrial areas, or a business district. You should also avoid a neighborhood with clear signs of deterioration (such as cluttered yards, rundown homes, and broken-down vehicles) or with an excessive number of homes for sale.

PRESERVE GOOD LOOKS: HOW TO PAINT LIKE A PRO

Keeping your house painted--inside and out--is one of the most sure-fire things you can do to maintain both its appearance and value. If you're willing to invest a little elbow grease, you can save a whopping amount of money: approximately 85 percent of what a professional charges you is for **labor.**

Arm yourself with the facts about paint, buy the necessary tools to do the job right, and you can end up with a professional-looking job at a fraction of the cost!

Choose the Right Paint

Where do most amateurs make the biggest mistakes? On the most basic step: choosing the paint!

If you've never paid much attention, you need to now. All paints are **not** alike. There are obvious differences in color, but that's just the beginning. There are also different kinds of finishes, and the one you choose will depend on the job you're doing. There are also different basic kinds of paint--and where the paint goes up on the wall will dictate the kind you should buy.

Begin by deciding what color you want. Paint stores feature an array of "chips" (samples of color on small strips of cardstock), but you need to understand that they are **close approximations only.** You need to understand, too, that the light inside your kitchen is different than the light inside the paint store--so what appears to be a creamy oyster color in the paint store may actually be a pale lavender on your kitchen wall.

For best results, you need to invest a little "front money". Buy the smallest amount of paint the store will sell you; some will let you buy a sample only. Take it home, paint it on the wall under a window or in another spot where it gets full light, and let it dry overnight. Do you like what you see? If so, have the paint store mix a full batch for you. If not, it's back to the drawing board--go back to the store, explain what was wrong, and try again. Keep trying until you get what you want. It sounds like a tedious process--and it can be--but the time you spend here is well worth it.

Before you have a full batch of paint mixed, you need to know how much you'll need to **finish the job completely.** (You should allow a little left over for eventual touch-ups, too.)

Why?

Because even though the paint store will use a precise formula to mix your color, no two batches are ever quite the same. You may run out of paint with half a wall left to go--and chances are good that you'll always be able to tell!

To figure out how much paint you'll need, measure the length and width of each wall; multiply the length by the width to get the number of square feet. Measure each wall individually, and then add the four figures for the total number of square feet. (Don't worry about subtracting out for doors and windows; you can use the extra paint later for touch-ups.)

Now divide the total number of square feet by 100. The resulting figure tells you **how many quarts of paint you need for one coat.** (Divide it by four to get the number of gallons you'll need.) Most painting jobs require two coats, so you'll probably need to figure two times the amount.

Now for choosing the paint type and finish. Paint comes in two general types: oil-base and latex. *Oil-base* must be thinned with turpentine or solvent, which means your brushes and other tools have to be cleaned with paint thinner. It has a stronger odor when wet, and it takes three or four times as long to dry. But you should take the time involved to use oil-base paint if the surface will get a lot of wear, if it will be exposed to dampness (such as in a bathroom), or if it has previously been covered by lots of layers of paint. You should also use oil-base paint on metal surfaces, on objects that have to bear weight (like chairs), or on surfaces that have to bear heat (like radiators).

Latex is a water-based paint that is fine to use on ceilings and walls that get a normal amount of wear and that are not exposed to unusual extremes in temperature or humidity. You can also use latex paint for furniture that is in good condition. Latex paint has little odor when it is wet, and it can be thinned with water--which also means that your brushes and other painting tools can simply be rinsed out with water for cleaning. One of its best advantages is drying time: in warm weather or in a heated room, it can dry completely within a few hours.

Paint finishes range from flat (with no sheen at all) to high-gloss (which is so shiny that it looks almost like lacquer). The finish you choose should depend on personal taste as well as where you will apply the paint. These guidelines give a good general indication:

Flat. Flat paint is usually used on ceilings so that the ceiling in a room won't reflect a lot of light. You can also use flat paint on walls, but you need to be aware that it picks up fingerprints much more readily and is more difficult to clean.

Satin. Satin is one step up from flat in the shine department. You should use satin-finish paint in areas where you want just a subtle luster or a light sheen; many people prefer satin-finish paint for interior walls.

Semi-gloss. Semi-gloss is the most widely used paint finish for interior walls. It can also be used to highlight: you could paint your walls with satin-finish, for example, but use semi-gloss on chair rails, mouldings, or woodwork. Semi-gloss is also preferred for use on bookshelves and wood furniture.

High-gloss. The paint with the greatest amount of shine is high-gloss paint; it is so shiny that it looks like lacquer. High-gloss paint is available only as an oil-base paint. High-gloss is recommended for metal surfaces and for surfaces that have to bear heat (such as radiators). High-gloss can also be used to paint furniture that you want to appear lacquered.

Take The Time For Preparation

Unfortunately, once you've selected color, type, and finish, you can't dash right home from the paint store and start splashing the paint on your walls. If you want a professional-looking job, you need to take the time to "prepare" the surfaces you are going to paint. The work involved in preparation depends on what is already on the wall.

Regardless of what's already on the wall, there are some basics you need to do. Use a dry cloth or a vacuum to go over all walls and remove any surface dust. Then get rid of any soil, grease, or mildew that is on the walls (use a no-rinse detergent to wipe down walls in the kitchen, which usually have a thin coating of grease on them from cooking residue). If there are mildew stains on the bathroom walls, wipe them off with liquid bleach. Remove all picture hangers, nails, switch plates, outlet cover plates, and other hardware (such as knobs or handles).

If you're starting from scratch with unpainted wallboard, you'll need to purchase a "primer" (a liquid that you paint on to help the regular paint adhere to your walls). If possible, your primer should be the same brand as your paint. Before you paint on the primer, sand all joints and pound in any protruding nails (nailheads should lie below the wall surface). If you're using a dark color, you can make your job easier by stirring half a pint of paint into every quart of primer; by darkening your primer, you should be able to cover your walls with one coat of paint.

If you're painting walls, ceilings, and woodwork that have already been painted before, you don't need primer, but you need to "rough up" the surface (it will help the paint adhere). If it's a small surface, you can rub it with steel wool or sandpaper. If you're doing an entire wall or a whole room, you can purchase "liquid sandpaper" that simply paints on with a brush.

Once you've sanded the surfaces, you need to fill in all holes and cracks. Use spackle (a white, putty-like compound available at paint stores) and a spackle knife (a flat, broad tool that smooths spackle) to fill in cracks and small nail holes. You'll first need to make the crack big enough so you can fill it with spackle: pull the point of a metal can opener down the length of the crack to "open" it. Slightly overfill cracks and holes with spackle, smooth them by wiping with the spackle knife, allow them to dry, and sand them to

Looking For Sandpaper? How To Make The Grade

If a home-repair job calls for sanding, you'll need to decide on a grade of sandpaper. It's really quite easy: the grade you choose will depend on the job you need done.

Coarse sandpaper is for intense sanding--for jobs that need a lot of material sanded down. Coarse sandpaper is perfect for removing heavy paint or taking heavy finishes off of wood.

Medium sandpaper takes off lighter finishes and smooths roughened wood.

Fine sandpaper should be used for the final sanding before you paint or apply fillers, such as spackling.

Very fine sandpaper should be used on very hard wood or to sand surfaces between coats of paint or stain.

Extra fine sandpaper should be used for the final polishing; extra fine or superfine sandpaper will give surfaces a mirror finish.

a smooth finish. You can clean up any excess with a damp cloth.

If you have large holes in the wall, they will need to be filled with plaster. Someone at the paint store can help you choose an appropriate plaster. For best results, keep it moist enough to work with easily. Wet down the area you're filling with a damp cloth, fill with plaster, wet the surface of the plaster, and smooth it. When dry, sand the patched area until it is smooth.

If you're painting metal, make sure you have cleaned up or prevented rust. Coat the entire surface of unpainted metal with a primer designed to inhibit rust; if the metal surface has been previously painted, use the primer to cover any spots that are already rusted.

Begin Painting Now!

With all the preparation completed, you're ready to start painting. As a general rule, you should paint in this order:

1. Ceilings
2. Walls
3. Doors
4. Window frames
5. Baseboards
6. Trim (such as mouldings)

Before you start, gather up your tools. For most room-sized jobs, you'll need brushes of varying widths, an angled brush, a roller, a pan, flat sponge applicators (for latex paint only), masking tape, a small ladder or stepstool, and razor blades. You'll need to move out as much furniture as you can, and drape the remaining furniture and floors with old sheets or dropcloths. You should wear old clothes and a hat--some paint **will** splatter, no matter how careful you are!

As you are painting, make sure you have enough paint on your brush. If you're using a roller, dip it about halfway into the paint, roll it **very gently** on the pan grid to smooth it, and press the edges against the pan to squeeze paint out of them (if you don't, you'll leave "trails" on the wall).

Never paint in uniform sections or "stripes". Instead, work in three-foot sections at a time and use large Ws and zig-zags to fill in each section. Go over each section several times as you fill in, smoothing out excess paint or ridges. Overlap each section to keep the whole job looking smooth.

The best strategy is to start painting at a window (or other source of light) and work away from it. As you finish each section, check it against the light. Did you miss any spots? Your new paint will look "wet" (it will glare in the light), while the old paint beneath it will look dry. Check carefully; you want to catch any missed spots while you're still painting. Once latex paint has dried, you can touch up spots you missed--but if oil-based paint dries, you have to repaint the entire surface.

"Tricks of the trade" for specific surfaces include these:

Walls. If you're painting the walls with different paint than you used to paint the ceiling, you need to carefully paint a border around the top of the walls where they join the ceiling. Use a brush that's between two and three inches wide. Don't leave a straight edge; you don't want the brush line to show when you paint the rest of the wall.

Work in three-foot sections of wall, using the "W" and zig-zag methods as you fill in each section. When you move to a new section, start three feet from where you left off and work toward the wet paint, not away from it.

Doors. Begin by painting the door frame; if you're using a different color than you did on the walls, you should wait until the walls are completely dry. Use a small brush; you can also use pieces of masking tape to mask off the wall adjacent to the door frame. After you've finished the door frame, paint the edges of the door; finally, paint the door itself. When painting a door, start at the top and move down to avoid dribbling paint on a surface you've already finished.

Window frames. Use a small, angled brush to paint window frames. If you want to, you can use masking tape on the glass panes to keep paint off the glass. If you do get paint on the glass, you can use a razor blade to scrape it off after it has dried.

Baseboards and trim. Wait until the walls have dried completely before painting the baseboards and trim. Protect walls and the floor with masking tape.

PAINTING THE EXTERIOR OF YOUR HOUSE

Now that you know the basics, feel like you're ready to tackle a bigger job? Then move on outside--and give your home new life with a fresh coat of paint (and maybe even a new color!).

Many of the principles are the same for any painting job, but you'll need some specific tricks if you take on the exterior of the house.

What About Color?

You can leave it the same if you like it. If you don't, there are plenty of options you can choose!

Painting the exterior of a house isn't as simple a proposition as painting a kitchen, so you need to take some time when choosing your color. What have you seen on other houses that you like? Would those same colors work on your own house? If you have trouble visualizing things, try taking some black and white snapshots of your house; you can experiment by coloring the photos. Remember that you have two or three different elements that need paint (the siding, the trim, and the shutters), so you can choose two or three different colors.

When you look at colors, take into consideration the existing factors that affect your home. You'll have to work around some permanent things, for example, such as your roof and any existing brick. You also need to consider your setting and the houses around yours. If your house is nestled in a wooded area, you should stick to earth-tone colors. If your home is surrounded by conservative homes, you probably don't want something too flashy or garish on yours.

A Tape By Any Other Name. . .

. . .might not do the same thing! There are at least fifteen different kinds of tape on the market, and you can use them in plenty of creative ways to make your home-repair and - maintenance jobs easier!

To get you started, try some of these:

- **Need to paint a straight line?** Line up two strips of masking tape, and paint between them.
- **Keep welcome mats and area** rugs from slipping with a few pieces of double-faced carpet tape.
- If a cupboard door keeps swinging open, put a few small pieces of magnetic tape on the door and frame.
- Have a picture that refuses to hang straight? Put a few pieces of double-faced foam tape on the back of the frame and affix it to the wall.
- Tired of the kitchen drawer that always sticks? Press a strip of nylon slick tape in the track.

Lots of factors will impact the color (or at least the intensity) that you choose. What style is your home? A contemporary home is a natural for dramatic splashes of color. A traditional colonial home, on the other hand, looks best in a conventional color with white at the window.

You also need to decide whether to use a light or a dark color. Light colors reflect the sun (thereby keeping your house cooler inside) and make your home look bigger. Dark colors make your home look smaller and absorb sunlight (thereby keeping your house warmer inside). If your house is perched on a windy knoll in Maine, then, you'll probably want a dark exterior for warmth; if your house is situated on the fringe of California's desert country, you'd do better with a cool, light-colored exterior.

If there are some architectural features you don't like, use little contrast on those; strong contrast emphasizes architecture.

If you've narrowed your choices but can't make a final decision, try it out! Get a small sample from the paint store and paint it on the house--paint a small area that is shaded and a small area that is exposed to direct sunlight. See how you like it. Keep mixing and working until you find what you want.

How much paint will you need? Repeat the formula you used on the interior: multiply the height by the width of each side of the house to determine the total square feet. If there are large areas that won't be painted (such as a double French door or an area that is brick), subtract that area. Divide your total by 400 to figure out how many gallons of paint you'll need.

Determining What Kind of Paint to Use

Your two options for interior painting--oil-based and latex paint--can also be used on the exterior of your house. In addition, you have two other options: stucco paint (applicable only if your home is stucco, of course) and exterior wood stain (applicable only if you want the natural color of wood).

What you choose will depend on your climate and what you want the paint or stain to do:

Oil-based paint adheres well to surfaces, so is less likely to peel. It also prevents water from penetrating into the wood and works as a good sealant. Oil-based paint will even seal hairline cracks to provide protection to your wood siding.

Latex paint lets moisture escape, thus reducing the likelihood of blistering. It also dries quickly, so blowing dirt, bugs, and other debris will be less likely to stick to it.

Stucco paint is specially formulated to coat stucco and fill in cracks; it is a thick coating that is available in various colors. Specially formulated stucco coatings will expand with the stucco in changing weather conditions.

Exterior wood stains are available in a range of colors and transparencies, ranging all the way from transparent (which lets the wood show through completely) to solid (which hides the color of the wood but lets the grain show through). You can also purchase "weathering" stains that give wood a silvery weathered appearance in as little time as six months.

Most stains last longer than paint because they enable moisture to escape without cracking or peeling.

Preparing the Surface for Paint

Basically, you need to do the same thing on the outside as you did on the inside: you need to clean off debris, patch up holes, and remove any hardware. Good preparation is crucial--it will help your paint last longer and will result in a more professional-looking job.

Start by repairing any damage to walls, trim, or shutters. Then you need to wash **all** the surfaces you will be painting; use a detergent to get rid of grease, chalk, mineral deposits, and dirt. If wood knots have oozed a resinous deposit, remove it with turpentine and seal the knots with a specially designed sealant. Then let the house dry; it takes about a week of clear, warm, sunny weather in order for the house to dry out completely. (Allowing time to dry is vital--moisture in the wood will cause blistering and peeling of the paint.)

Make repairs much as you did on the surface of your interior walls. Fill in cracks and holes with caulking. Scrape away any peeling paint. Sand out patches of rust, and coat rusted areas with primer. Remove mildew by scrubbing it with a bleach solution (one cup of household bleach in a gallon of water). Pound in nails that are protruding above the surface. If there are rusty nails, pound them in to slightly beneath the surface, coat them with primer, and cover the hole with putty. When the putty has dried, sand it smooth.

Finally, Begin Painting Now!

Follow the basic guidelines you did when painting the interior of your house, and keep these additional ones in mind:

- Paint only during good weather. The ideal is moderate temperature with indirect sunlight. **Never** paint the exterior of your house when it is raining or snowing or when the temperature dips below 50 degrees F. (It's not your comfort you should be concerned with: paint won't penetrate or cure if the weather isn't right.)
- Make sure you are using the right kind of brush for the job. Use nylon brushes for latex paint, natural-bristle brushes for oil-based paint, long-napped rollers for rough-textured surfaces (such as masonry), and short-napped rollers for smooth surfaces.
- Apply two coats of paint on the exterior, letting the first dry completely before you apply the second. For best results, apply the first coat with a paint brush and the second coat with a roller.
- To avoid painting windows shut, open them before painting the frames and casing. Leave the window slightly open, opening and closing it several times a day until the paint dries.

NO TIME FOR SPLASHING: HOW TO SOLVE COMMON PLUMBING EMERGENCIES

Water drips. It runs. It splashes. And it's **inside** your house.... What can you do?

Start with shutting off the water! As soon as you see water leaking from a pipe, coming through a wall, dripping through a ceiling, or running across a floor, shut if off so your damage will be kept at a minimum. Sinks and toilets have individual shut-off valves; they're usually just under the fixture, but they might be located in the basement, utility room, or crawl space.

If you can't identify which fixture the leak is coming from, you need to quickly shut off all the water to the house. The main shut-off is usually located on the outside wall where the main enters the house or next to the water meter. Turn shut-off valves clockwise to turn off the water.

The most common plumbing emergencies, with their solutions, include the following:

Stopped-up sink drain. If water is sluggish or won't drain at all, use a rubber "force cup" (similar to a toilet plunger). If that doesn't work to dislodge the clog, use a chemical drain opener (make sure you follow label directions carefully). If you still can't free up the drain, get under the sink. Put a bucket under the trap, and open it. Fish a wire up the pipe and pull out any debris you can reach (it will usually be a combination of hair and grease). Replace the trap and run scalding hot water through the pipes.

Restricted water flow. If you don't seem to have enough water pressure, it's time to do a simple test: you may have hard-water scale buildup in your pipes. To find out if you might have such a problem, turn the water on full force, making sure all valves are fully open. If water courses out at first and then slows down to a small stream, your pipes are restricted. This isn't something you can solve on your own; a professional plumber will need to replace the pipes involved. If you can afford it, avoid galvanized steel pipes--they tend to encourage scale buildup.

Leak in a wall. A leak in a wall is usually caused when the pipe behind the wall gets damaged. Turn off water immediately and call a professional plumber. In some cases, the pipe can be repaired or replaced without the wall being cut.

Leak in a pipe. The most common cause of leaking from a pipe is a corroded pipe or a frozen pipe. If the pipe's joints are threaded (that is, if they screw together like a lid on a bottle) you might be able to repair the leak yourself by tightening the joint. You might also be able to repair a burst pipe with a clamp-on pipe patch, available in home center or plumbing supply stores. If neither of those approaches work, you need the help of a plumber.

Overflowing dishwasher. The most common cause of an overflowing dishwasher is simple: a large piece of food, built-up grease, or a dishrag may be clogging the screen around the drain. If so, simply remove the source of the clog. Other possible causes include a fault in the electric controls or damaged pipes. You should turn off the current to the dishwasher (unplug it if it's a portable model) and call a repair service.

Overflowing toilet tank. If the water keeps running (sometimes without ever stopping) after you flush the toilet, the toilet tank is probably overflowing into the bowl. Lift the float ball in the tank; if the water stops running, try bending the arm of the float ball so that it will sit a little lower in the tank. If that doesn't work, turn off the water shut-off valves located between the toilet tank and the floor, and call a plumber.

244

KEEP AN EYE UNDERFOOT: TAKING CARE OF YOUR CARPETS

The carpets in your home represent a substantial investment: they are probably one of the single greatest expenses in a home. Unfortunately, the carpets in your home can also be the victim of unusual wear and tear, damage, and stains.

Some preventive care on your part and prompt removal of stains can prolong the life of your carpet and preserve your investment in its beauty.

General carpet-care rules include the following:

- Vacuum your carpets thoroughly and regularly. Heavy traffic areas should be vacuumed every day, and other areas should be vacuumed every four to seven days. Regular vacuuming does **not** wear your carpets out more quickly--on the contrary, it removes particles that can cut your carpet fiber if they aren't removed.
- Vacuum carpeted stairs daily if they get daily wear. Use the brush attachment or upholstery nozzle if your vacuum cleaner has accessories. If your stairs get extremely heavy use, consider covering them with a vinyl or nylon runner to protect your carpeting.
- Clean your carpets regularly to get rid of the deeply embedded dirt fibers that aren't removed by vacuuming; you should clean carpets three to four times a year, more often if traffic is heavy or heavy soil is tracked into the house. You can rent carpet shampooing machines for a nominal fee; the place where you rent the machine will also sell you shampoo. You can also clean your carpets yourself by spraying on a shampoo foam (available in grocery stores and home centers), working it into the carpet with a damp sponge, allowing it to dry, and vacuuming it out. You should hire a professional carpet cleaner once a year to thoroughly clean all residue from your carpets.
- Remove any stains promptly; the longer they sit, the more difficult they are to remove. The most common method is to remove excess material by blotting it up with a light-colored clean towel or by scraping it with the dull edge of a knife; clean the stains by rubbing in the solution recommended on the chart below; gently brush the pile to restore the carpet's original texture once the stained area has dried; and finish up by vacuuming.

Use the following guide to remove stains from specific sources in your home:

Stain	Stain Remover
Asphalt	Detergent and volatile solvent
Beer	1 tsp. liquid detergent and 1 tsp. white vinegar in 2 C. lukewarm water
Berry stain	1 tsp. liquid detergent and 1 tsp. ammonia (3-6%) in 2 C. lukewarm water
Bleach	Liquid detergent and lukewarm water
Blood (wet)	Liquid detergent and cool water
Blood (dried)	Warm detergent, ammonia (3-6%), and lukewarm water
Butter	Cleaning fluid and cornmeal (enough to make a paste); leave for 2 hours, vacuum
Catsup	Liquid detergent
Chewing gum	Volatile solvent
Chocolate	Liquid detergent/ammonia/water
Coffee	Liquid detergent/white vinegar/volatile solvent
Cola drinks	Liquid detergent
Crayon	Paint remover
Food dye	Liquid detergent and water
Furniture polish	Paint remover and liquid detergent
Grape juice	Salt (rub it in, let it sit, vacuum)
Gravy	Liquid detergent
Ink (permanent)	Paint remover/volatile solvent/detergent
Ink (washable)	Liquid detergent and water
Lipstick	Paint remover
Mascara	Paint remover/volatile solvent/detergent/water
Milk	Liquid detergent
Nail polish	Volatile solvent
Paint (oil-based)	Paint remover

246

Paint (latex, wet)	Liquid detergent and water
Paint (latex, dry)	Paint remover
Shoe polish (liquid)	Volatile solvent/detergent/water
Shoe polish (wax)	Volatile solvent/apply heated iron through a clean white rag
Tea	Liquid detergent
Urine	Liquid detergent and white vinegar
Vomit	Warm detergent/white vinegar/water
Wax	Volatile solvent/apply heated iron through a clean white rag
Wine	Liquid detergent/ammonia (3-6%)/white vinegar/water

PUBLIC ENEMY NUMBER ONE: GETTING RID OF MILDEW

Don't think you have to live in a humid climate to have a mildew problem: mildew thrives in all parts of the country. It's not limited to a single season, either--and if you don't spot it and get rid of it, it can literally rot whatever it's growing on.

What is mildew?

Simply stated, it's a mold. It thrives on moisture and does best where there is little or no ventilation. It's stubborn, it spreads, and it causes a characteristic musty odor that is extremely difficult to get rid of.

Mildew causes a brownish stain that looks a lot like dirt. So how do you determine whether it is actually mildew? Simple. Wet the corner of a rag with household laundry bleach and hold it against the stain for one minute without rubbing. If the stain looks the same when you peek under the rag, it's dirt. If the stain has disappeared or gotten a lot lighter, it's mildew.

The key to getting rid of mildew is to **kill the fungus** and to make your home an inhospitable place for mildew to grow. It's not enough to just wipe mildew away; you have to kill it, or it will come back (even if you can't see a trace after you've cleaned).

Killing Mildew in a Bathroom

Commercial mildew removers for use in the bathroom are widely available; you will find them in the same area of the grocery store where bathroom cleansers and toilet bowl cleaners are found.

You should follow label directions carefully, but, in general, you should spray the mixture on, wait a few minutes, rub it in with a soft brush, rinse it off, and wipe the area dry.

If mildew is growing on the grout between bathroom tiles, mix one-half cup of liquid laundry bleach in two cups of warm water. Use an old toothbrush to scrub the solution into the mildew. Wait a few minutes, rinse with clear water, and wipe the area dry.

Removing Mildew From Painted Surfaces

To get mildew off painted surfaces without damaging the surrounding paint, make a mix that contains the following:

1 C. liquid laundry bleach

2 T. powdered cleanser containing trisodium phosphate (such as Spic 'n Span)

2 qts. water

Scrub the solution on the mildewed area, allow it to dry completely, and rinse off with plenty of clear water. As soon as you can, repaint the area to discourage further mildew growth.

An Ounce of Prevention. . .

To prevent mildew from growing in your home in the first place, follow these guidelines:

• Keep outside walls free from foliage (such as shrubs and trees) that keep the house shaded and damp. Trim shrubbery so that sun can reach the foundation, siding, or brickwork.

• Check your lawn watering habits: don't allow sprinklers to keep your siding or foundation wet all the time.

• Keep damp areas in your house (such as the bathroom, closets, crawl spaces, and the basement) well ventilated to discourage mildew growth. If there is a window in the bathroom, keep it open at least partway; if not, install and run a fan periodically. After you have finished showering, extend the shower curtain and let it dry. Install vents in closet doors or replace them with louvered doors.

• Use mild heat in stuffy areas, such as closets. You can leave a 25-watt bulb on in a closet, and it will provide enough heat to keep the closet dry. You can also buy electric heating cables that can be taped to the walls of closets and other closed-off areas.

- Try to keep things dry, and avoid situations that could encourage mildew growth. Never leave damp or wet towels in a heap; hang them up immediately after showering or bathing.
- If you live in a humid climate, do what you can to dehumidify. If you can afford it, purchase a dehumidifier. Vent your clothes dryer to the outside. Dehumidifying chemicals are available in sealed bags; you can hang them in closets or other damp, closed areas until they get damp. By drying them in a low-heat oven, you can reuse them.

RIGHT AT YOUR FINGERTIPS: COLLECT THE TOOLS TO DO THE JOB!

You're out on your own. You've stocked the kitchen with pots and pans, the cupboards with spices, and the medicine chest with handy first-aid remedies.

All set?

Not at all!

Anyone who lives in a home--whether it's a city apartment or a two-story country manor--needs a set of basic tools to take care of minor repairs, hang up pictures, or measure the spot for a new chest of drawers. If you'd like an idea of the basics you should collect, stock up on the following:

Hammer. Buy a solid 14- to 18-ounce claw hammer. You can use it to pound in nails as well as to remove them.

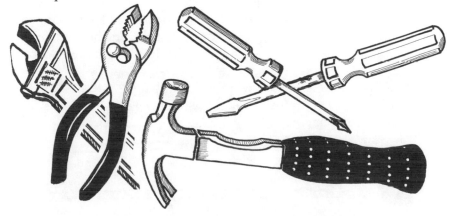

Screwdrivers. You'll need one with a flat head as well as a Phillips screwdriver, and you should get them with several different-sized heads to handle various jobs. One good idea is to buy a single screwdriver that has six interchangeable magnetic heads.

Variable-speed electric drill. This will undoubtedly be your most expensive tool, but it's worth the money you'll pay! Look for a drill that has attachments for buffing, polishing, and sanding, and make sure the drill has a reverse speed that allows you to remove screws. You can purchase additional drill bits and screwdriver bits if you want to. For an extra investment, you can buy a cordless drill.

Pliers. Make sure they include a wire cutter.

Channel-lock pliers. Channel-lock pliers are the ones that are adjustable (they look more like a wrench than pliers). You should get ones with five or six adjustable widths.

Needle-nose pliers. Needle-nose pliers (which also cut wire) can be used to work in tight places, hold tiny screws, and strip the insulation away from electrical wires. Check the quality by closing the blades; you shouldn't be able to see any light between them.

Saw. Get a basic, all-purpose saw with medium teeth; you can purchase shorter, more lightweight saws that are more convenient to keep in a tool box.

Hacksaw. A hacksaw will saw through thin metal, unlike an all-purpose saw.

Utility knife. A utility knife with a retractable blade can be used to cut wallpaper, cardboard, picture mats, plastic floor tile, and other things you can't cut with scissors.

Putty knife. Use a 1 1/4-inch putty knife to patch holes, to scrape putty, and to remove peeling paint or wallpaper. The best quality putty knives flex easily and have a firmly screwed wooden handle.

Tape measure. Get a self-winding metal tape measure that measures at least eight feet (preferably ten feet) and that locks at the right measurement.

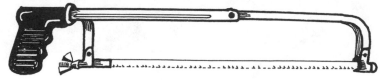

Rubber toilet plunger. The most convenient kind have a removable wooden handle that screws into the rubber head.

Staple gun. A good-quality staple gun enables you to tack things with ease. They are available in different models and sizes; make sure the staples you purchase fit the gun you buy.

Nails. The most commonly used sizes are 1- and 1 1/2-inch nails; keep some on hand for repairs.

Screws. Get a variety of sizes!

Wood glue.

Four-inch C-clamps. C-clamps can be used to hold things together while glue is drying, or to anchor items that you are sawing or nailing.

Tool box. Finally, get something to hold it all! Tool boxes are

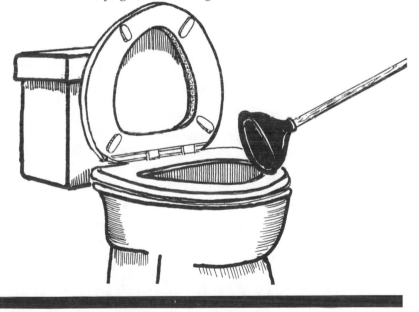

Glue: A Pretty Sticky Subject

Confused about which glue to use for the job?

A few simple guidelines can clear things up. Use the following glues on the materials listed:

Rubber cement: paper, leather, cardboard, small pieces of fabric.

White glue: cardboard, leather, wood.

Yellow wood glue: wood.

Instant glue: glass, ceramics, hard plastics, and metal.

Hot glue: cardboard, tile, ceramics, wood, and craft projects.

Epoxy: glass, tile, metal, and masonry.

Spray adhesive: paper, small areas on cardboard, small pieces of fabric.

available in all price ranges, and they can be very simple or extremely complex (featuring different levels and separate compartments for nails, screws, bolts, and so on). You don't really need anything fancy; something lightweight that can help you organize things will do the trick!

It Pays To Call For Help . . .

If you're a beginner handyman, there is plenty you can do around the house--but there are some things you should not try on your own.

Why?

Some things look simple on the surface but can lead to major problems--problems that will be expensive and time-consuming to have fixed later on.

As a general rule, follow these guidelines:

- Never try to repair an appliance or other item that is still under the manufacturer's warranty; you'll invalidate the warranty and end up having to pay for service.
- Don't take down a wall until you have checked with a reputable contractor; the wall could be a structural support, and you could end up with more than you bargained for.
- Don't do your own roofing or roof repairs. You could ruin the roof and necessitate a full replacement--and, even worse, you could fall off and critically injure yourself.
- Never attempt to do internal wiring unless you are a licensed electrician. Faulty wiring repairs can cause home fires (if you don't electrocute yourself first).
- Never attempt major plumbing unless you are a licensed plumber.
- Don't start any project that opens up part of your house unless you can complete it **the same day.** You'll face weakened security and possible inclement weather.
- Finally, don't try to fix an appliance until you've unplugged it, and don't unscrew a faucet handle until you've turned off the water!

YOUR CAR: BUYING IT, DRIVING IT, AND KEEPING IT IN GREAT SHAPE

CHAPTER 7

C ars: you can't live with 'em, and you can't live without 'em!

Found yourself muttering that sentiment quietly--or maybe not so quietly--under your breath?

Believe it or not, there **are** things you can do to make owning a car a lot of fun! The key lies in buying right, driving right, and staying on top when it comes to repairs.

BUYING A CAR: GETTING YOUR MONEY'S WORTH

Okay. You've decided it's time to take the plunge and buy a new car. If it's your first time, you probably haven't done much yet--except maybe drive around a few flashy new-car lots after closing time, when no salespeople were around.

Right?

Well, it's time to get over the jitters and take some positive steps toward owning your first new car! Whether you're in the market for a new or used car, some guidelines are pretty basic:

Do your research. Simply stated, find out which car is best for you!

How?

Easy! Visit your local library, and grab some of the annual publications that rate the cars currently on the market. **Consumer Reports** publishes an annual buying guide that lists the latest statistics on most cars on the market. The information desk at the library can guide you to others that will give you breakdowns on price, safety, reliability, and repair records.

Narrow your choices down to several makes and models based on what you want and need in a car...and you're ready to rally get started!

Figure out where the best dealers are. How? Start by asking some local mechanics; they can tell you which dealers have the best parts and service departments (an essential if you leave the lot with a car). Ask friends. Call the local chamber of commerce and find out which dealers have been in the community the longest--usually a key to excellence. And, finally, contact your local Better Business Bureau to find out what, if any, complaints have been lodged against dealers in your community.

Go shopping! Don't buy the first car you see at the first dealer you visit. Shop around--you're making a big investment!

Stick to the makes and models you decided on earlier, but use the time at the dealer lot to check out various options that are available. You can buy some makes that are stripped-down copies of their more expensive counterparts--and you may not miss the "standard equipment" that's been removed. Or you might decide that life isn't worth living without factory air conditioning and a high-quality sound system.

Ask the sales personnel for specific dollar figures, and determine what you can realistically afford. Find out, too, which options can be added later and which must be done now.

When you shop can be as important as **where** you shop. The best time of year to shop for current-year models is August through December; dealers will be eager to clear out as many cars as possible to make room for next year's models. The best days to shop are Tuesday, Wednesday, and Thursday between 8 a.m. and 5 p.m.--there are fewer customers then, and salespeople will have more time to spend with you.

Resist high-pressure sales tactics. You'll know them when you get them--and they're mighty unpleasant. Avoid any salesperson who tries to pressure you into an immediate decision, regardless of the reason. A good salesperson will allow you the time you need to make a good choice. If yours won't, leave the lot. Period. Don't stick around and get badgered.

Take it for a spin. With your options narrowed, take your prospective car for a test drive. If your salesperson is a good one, you'll be able to really put the car to the test.

How?

To begin with, drive it for at least half an hour; moseying around one city block won't cut it. Aim for as many different road and traffic conditions as you can while the car is out. If you can, take it for a short stretch on a freeway; check acceleration and passing power. Climb hills. Take some turns. Do some stop-and-go driving.

Try parking it in a few tight spots. Notice the ride, the sound of the engine, the efficiency of the ventilation system. If a salesperson balks at letting you test the car that extensively, leave. Find someone else who will.

Negotiate on price. Found what you want? Then start bargaining! Tips for negotiating on new and used cars follow. Don't pass up this vital step. . .you should **never** shrug your shoulders and give the dealer his asking price without at least trying to get a discount. Take a pocket calculator with you, and let the salesperson see you using it.

Before you agree to buy any car, get at least three dealers' price quotes on the car. You might be amazed to find out that you can save a substantial amount of money just by shopping around!

Sign on the dotted line. When everything is to your satisfaction, it's time to sign the sales agreement.

Stop! Before you sign anything, read it over **very carefully**. Make sure you know exactly what you are committing yourself to. Your sales agreement should list the **exact price of the car--** including all the options, the sales tax, the dealer prep, the shipping charges, and any other fees that apply. These should be itemized clearly so you understand each one.

Buying A New Car: How To Get The Best Loan

Looking for a new car loan? Here's how to find the lowest rates with the least amount of hassle:

- Find out if the car manufacturer is offering a "pre-approved loan" on the model you want. If so, your credit is preapproved, and it's the easiest way to get a loan.
- Always check to find out if the car manufacturer is offering any incentives. Many of them periodically run "specials" that offer a significantly lower interest rate to car buyers.
- Belong to a credit union? Check there first. Rates are usually lower, and could be up to a percentage point lower than that if you're a member.
- To avoid last-minute hassles, check with your bank or credit union about a preapproved loan. Some will go ahead and process your loan for a specified amount, and then hold the loan for sixty to ninety days. When you find the car you want, you know you already have financing approved.
- Borrow for as short a period as possible. You'll always pay less in total financing charges if you take out a three-year loan, for example, than if you take out a four- or five-year loan.

If you're financing through the dealer, the sales agreement should also list the financing costs. If you are expected to find your own financing, make sure that the sales agreement allows you to cancel without losing your down payment if you are unable to arrange outside financing.

If you're trading in another car, make sure the sales agreement lists the price you were quoted. If it doesn't, speak up. . .it will affect the final price of your new car.

Negotiating on a New Car: How to Get the Best Possible Price

When you're looking at a new car, you need to do some fast fingerwork on your pocket calculator: once you know what the **dealer** probably paid for the car, you'll know what your rockbottom price will be!

Here's how:

Some publications list dealers' actual cost; they are available at newsstands. If you can't find one, you can get a pretty good idea of what a dealer paid for the car you're looking at by using some standard formulas.

While individual dealerships can vary, of course, most mark up a new full-sized car by 15 to 20 percent. The usual markup on compacts and mid-sized cars is 13 to 15 percent, and the common markup on subcompacts is about 12 percent. Most dealerships mark up options by 18 to 20 percent.

How far down will a dealer come on price?

Obviously, it depends on the dealer--but if you're shopping at the right time of year, you can usually get a dealer to give you a car for $300 to $500 more than he paid for it.

Before you start negotiating, then, figure out what the dealer paid for the car; make sure you include all options. Then subtract another $200 or $300--that's to make room for bargaining!

Now approach the salesperson and state what you are willing to pay for the car. Hold on--don't be surprised to get an emotional reaction ("We couldn't **POSSIBLY** give this car away for **THAT AMOUNT OF MONEY!**" may come close to the response you'll get). Don't back down. Stay calm, and ask for a counteroffer. Keep the bargaining process going until you get the price you want (or until the dealership refuses to go any lower).

Don't let down your guard once you've agreed on a price, however. Taxes, freight, and some other dealer fees will be added-- but make sure the sales agreement you sign reflects the price you both agreed on. (Some unethical dealers have been known to boost the price back up after a fervent bargaining session, and the unwary buyer, smug from a supposed victory, never notices.)

BUYING A USED CAR: HOW TO AVOID GETTING BURNED

If you can't afford a new car or have decided on a reliable used one, you can get a good, reliable car--if you take some basic precautions along the way.

When buying a used car, you have an option you don't have with a new car: you can buy your car from a dealer, or you can make your purchase from a private party. You'll usually save money by purchasing from an individual; dealers obviously need to mark up their cars to cover the overhead costs of operating the dealership. But, on the other hand, you can often get a limited warranty for a used car through a dealer--and a private party will rarely make any guarantees. And because a dealer's business depends on repeat business, he can't afford to pass on a "lemon" or to risk an unsatisfied customer. Finally, a reputable dealer will usually back you up with a service department--something you can't get from a guy across the street.

Whatever you decide, some basic tips can help you get the best for your money when buying a used car:

• Check the most recent April issue of *Consumer Reports,* the issue dedicated to cars. Look up the "frequency of repair" records for the makes and models you're interested in. Modify your choices, if necessary--aim for a make and model that has a low rate of needed repairs.

• If you decide to buy from an individual, try finding a car you're familiar with (your sister's car, for example, or a friend's car). You'll know how much wear-and-tear the car has had, what the maintenance has been like, and whether the car has been a chronic repair headache.

• If you decide to buy from a dealer, look for an "off-brand" car on the lot. If you're at a Chevrolet dealer, for example, look for a Chrysler or a Toyota. A dealer may be willing to work a better deal on a car he doesn't usually stock or that he is not as familiar with.

- If you decide to buy a car through the classified ads, consider only those cars that are currently registered and that are owned free and clear by the seller. You'll have financial entanglements you never dreamed possible if you buy a car that someone still owes money on or that can't be registered for some reason.
- Steer away from exotic models (they are more costly and difficult to repair), sports cars (they usually get more abuse), and luxury cars loaded with options (there are simply more things to go wrong!).
- Aim for the lowest mileage you can get. You are better off to buy a car that's a year or two older if it has lower mileage than its newer counterpart.
- Insist that a reputable mechanic inspect the car before you make a final decision on the car; if you're buying from a dealer, take the car to an independent mechanic for an inspection. (You may need to leave a small deposit with the seller before taking the car, but it's a wise investment.) If the owner or dealer won't allow an inspection, close off negotiations right then: there's obviously something to hide, and you don't want to find out about it later! Your mechanic should know what to check, but you should ask for a report on the brakes, suspension, engine compression, frame, battery, alternator, radiator and hoses, transmission fluid, and electrical system.
- If your mechanic says that the car needs repairs, get an estimate on repair costs. Add them to the sales price of the car to find out whether you're still getting a good deal.
- Check the car out yourself, you should reject a used-car candidate if you find rust spots anywhere on the body, uneven tread wear on the tires, uneven engine idling, brakes, a noisy engine, sticking squealing or grinding gears, a jerking clutch, too much free play in the steering wheel (more than about three-fourths of an inch), or smoke pouring from the exhaust pipe.
- To figure out what you should pay for a used car, scan the classified ads. Circle all the ads for the make and model you want. Then average the prices. Regardless of the car's condition, refuse to pay more than that average.

- Arrange for your financing ahead of time when buying a used car. First of all, you need to find out how much your bank or credit union will loan on the car you want to buy (financial institutions have strict guidelines, and you'll need to fall within these.) Be sure you figure in interest charges, finance fees, and other "hidden" costs--you might find out you're not getting a good deal after all.

BEHIND THE WHEEL: DRIVING LIKE A PRO

You pull around a corner one December morning and find yourself skidding across a sheet of black ice. . .or you're heading for an important appointment in rush-hour traffic when a radiator hose splits open. . .or you turn the key in the ignition and **nothing** happens. . .or you get broad-sided as you sail down a narrow roadway.

Getting More From Your Gasoline Dollar: How To Increase Your Gas Mileage

Regardless of what conditions you're driving in, you can use a few simple tricks to increase the gas mileage you get. If you live at an altitude above 5,000 feet, have your carburetor adjusted by a mechanic. Then try some of the following:

- Plan your route ahead of time, especially in city traffic. Try to avoid areas of heavy congestion where you spend a lot of idling time.
- Try to maintain a constant speed, especially on freeways.
- Avoid the temptation to weave in and out of lanes; lane changing is a real gas guzzler.
- Stick to streets with good pavement whenever possible. The constant speed variations involved in dodging ruts and potholes will gobble up gas.

- If you're approaching a long uphill climb, gradually accelerate *ahead of time* so your speed is built up when you start climbing. When you hear the car start to strain, shift to a lower gear.
- Air conditioners cut gas mileage by as much as 20 percent, so use them only when necessary--and then only long enough to cool off the car. Park in a garage or a shady spot to keep the car as cool as possible during hot weather.
- When the weather's hot, fill your gas tank early in the day. Why? Gas expands when it gets hot, and if you fill up later you'll get less gas for your money.
- Park in a garage in the winter if you can; if not, cover the engine with a blanket while the car is parked. Why? A warm engine will start up more easily--and most of your fuel is used when you're trying to crank up the engine.
- Use snow tires and/or chains only while necessary; remove them as soon as you can in the spring. They cause more friction, which in turn burns up more gas.

Recognize these driving nightmares?

Driving a car can be a hazardous business these days: the National Highway Traffic Safety Administration says that one in every eight people is involved in some kind of a collision every year--and exactly half of us will be injured in a car accident during our lifetime.

Want to reduce the odds that you'll be one of the unlucky ones?

Then learn some basics about defensive driving, and become familiar with the tricks associated with driving in your specific climate!

AVOIDING ACCIDENTS: LEARN TO BE ON THE DEFENSE

Being in an automobile accident is often not merely a matter of "dumb luck." By keeping on the defense and sharpening your

---

Silence Is Not Golden: What To Do When Your Car Won't Start

Sooner or later, it happens to everyone. You slide into the driver's seat, turn the key in the ignition, and nothing happens. Dead silence. Or maybe there's a little choking, clicking, or gasping.

What can you do now?

If you left your lights on or it's an especially cold morning, your battery may need recharging. Follow the jump-start instructions included with this chapter.

Follow these guidelines to correct other possible problems and get your car going again:

Check the Battery

Even if your battery is charged, it might not power your car if it's dirty or low on water. Do the following:

[ ] Check the water level. If it's low,

add distilled water.
[ ] If the battery is very dirty, wipe it off.
[ ] If the cables are corroded, use a wire brush to scrub them until they are clean.
[ ] If the cables are loose, tighten them with a wrench.

Check the Choke

If it's a cold morning, your choke may be stuck open. Here's how to find out, and how to correct the problem:

• Find the air filter; it looks like a large, round, flat "can" with pleats in it.

• Remove the air filter. It will probably be held in place with a clip or a wing nut.

• The carburetor lies just under the air filter; in the center of the carburetor you'll see a round opening that has a metal disk in it. That's the choke.

• The metal disk should be closed-- in other words, it should lay flat so driving technique, you can greatly boost your ability to avoid a smash-up.

First of all, you need to practice defensive driving from the minute you pull out of your driveway. Why? Regardless of what you might have believed, most serious accidents don't happen to drivers who are speeding down interstate highways. In fact, most serious accidents happen within twenty-five miles of home. And you're three times as likely to be involved in a serious accident on a rural road as on an interstate--and twice as likely on a three- or four-lane city street.

To improve your driving defenses, follow these tips:

Sit Up!

Start by sitting right. Sit squarely in the driver's seat with your back against the seat. Place both feet firmly on the floor, and adjust the seat so you can easily reach the pedals. In this position, you

---

it covers the round opening. If it's stuck open, try wiggling it with your finger to close it. If it won't close, try using a spray lubricant (such as WD-40) on it.

• Replace the air filter, and make sure you fasten the clip or tighten the wing nut.

If you develop a chronic problem with a sticky choke, have a mechanic check your carburetor thoroughly; there could be other problems that need repair.

Check the Distributor Cap

That sounds complicated, but it isn't! If you have driven through standing water or if it has been raining, you may have moisture under the distributor cap--and moisture prevents the spark plugs from doing their job.

Here's how to solve the problem:

• Lift the hood and find the distributor. Its round, plastic cap has one cable in the middle and smaller cables branching out to the spark plugs.

• Remove the cap. If it's held in place with two clips, simply pry them loose. If it's held in place with two small screws, use your screwdriver to remove them. (Make sure you put the clips or screws in a safe place so you won't lose them!)

• *Do not remove any of the cables.*

• Lift up the cap, and look inside it. If you find condensed moisture, spray some mechanic's solvent into the cap. (Any auto supply store carries solvent in spray cans.)

• *Never use any other solvent, such as gasoline, to try to evaporate the moisture under a distributor cap.*

• Using a clean soft rag, dry the distributor cap.

• Replace the distributor cap. Make sure you replace the clips or the screws.

should be able to see clearly out the windshield; adjust your rearview and side mirrors to give you full vision of what's behind and to the side.

Imagine that the steering wheel is the face of a clock: now place your hands at 9 and 3. Keeping this grip--with **both** hands on the wheel--allows you to react with split-second speed if you begin to lose control of the vehicle.

This should need no reminder, but **always fasten your seat belt.** It's a law in many states--but even where it isn't required, you should make it a personal "law." Use both a lap belt and shoulder strap to minimize injuries in case of accident. The lap belt should be snugly fastened across the tops of your thighs and your hips, **not** across your abdomen (in a sudden stop, you can rupture abdominal organs with a lap belt that is improperly positioned). There should be no more than one to two inches of "play" in your shoulder strap as it lies across your chest.

Stay Alert

Cut down on the number of distractions you have. If you need the heater or the air conditioner, adjust them while you're idling in the driveway--not after you're headed down a highway at 40 m.p.h. Find the radio station you want before you leave the driveway, too. If you'll need sunglasses, take them out of the glove compartment before you start out: in the few seconds you are fiddling in the glove compartment, your car can travel a hundred yards!

Even if you're talking to a passenger or listening to the radio, keep your thoughts centered on what's going on around you. Focus on the "big picture," a 360-degree circle around your car.

While you're driving, keep your eyes moving. Resist the temptation to read billboards or focus on something else that grabs your interest. Your eyes should be in constant motion: you should check your rearview and side mirrors every five seconds. The rest of the time, look ahead--**far** ahead. You should be watching the scene you'll be in fifteen seconds from now, a practice that gives you plenty of warning if there are impending dangers.

Make sure, too, that you keep your eye on what other drivers are doing. You can expect that somebody else will do the unexpected--and you'll be as ready as possible if you are watching.

Make Sure You're Seen

Do whatever you can to boost your own visibility to other drivers. Turn on your headlights at dusk; don't wait until it really gets dark. Use headlights, too, if it is raining or snowing. If your car has fog lights, use them; if not, parking lights (the ones with a yellowish hue) work well in the fog to alert other drivers to your position.

If you're going to change lanes or turn, signal. Sounds basic, but it's amazing how many people neglect it. By letting other drivers know your intentions, you can cut down significantly on problems.

When you need to slow down because of an obstacle in the roadway ahead, start slowing as soon as possible--and **use your brakelights to your advantage.** Start slowing by lightly stepping on your brakes as a warning to cars behind you.

If you can see that another driver hasn't noticed you, tap the horn lightly. All you need is enough to spark eye contact-not a loud, annoying blare that will irritate the other driver.

Allow For Extra Room

When you can, surround yourself with space. Start by allowing enough space between you and the car ahead of you. Why? If you're going 55 m.p.h. and suddenly need to stop, your car will travel about 60 feet **before your foot even reaches the brake pedal.**

The National Safety Council recommends what it calls the "two-second rule" for gauging safe distance. Here's how it works:

Pick out a stationary object on the side of the road, like a telephone pole, a road sign, or a bus bench. Watch to see when the rear bumper of the car ahead of you passes the object. Then count out loud, "One thousand one, one thousand two." Your front bumper should not reach the object until after you have finished counting.

When you can, leave at least one side open. It's best to drive in the right-hand lane when you can; that way, you at least have the shoulder of the road in case of an emergency. (Studies have shown that the left-hand lane is the most hazardous, with more tailgating, more haphazard lane changing, and higher speeds than in other lanes.)

What happens if someone starts tailgating you? If you can, get out of the way. Change lanes if that's possible. As a last resort, signal and pull off onto the shoulder of the road to let the offender pass. Exercise care when pulling back onto the road, of course.

Follow Good Driving Rules

Most accidents in free-flowing traffic are caused by one of three things: 1) a driver changes lanes without looking; 2) one car follows another too closely and can't stop soon enough; and 3) a car skids or spins out of control (usually because of wet or icy pavement) and is struck by another car.

Keeping those accident causes in mind, you can figure out some basic driving rules. We've already talked about one: leave plenty of room between you and the car ahead of you.

What if you try to stop suddenly and your brakes lock? You'll know the brakes have locked if you hear tires squealing against the pavement or you feel the car skidding. The trick is to let up on the brake and then start pumping it on and off; you'll achieve the shortest stopping distance that way.

When you get ready to change lanes, check your rearview and side mirrors first--before you even signal your intentions. **Then turn around and check the "blind spot" at the rear side of your car.** Once you're assured the coast is clear, turn on your signal. That lets other drivers know where you're going. Then accelerate slightly and smoothly as you change into the other lane to avoid cutting off a car that's behind you.

Tips on how to drive on wet pavement follow later in this section.

The top three accident-causers in city traffic are these: 1) a driver turns left in front of oncoming traffic; 2) a driver rear-ends another car waiting at a stop light or sign; and 3) a driver runs through a red light or stop sign.

Knowing these, you can drive defensively. The number-one rule in city driving is **never assume anything.** Never assume that just because someone has on a turn-signal indicator, he's going to turn. Never assume that just because someone has started to turn, he's going to complete the turn. Never assume that just because the light is red, the other driver will stop.

Your best defense is to slow down and wait. If someone ahead of you is signalling to turn, slow down; don't proceed until he's actually turning. When you approach an intersection, slow down

slightly and check traffic in both directions. If someone is coming from the side, don't assume he'll stop--even if he has a stop sign or red light. Don't enter the intersection until you clearly see that he's braking for a stop.

What if someone comes racing into the intersection? Your best defense is to steer **away** from the collision and pump your brakes to get as quick a stop as possible.

Finally, when you're stopped at a red light, stop a comfortable distance behind the car stopped in front of you. Keep your eye on the traffic that approaches from behind. If you can clearly see that someone isn't going to stop, rapidly accelerate and steer sharply to the side if there is an opening (such as onto the shoulder of the road). If you have no route of escape, quickly stretch out on the front seat to reduce your chances of serious injury from a rear-end collision.

Ease Into Curves

When you're approaching a curve, take a good look at it. Is it long? Short? Sharp? Gentle? Visualize what you'll have to do to handle the curve safely.

Slow down slightly **before** you get to the curve. As you enter the curve, gradually release your brake pressure. While you are still in the curve, begin accelerating gradually and smoothly to regain your driving speed and come out of the curve with more control.

Coping With Car Trouble: Essentials To Have On Hand

Anyone can have car trouble now and then, even with careful maintenance. To be prepared for anything, keep the following essentials on hand in your car at all times:

[ ] Fire extinguisher (dry chemical extinguisher)
[ ] Jumper cables
[ ] Tow rope
[ ] Spare tire
[ ] Jack and lug wrench
[ ] Screwdrivers (one Phillips, one regular)
[ ] Pliers
[ ] Flares and/or reflectors
[ ] First-aid kit
[ ] Empty gas can
[ ] Jug of water
[ ] Old blanket
[ ] Rags (at least one white)
[ ] Flashlight with long-life batteries
[ ] Pocket knife
[ ] Four quarters (for emergency phone calls)

Recover From Skids and Swerves

If you suddenly have to change direction to avoid an accident, follow this hard-and-fast rule: **stay off the brakes.** Your natural instinct may be to slam on the brakes--but that's where you'll get into trouble. In fact, you should try to avoid using the brake at all. Here's how:

As soon as you spot trouble, take your foot off the gas pedal. Turn the steering wheel quickly but slightly in the direction you need to go. As soon as you're out of danger, steer the wheel straight ahead. Then ease the accelerator back on as you return to your original lane and direction.

If, despite using this method, you start to skid, **continue to stay off the brake.** Ease off the gas and quickly turn the steering wheel in the direction that the car's rear end is sliding. If you go too far in one direction, turn the wheel in the other direction. Continue turning your wheel gradually (no abrupt angles!) until you've regained your direction **without stepping on the brakes.**

Take Care on Rural Roads

Of all the places you can drive, rural roads are the riskiest. Why? Since they are in sparsely populated areas, they tend to have high speed limits. They tend to be narrow and poorly lighted; many have unmarked intersections. You also run the risk of slow-moving farm machinery coming on to the road from a field instead of at an established intersection. When traveling on rural roads, keep a sharp eye out for vehicles and farm machinery entering the road

---

Your Car: Which Oil Is Right For You?

Buying oil for your car can suddenly become pretty complicated when you look at the label: you're likely to find a whole smattering of letters and numbers.

The numbers you're looking at indicate *viscosity:* the oil's relative thickness and its ability to flow at outside temperatures. If it gets too thick in cold weather, your car will be hard to start; if it gets too thin in hot weather, your engine parts won't be lubricated enough.

Here's a general guide to the ones you should pick:

5W-30   Four-cylinder engines

10W-30   Six- and eight-cylinder engines and all General Motors diesel engines

10W-40   Everything else! (it's the most widely used engine oil)

from the side. Reduce your speed and be on the alert if you see a vehicle even **sitting** on the side of the road.

Travel at a speed that seems comfortable to you, and don't exceed it--no matter what the posted speed limit says.

If you develop any kind of problem (a stalling engine or a flat tire, for example), pull well off the roadway before coming to a complete stop. If possible, stop on a straight section of roadway; if you can, avoid parking on hills or curves where you might not be seen by oncoming traffic.

A Checklist of "Don'ts". . .

Finally, there are some things you simply shouldn't do if you want to avoid an accident. According to the Highway Users Federation for Safety and Mobility, don't:

• Double-park
• Stop behind a car that is double-parked
• Drive in another motorist's "blind spot"
• Drive next to another vehicle for long distances, blocking two lanes of traffice
• Hold up traffic in the fast center lane while you wait to make a left-hand turn

---

In An Accident? Quick Tips For Safety

Statistics show that you've got a one in four chance of being involved in at least a minor fender-bender this year. If you *do* become a statistic, do these quick things to help protect yourself and others involved in the accident:

[ ] If you can, move out of the pathway of oncoming traffic.
[ ] Turn off the car's ignition.
[ ] Activate your car's emergency flashers to alert oncoming traffic of your plight.
[ ] Set out flares--one immediately behind your car, and one about

400 feet behind that one. Always keep flares away from spilled gasoline.

[ ] Ask a bystander to call the police or highway patrol, and let them know how many people seem to be injured. *Never leave the scene of the accident yourself.*

[ ] If someone is injured, don't move him unless he is in danger from fire; if he has a neck or back injury, moving him could permanently injure him. Cover all victims with a coat or blanket to prevent shock, and use direct pressure (with the heel of your hand) to control bleeding until help arrives.

- Drive so slowly that you lag behind all the other traffic on the road
- Drive so fast that you pass all the other traffic on the road
- "Jump the gun" when the light turns green
- Speed up to get through a yellow light
- Finish making a left turn long after the light turns red
- Try to bolt across railroad tracks before the train reaches you
- Try to dash across a through street before there's a clear break in the traffic

NO TIME FOR SNOOZING: HOW TO STAY AWAKE BEHIND THE WHEEL

Ideally, you shouldn't drive unless you are feeling good and are well-rested. Unfortunately, though, we all have to drive under less-than-ideal situations--times when we are under stress, coping with illness, or "running on empty" in the sleep department.

Use these tips to keep from getting drowsy behind the wheel:
- Avoid all drugs if you need to drive. That includes tobacco and coffee: the caffeine in coffee and some soft drinks has a greater letdown than the temporary "up" it provides!
- Eat light foods and snacks that are easy to digest. Oily, greasy, or heavy foods are hard to digest and make you sleepy.
- Keep plenty of fresh air flowing through the car. You'll stay more alert if your car is slightly on the cool side. Turn your vent to "fresh" to draw fresh air into the car, and open a window occasionally (even in winter, crack a window now and then).
- Stop often. Get out of the car and walk around briskly at rest stops, gas stations, or shopping center parking lots. If you're traveling with others, have a quick "race"--the run will boost energy and help combat fatigue.
- Wear sunglasses to cut down on glare, which makes you squint, which eventually makes you want to close your eyes. If you'll still be driving at nightfall, protect your night vision by wearing polarized sunglasses during the day.
- Change your posture or position for a refreshing break. Move your seat closer to or farther away from the pedals; if you can adjust the back of your seat, do it.
- Turn on the radio or cassette player, and find something interesting. You might like a stimulating talk show, or might be revived by some fast-paced jazz.

If you try all these tricks and still find yourself dozing, **pull off the highway as soon as you can.** Get out of the car and walk around. If you can, find a protected area in which to park your car, lock the doors, and take a short nap. If you still have hours to go, play it safe: find a motel and stop for the night.

IF YOU DO GET IN AN ACCIDENT. . .

If you've taken all possible safety precautions and still get in an accident, there are a few basics you should know. Assuming you are not badly injured, do the following:

• **Never leave the scene of an accident** before proper law enforce-

---

How To Change A Flat Tire

It's happened: your tire has blown out or gone flat. Here's a simple step-by-step guide on how to change the tire safely and properly:
• **Pull as far off the road as you can.**
• **Activate your flasher lights to alert other drivers.**
• **If you have a manual transmission, put your car in first gear; if you have an automatic transmission, put your car in park.**
• **Set the emergency brake.**
• **Put rocks or some other kind of block on both sides of the wheel that's diagonally opposite the flat tire.**
• **Use a screwdriver or the end of the lug wrench to remove the hubcap or wheel cover.**
• **Loosen, but don't yet remove, each lug nut with the lug wrench. (If the lug nut is marked "L," turn it clockwise; if it's marked "R," turn it counterclockwise.)**
• **Get the spare tire and the jack out of the trunk.**
• **Jack up the car (refer to your owner's manual for specific**

instructions on how to operate your jack). The jack should be completely perpendicular to the ground and should be firmly under the car.
• **Jack up the car until the flat tire is at least three inches above the ground.**
• **Completely remove the lug nuts; put them in the hubcap or wheel cover so they won't get lost.**
• **Remove the flat tire from the wheel axle.**
• **Put on the spare tire; make sure all bolt holes are aligned.**
• **Replace all lug nuts, tightening them by hand.**
• **Lower the car until the tire touches the ground firmly.**
• **Use the lug wrench to tighten the lug nuts completely.**
• **Finish lowering the car.**
• **Remove the jack and check the lug nuts again to make sure they are completely tightened.**
• **Replace the hubcap or wheel cover.**
• **Put all your equipment (including the flat tire) back in the trunk. Make sure you turn off your flasher lights before you get back on the highway--and take care as you reenter the flow of traffic!**

ment officials arrive. It's against the law.

- Be prepared to produce your driver's license and proof of insurance coverage.
- Quickly enlist the help of anyone who witnessed the accident. Get names and telephone numbers in case you need some support later on.
- Exchange names, driver's licenses, and telephone numbers with the other driver. Find out who the other driver is insured by.
- Cooperate fully with police, highway patrol, or sheriff's officials who arrive to investigate the accident.
- As soon as possible, contact your insurance agent to arrange for filing a claim and getting an estimate on damages.

IN ALL KINDS OF WEATHER: HOW TO BEAT THE HEAT

You're driving on one of those "dog days" when the air hangs hot and heavy and not a breeze offers relief. You watch the temperature gauge creep steadily up...and finally you hear the hiss of steam under the hood.

What now?

There are some tactics you can use to prevent an actual overheating when you see the temperature gauge rising. First, turn off the air conditioner. You might find that simply turning off the air conditioner solves the problem. If that doesn't work, turn on the heater: it will help to cool off the engine.

If the gauge still creeps up or steam actually starts to hiss, do the following:

- Pull off the road as far as possible, well out of the way of oncoming

---

Trip Tips: What To Check Before You Leave

Taking off on a trip? Before you leave, check the following:
- [ ] Tire pressure (including the spare).
- [ ] Engine oil level.
- [ ] Radiation water level.
- [ ] Transmission fluid level.
- [ ] Brake fluid level.
- [ ] Power steering fluid level.
- [ ] Windshield washer fluid level.
- [ ] Windshield wiper blades.
- [ ] Lights.
- [ ] Hoses (look for bulges or cracks).
- [ ] Belts (look for excessive wear or cracks).
- [ ] Battery fluid.

traffic. If you can, avoid stopping on a hill or curve. If that's not possible, protect yourself by getting out of the car and asking all passengers to get out and away from the car. Put on the emergency brake. Place one flare directly behind the car, and another about 400 feet behind that. If it's dusk or dark, leave your headlights on low beam, activate your emergency flashers, and leave on your interior lights.

- You have to wait for the radiator reservoir to cool down **before you touch the cap.** If the radiator is hissing steam or is too hot for you to comfortably place your hand on, you should not touch the cap. (If your car doesn't have a radiator reservoir, you simply have to wait for the engine to cool down.)
- After at least thirty minutes (the minimum cooling time), use a large, heavy cloth (such as a thick terrycloth towel) to turn the radiator cap. Turn the cap **away** from your face to avoid getting burned by steam.
- Add enough water to fill the radiator to the top. Replace the cap; make sure it is screwed on tightly.
- As soon as you can, stop at a service station to have the radiator, hoses, and pump checked.

THE WEATHER OUTSIDE IS FRIGHTFUL: COPING WITH ICE AND SNOW

Even the best and safest driver can encounter problems in winter, when coping with rain, fog, ice, and snow become critical.

Summertime, and the Driving Is Easy!

It's fun to travel in the summer-- even if it's just a trip around town! To get your car ready for summer's heat, use the following checklist:

[ ] Start up the engine; make sure all warning gauges are working (they all light up when you first turn the ignition key)
[ ] Check the spare tire for air and tread wear.

[ ] Have the exhaust system checked.
[ ] Check all belts for cracks or excessive wear.
[ ] Check all hoses for bulges, cracks, or loose connections.
[ ] Check the water level in the radiator; carry an extra plastic jug filled with water.
[ ] Check the windshield wiper blades.
[ ] Check the windshield washer reservoir; fill it and keep extra on hand.

271

The basic rules for driving in stormy weather are to reduce your speed and increase the space between you and other cars. Boost visibility by turning on your low-beam headlights (even during the day) and fog lights, if you have them. Use your defroster to keep the inside of the windshield clear, and use your wipers and windshield washer to keep the outside clean. Depending on what specific elements you're facing, use the following guidelines to increase your safety:

Driving in Rain

The biggest hazard from rainfall, of course, is the water: collected in puddles it can short out your spark plugs, and mixed with oil deposits on the road it can create a vicious slick. To drive safely in the rain, try the following:

- Before you turn on your windshield wipers, splash the windshield with your windshield washer to remove surface dirt and grit-- your wipers will do a better job of keeping the windshield clean, and you'll run less chance of scratching the glass.
- Cut down your speed, especially on curves.
- If you can, drive in the tracks left by the car ahead of you; they will be slightly drier than the rest of the road surface.
- Go very slowly through deep puddles; water can splash up under the hood and short out your spark plugs. After you've gotten through the water, pump your brakes lightly a few times to dry out the brake linings and make sure everything's still in working order.
- Unless absolutely necessary, avoid making sudden steering moves, sudden stops, or sudden acceleration.

Driving Safely in Ice and Snow

- Before you ever drive on ice or snow, check your tires. They should be fully inflated and have plenty of tread (at least one-eighth of an inch). If you live in an area where snow is a continual problem throughout the winter, you might consider investing in snow tires for added traction in winter driving.
- Keep all windows clear of ice and snow at all times while driving. If you need to pull over occasionally to clean off slush or heavy snowfall, do it--but choose a safe place well off the traffic area.
- Drive as slowly as you can and maintain as much distance as you

possibly can between you and the driver ahead of you.

- Be especially cautious when driving over shaded areas (such as those beneath overpasses) and over bridges (the wind beneath them ices the surface quickly).
- Slow to a minimum speed when approaching hills, going down hills, and when entering and taking curves.
- To stop safely on icy or snowy roads, take your foot off the accelerator well in advance (far before you usually would). Pump your brakes slowly and lightly to come to a gradual stop instead of applying firm pressure to the brakes.
- To start out without getting stuck, don't punch down the accelerator. Instead, use gentle and gradual acceleration. If you do get stuck, rock the car back and forth (using the reverse gear) while keeping your wheels pointed directly ahead.

If you do get stuck in a blizzard, don't panic! The American Red Cross advises that you pack some precautionary gear in your trunk before any winter driving (see the accompanying sidebar for their checklist), and gives these tips for anyone who's stuck in a storm:

- **Never try to walk for help.** You're more likely to be found in your car, and you risk hypothermia (general body cooling) if you try to walk any distance.
- Tie something bright (such as a red bandanna or a bright piece of clothing) to the car's antenna to make your vehicle more visible.
- Preserve body heat as much as you can. Don't move around. Never try digging your car out--you'll perspire, and that lowers body heat to dangerous levels. Don't eat snow or drink alcohol,

Checklist for Winter: Cold-Weather Emergency Kit

If you live in a cold climate or will be driving in snowy weather, the American Red Cross suggests you keep the following in your trunk at all times:

[   ] Matches
[   ] Candle stubs
[   ] Sterno
[   ] Nonmetallic flashlight with batteries
[   ] Small, sharp knife
[   ] Plastic garbage bag (use as a poncho)
[   ] Mittens, hat, and scarf
[   ] Blanket (wool if possible)
[   ] Red bandanna or other strip of red cloth
[   ] Plastic whistle
[   ] Facial tissue
[   ] Thirty feet of heavy twine
[   ] Snack food (raisins, nuts, granola, small candy bars)

both of which cause body temperature to plunge.
- Use your engine and heater sparingly; run them no more than fifteen to twenty minutes out of each hour.
- Once each hour, get out of the car and check the flashers and the exhaust pipe to make sure they are not being blocked by snow. If you are in a blizzard, anchor yourself to the steering wheel or the door handle with a length of heavy twine before you walk around the check the exhaust--you can get lost or confused in just a few feet in a heavy blizzard.

GETTING YOUR CAR REPAIRED: FINDING A MECHANIC YOU CAN TRUST

When should you look for a good mechanic?

Before your car breaks down!

Standing on the side of the road, wiping your brow as your car is being hitched to a tow truck, is **not** the time to start looking for a good mechanic. The time to start is the minute you buy your new car--and here's how to find a great mechanic:

- Find a shop that has been approved. Start by looking at independent garages, service stations, auto dealerships, specialty shops (such as AAMCO), or nationwide department or specialty stores (such as Sears). Look for a shop that has been approved by the AAA (American Automobile Association) and that employs at least one mechanic certified by the National Institute for Automotive Service Excellence. These mechanics have to pass tough tests to prove their competence in a variety of areas before they are certified. (If you own a diesel car, look for a shop bearing the Association of Diesel Specialists logo; these shops have

---

Let It Snow, Let It Snow. . .If You're Ready!

Feel that first hint of winter in the air? Here's a quick checklist to get your car ready for what's ahead:

[ ] Have the exhaust system inspected for worn parts or leaks that could cause carbon monoxide poisoning

[ ] Test the heater to make sure it works

[ ] Check windshield wiper blades; replace them if they streak

[ ] Fill up the windshield washer fluid and test to make sure it works

[ ] Test the hazard lights

[ ] Have at least one ice scraper at hand

mechanics versed on the latest diesel techniques.)

- Ask for recommendations. Ask your friends, neighbors, or family members which shops or mechanics they like--and which they don't.
- Check with the Better Business Bureau to find out if any complaints have been registered. Because of the nature of the business, most car repair shops will have an occasional complaint registered--but steer clear of one with many unsatisfied customers.
- Visit the shop yourself. Is it reasonably clean? That's a good indication that the owners take professional pride in their work. Is it busy? That's a good indication, too. If you can, talk to a few people who are waiting for service--if they're repeat customers, find out whether they were satisfied with the work, costs, and reliability.
- Talk directly to the owner, the manager, or the mechanic who does the work. You'll notice attitude right away; a person who seems concerned, friendly, and willing to listen to **your** concerns is the best one to deal with. Ask what services the shop provides; these vary, so you should know what is available. Then ask for the price of a few basic services (such as a front-end alignment or an electronic tune-up). You should do some comparison shopping, even though price is not always as important as quality.
- Ask about any extra services. Some repair shops offer loaners while your car is being repaired; others run extra diagnostic and road tests to pinpoint any potential problems.
- To be on the safe side, try out a new mechanic for the first time on a small inexpensive job. If you're satisfied, you'll feel more secure when the big ones come along.

When the time actually comes for repair jobs, you can avoid repair rip-offs by using the following strategies:

Steer clear of "specials." Some shops attempt to lure in customers by offering "specials"--but once you get there, you are persuaded to do something that costs significantly more.

Get clear on warranties. If you have any questions about what your warranty covers, clear them up **before** you take your car in for repairs.

When you take your car in, insist on talking to the mechanic who will be doing the repair work on your car. Some shops hire people who write up service orders and pass them on to the mechanic--but these people are rarely qualified to make judgments about what is needed.

Instead of asking for a specific repair, describe to the mechanic what is wrong with the car. Then let the mechanic make the "diagnosis" and determine which repairs are needed. Find out which repairs are necessary right now, and which are considered "maintenance"--then do what you can afford to do.

Get a second opinion on any major job. Take the car to a different mechanic, describe the problem, and ask for a diagnosis as well as a price estimate. You should also seek a second opinion on smaller jobs if you feel uncomfortable with the first mechanic's assessment or price.

Always get a written estimate for repair work, and do not authorize the shop to exceed the estimate without your approval. If a repair shop charges you more than 10 percent over what they cited in a written estimate, you can initiate legal action.

Read the repair order carefully to find out exactly what you are authorizing the shop to do. Find out what will happen if the repair is not done right--will it be corrected at no cost to you? **Never authorize a shop to do "any necessary repairs"**--chances are good that you'll pay a small fortune for work that didn't need to be done.

Be wary of a mechanic who calls later and says that additional work is now necessary. If you feel uncomfortable, tell the mechanic to fix only what was agreed on until you can get some more information.

When you get the bill, read it over carefully; if you don't understand something, ask for an explanation. Refuse to pay the repair bill unless it is itemized and all appropriate breakdowns are made.

KEEPING THINGS IN TOP SHAPE: HOW TO MAINTAIN YOUR CAR

While you'll need a mechanic for the big stuff--like transmission repair--there is plenty you can do on your own to maintain your car so you won't need as many repairs! If you start by breaking your car in the right way and giving it regularly scheduled maintenance, you can save a lot of money--and make your car road-worthy for many, many miles.

BREAKING THINGS IN: USE A GENTLE TOUCH

What's the most critical time for any car?

Easy: the first 2,000 miles! That's when a new car is "broken in," and if it's done the right way, it will ensure minimum wear and tear.

Before you take your car out on the road, read through the owner's manual. It contains information on what kind of fuel you should use, as well as whether you can use gasoline additives. It will also help acquaint you with all the car's systems--how to run the air conditioner, which knob controls the stereo, what the warning lights mean.

If your car is equipped with a standard transmission, consult the owner's manual to find out the maximum break-in speeds for each gear. Be sure to keep within these limits for the first 2,000 miles.

Check the manual's recommended tire pressures, and make sure you run your car accordingly. You should check the tire pressure at least once a week during the first 2,000 miles. (A weekly check throughout the life of the car isn't a bad idea, either.)

Make sure you don't try to tow anything until you've driven at least 2,000 miles.

Once you're familiar with the car, you're ready to start breaking it in. Follow these pointers:

For the First 100 Miles

- Keep your speed under 50 m.p.h.
- Make sure your car has plenty of oil. Use the right viscosity for your car and the climate you're driving in; the accompanying sidebar can help you choose the right oil. (Many new cars need extra oil for the first few hundred miles, but that should gradually diminish until the engine reaches a normal level at about 2,000 miles. If your car continues to "burn oil" at 2,000 miles, let the dealer know.)
- Get your car rust-proofed if you live near the ocean, in a humid climate, or in an area that gets snow during the winter. This is done by the factory in some cases; if your car was not rustproofed by the factory, get it done during the first 100 miles.
- Avoid "jackrabbit" starts--not only during the first 100 miles, but always.

- If your car has a high-efficiency gear (fifth speed or overdrive), wait until you've been on the road at least ten minutes before you use it. To avoid unnecessary wear, these gears should be completely warmed up before they are used.
- Try to avoid very short or stop-and-go trips at first; ideally, each trip should be between twenty and thirty miles. (You should continue to avoid short trips when you can for about the first 500 miles.)
- Help smooth out any irregularities on the brake surface by breaking them in every twenty miles or so. Here's how to do it: press down on the accelerator enough to keep the car moving while you put a moderate amount of pressure on the brake pedal. Hold down the brake pedal for about thirty seconds at a time for the greatest effectiveness.
- Help your paint job "harden" by washing your car frequently with cool, clear water in a spot protected from direct sunlight.

- Don't wax your car right away--it prevents the paint from drying and hardening. You should wait to wax your car until water no longer beads up on the paint (usually about six months).
- If you live in a snowy or icy area where salt is used on the roads, you need to rinse the salt off your car whenever the outside temperature is above freezing but below 42 degrees F. Between those temperatures, the salt will corrode the finish on your car.

Between 100 and 500 Miles

- Vary your speed as much as you can so that all engine parts get

thoroughly and evenly broken in. If you have cruise control, don't use it for the first 500 miles--try to avoid driving at the same speed for longer than five or six minutes at a time.
- Smooth down uneven parts on the engine by using sudden acceleration once every twenty-five miles or so between 100 and 500 miles. To do it, get your car cruising between 35 and 40 m.p.h. (**Never** try this technique from a standstill.) Then quickly step on the accelerator and leave it floored until the car is traveling at 55 m.p.h. At 55, start gradually easing off the accelerator.

At 1,000 Miles

- Take the car in for its first maintenance: have the transmission fluid, the engine oil, and the oil filter changed. Why so soon? As a new car breaks in, engine parts start rubbing together for the first time, and particles of metal drop into the oil and fluid. By changing oil and fluid now, you get rid of the debris that could cause problems later.

FOLLOW RECOMMENDED MAINTENANCE SCHEDULES

You can save money, prevent inconvenient breakdowns, and prolong the life of your car by doing one simple thing: follow the recommended maintenance schedule for your car. You'll find it in the owner's manual.

If for some reason you don't have your owner's manual, follow these general maintenance guidelines. These guidelines are designed for a car that's a few years old; newer cars need slightly less frequent maintenance, while older cars need more.

Every Two Weeks:

- Check the engine oil. Add some if necessary.
- Check the radiator. Add antifreeze (in cold weather) or water (in hot weather) if necessary.
- Check the paint job for any chips, gouges, or deep scratches. Have damaged paint repaired before rust starts.
- Check the air pressure in all tires (including the spare). Add air if necessary.

Once a Month:

- Check power steering fluid. Add fluid if necessary.
- Unless you have a no-maintenance battery, check the battery fluid and add water if necessary.

Every 3 Months or 3,000 Miles:

- Change the engine oil and oil filter.
- Check all belts on the engine. Replace any that are worn.
- Check the automatic transmission fluid. Add fluid if necessary. If the fluid is cloudy or contains metallic particles, have a mechanic check the transmission.

Every 6 Months or 6,000 Miles:

- Wax the car's body.
- Rotate the tires.
- Lubricate all hinges and locks on doors, hoods, and trunks.
- Replace all spark plugs.

   Have a mechanic do the following: check brake fluid level in the master cylinder; adjust brake drums; check oil in the differential and manual transmission; check the air conditioner; check and adjust the clutch; grease all chassis fittings; and check the carburetor.

The Ten Things A Tune-Up Should Include

Taking your car in for a major tune-up? Your mechanic should do the following ten things:

1. Change and adjust the spark plugs--all of them.

2. Check the hoses for bulges, cracks, or loose connections; replace them if necessary.

3. Clean or replace the PCV valve (an emissions control valve that boosts fuel economy and cuts down on pollution).

4. Check the brake fluid.

5. Change the fuel filter.

6. Change the air filter.

7. Check the battery fluid level and the battery's ability to hold a charge. Clean the cables and connectors.

8. Check the fan belts for cracks or excessive wear; replace them if necessary.

9. Inspect the distributor, including checking, adjusting, or replacing the old points and checking the condenser.

10. Check the wiring and replace it if necessary.

Every 12 Months or 12,000 Miles:

• Replace the air filter.
• Replace the fuel filter.
• Replace windshield wiper blades.
• Flush out the radiator and replace the antifreeze.
Have a mechanic do the following: tighten engine manifold bolts; inspect and replace brake linings; repack wheel bearings; align front end; perform a major tune-up (including spark plugs, points, filters, pollution-control equipment, and ignition system).

Every 2 Years or 24,000 Miles:

In addition to performing regular maintenance, you can prevent costly breakdowns by **anticipating** when major parts will wear out. Use the information below to estimate the life of major car parts, and then keep your own mileage chart. Then, before you anticipate trouble, have your mechanic check these parts. A part that shows excessive wear should always be replaced instead of left to chance!

How long they last:
Batteries, 3 to 5 years
Fuel pumps, 50,000 miles
Water pumps, 60,000 miles
Brake linings, 50,000 miles
Shock absorbers, 2 years

Remember that these estimates are based on common-sense driving. If you have a lead foot or drive like you're at the Indy 500, you'll need to replace major parts more often.

TIRE TREAD WEAR: HOW TO SPOT TROUBLE

Want a clue about how your car is running?
It's as easy as taking a good look at your tires!
To start with, the tread depth should be at least an eighth of an inch; in many states, less than one-sixteenth of an inch is illegal. To test yours, stick the end of a ruler between the treads. For a simple on-the-road test, use a penny. Insert the top of the penny between the treads: if the top of Lincoln's head shows, your tire needs to be replaced.

Take a good look at the **way** your tires have been wearing. Different patterns in the way your tires wear give clues about what might be wrong with your car. Normal wear causes smooth strips to appear across the tread. If you see one of these patterns, be alert for mechanical problems:

The Tread Wear Pattern	The Problem
Tread in the center wears first	Overinflated tires
One edge of tread is "feathered"	Poor alignment
Tread worn on only one edge	Poor alignment
Tread on the edges wears first	Underinflated tires
Uneven wear at two or more places	Wheels out of balance
Scalloped wear at even intervals	Worn suspension
Flat spot at one place	Long skid on dry pavement

NEED TO GET UP AND GO? MAINTAIN YOUR CAR'S BATTERY!

Your car's battery converts chemical action into the electrical energy that makes your car run. If it's kept clean and filled with water, it will continue to hold a charge--and will keep things running smoothly!

Keep it filled. To properly hold a charge, your battery needs to be filled with water. Check the water level in your battery once a month. To check the level, pull the covers off the top of each cell and look inside. The water should cover the metal plates inside and come to within one-fourth of an inch of the top.

If your battery fluid is low, add enough **distilled** water to fill it to the proper level. Replace the covers and wipe the top of the battery dry. If the weather is cold, never add water to the battery unless you will be driving the car for at least five miles immediately afterward.

Keep it clean. To clean dirt from the top of your battery, cover the vent holes with tape. Mix one part of baking soda with two parts of water, and use a scrub brush to clean the top of the battery with the baking soda mixture.

Rinse the battery with clear water, and wipe it dry. Make sure you remove the tape that's covering the vent holes!

Battery posts and clamps can get corroded, making it difficult to start your engine. To remove corrosion, use a wire brush; scrub posts and clamps until they shine and all signs of corrosion are gone. To prevent more corrosion, coat the clamps lightly with petroleum jelly.

Keep it warm. If the weather is really cold, try to park your car in a garage--or at least in a sheltered area. If temperatures really dip low, your battery might need some help to stay warm. Fold up an old blanket and tuck it around your battery, or run a low-wattage light bulb on an extension cord and put in under the hood near the battery.

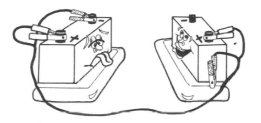

Dead as a Doornail: How To Jump-Start A Car

It's easy--and safe--to jump-start a car if you know what to do. Your owner's manual will state whether it's safe to use jumper cables on your car (a few with "electronic brains" can be damaged by jump-starting). If your owner's manual gives you the go-ahead, make sure you follow this procedure to get the cables attached in the proper order:

- Both cars should have ignition switches off and emergency brakes on. Automatic transmission cars should be in park, manual transmission cars should be in first gear.
- Remove the caps off the batteries in both cars. (If the batteries are "no-maintenance" batteries with sealed caps, don't try to remove them.)

- Attach one of the red clips on the jumper cables to the positive terminal of *your* battery. (The positive terminal is the largest of the two and will be marked *pos* or *+*.)
- Attach the other red clip to the positive terminal of the other car's battery.
- Attach one of the black clips to the negative terminal of your battery.
- Attach the other black clip to an *unpainted metal part* of the other car, *away from the battery.*
- Start the other car up first; let it run for about one minute.
- Turn your ignition and start your car.
- *Without turning off your ignition,* disconnect the cables from both cars.
- Drive your car continuously without turning off the ignition for at least fifteen minutes after jump-starting it so that your battery will recharge.

TAKING A BITE OUT OF CRIME: CHAPTER 8
HOW TO AVOID BECOMING A VICTIM

Statistically speaking, too many Americans run the risk of being victimized by crime--of being robbed, burglarized, mugged, raped, or assaulted. In any average year, in fact, more than two million American households will be burglarized, and the thieves will get away with almost $3 billion in stolen property.

Will you be one of the unlucky ones?

You don't have to be! There is plenty you can do to protect yourself from becoming a victim of crime--all the way from making your home a safer place to practicing some common-sense behavior in parking lots and on the streets.

SAFETY BEGINS AT HOME

There are plenty of things you can do to secure your home against a burglar--and lots of tricks that will discourage a would-be burglar from approaching your house in the first place.

You've probably heard lots of myths about burglars--who they are, what they take, when they strike. Now for the facts: Most burglars are under the age of eighteen. Most live within five or six blocks of the homes they burglarize. Very few burglars "case out" a place; they simply watch for signs that homeowners are gone, and they usually strike on impulse.

Most burglaries happen during daylight hours--not at night, as you might have suspected. Peak burglary hours are between 10 a.m. and 2 p.m. and again from 4:30 to 8 p.m. on weekdays, and between 6 and 7 p.m. on Fridays. Fewer burglaries happen on weekends, because most people are home from school or work then.

What do burglars go after most often? Small things they can easily carry that are also easy to sell. Cameras, small color television sets, video cassette recorders, sterling silver flatware, and good jewelry are popular targets. Cash (including coin collections), of course, is always top on the list.

285

There are two general strategies for preventing burglaries: discourage burglars from approaching your house in the first place, and make sure it's well secured in case they do try to get in.

Discourage a Burglar From Taking the First Step

How do you discourage a burglar from approaching your house in the first place?

Easy: make your house look occupied. Never let it look like you're not home. There are plenty of things you can do:

During the day, play a radio in the house; if you can, turn on an all-talk station. The sound of voices makes it seem that there are people inside. Even if you have a garage, park a car (with its doors locked, of course) in the driveway to make it look like someone's home. Turn the ringer on your phone down so that an incoming call won't ring incessantly, alerting passersby that no one is inside. Leave sheer draperies shut or blinds slanted to discourage "window shopping."

If you won't be home until after dark, purchase automatic timers for your lamps. Stagger them so that lamps in different

If You're Home When a Burglar Strikes: How to Protect Yourself

Chances are, you won't be home when a burglar strikes: burglars don't want to get caught, so they try their best to enter homes only if they are convinced no one is home.

If you do happen to be home, a few pointers can keep you from getting hurt:

- If you hear noise or a burglar alarm goes off, turn on the lights, lock yourself in a room, and call the police immediately.
- Start making noise! Chances are great that if a burglar hears someone is at home, he'll leave as quickly as he can. If nothing else, shout something like, "John, there's a burglar downstairs!"
- Never try to confront a burglar or find him yourself. Stay behind locked doors, and let the police do the searching. You will always be safest if you avoid actual contact with a burglar.

When you've been away from home--even if it's only for an hour-- be alert when you return. If you notice something out of place (a door or window open, a light on in the wrong room, or a light off that you left on, for example), *do not go into your house.* Someone may still be inside. Instead, go to a neighbor's house, call the police, and wait there until they have arrived. As a general rule, never enter your house if you suspect you have been burglarized until the police are there.

rooms turn on and off at varied intervals (it will look like people in the house are moving from room to room). Put a timer on a radio so it will turn on and off while you're gone. You might also put a timer on your television set--no one would suspect the house is empty with a television set on!

If you like pets, a good strategy is to get a well-trained dog. Sometimes the barking alone will keep a potential burglar from getting too close--he doesn't even get close enough to see if it's a very big dog!

If you have a telephone answering machine, don't state your name on it ("This is the Robinson residence. . . ") and don't say that you are not at home. Say something like, "We can't come to the phone right now, but we'll return your call as soon as we can."

If you will be gone for more than a day, enlist the help of your neighbors in protecting your home. Ask someone to park in your driveway. Either have your mail and newspaper delivery stopped, or ask a neighbor to collect mail and papers daily. Make arrangements for any other type of delivery, too (such as milk delivery). Even if you stop your newspaper and mail delivery, ask a neighbor to watch out for flyers, posted notices, and other things that could advertise your absence.

Ask a neighbor to do some simple yard maintenance, too. A would-be burglar will figure out you're gone right away if your lawn is drying up, your flowers are wilting, or the snow has piled up on your driveway and walks. Have someone keep your yard watered or your walks shoveled. If you'll be gone for an extended period, hire someone you trust to mow the lawns and do some basic yard care.

If you can't find a willing neighbor to watch out for you while you are gone, hire a reputable "house-sitting" service; they are usually listed in the classified ad section in newspapers.

It's always a good idea to organize a "neighborhood watch" in your area. Basically, neighbors watch out for each other and phone the police if they see any suspicious activity. Your local police department can help you organize such a group, and will provide you with warning stickers to post in the window.

Tighten Up Home Security

If all your strategies for discouraging a burglar fail and he approaches your house, you're not necessarily a victim: research shows that the average burglar will move on to easier turf if you can delay him by as few as three or four minutes. There are plenty of things you can do to boost home security, and many can be done with little cash output.

You should start with the outside of your home. Keep shrubs near your doors and windows trimmed low enough that a burglar couldn't hide behind them.

Don't put your name on your mailbox, on decorative plaques near the door, or on welcome mats. Why? A would-be burglar can jot down your name and address, look up your telephone number in the phone book, and call from a nearby pay or business phone to make sure no one answers. He can also ask neighbors about your estimated time of return--and if he calls you by name, neighbors may volunteer information since they assume he's a friend.

Install bright outdoor lights on each side of your house to provide plenty of illumination after dark. The lights should be as high off the ground as possible to prevent burglars from breaking or stealing them; high up under the eaves of the house (especially if the house has a second floor) is ideal. Lights should be photosensitive or connected to a timer so they go on automatically at dusk.

The most critical step is free: lock your doors and windows. Amazingly, a high percentage of burglars walk into homes through unlocked doors. Make it a general practice to keep your door locked, even if you are just walking the dog around the block or visiting a neighbor for a few minutes. Remember to lock your front door, too, if you are doing yard work in the backyard: plenty of burglars have "cleaned out" a house while the unsuspecting owners weeded a backyard vegetable garden.

Remember to lock your windows, too. A burglar with a razor blade can cut through a screen in about five seconds. And don't make it easy for a burglar to get in through a window--keep ladders, lawn chairs, picnic tables, or anything else he could climb on locked away in a shed or garage.

If the locks on your doors and windows are flimsy or broken, replace them. Install dead-bolt locks that have at least a one-inch bolt; the strike plate for the dead-bolt lock should have at least three-inch screws that pass through the doorframe and into the structural frame of the house. Double-keyed deadbolts are best because a burglar who squeezes in through a small window won't be able to carry out your television or stereo through the back door. You should always install a double-keyed deadbolt lock on a door that has a window in it; you'll prevent a burglar from breaking the glass, reaching in, and unlocking the door. Solid brass locks are the best; they can't be easily pried off with the kind of screwdriver that most burglars use.

If you have recently purchased or rented your house or apartment, have the locks changed; you never know who the previous owners or tenants entrusted their keys with.

Never attach an identifying tag with your address on it to your keys. If you lose them, a thief can pick them up, drive to your house, and simply wait for an opportune moment. If you do lose your keys, immediately have your locks changed as a safeguard.

Never rely on a security chain for protection. Even a teenager can kick a door with enough force to rip it out of the wall or door.

When you can, replace all hollow-core exterior doors with solid

---

Where to Hide Valuables at Home: The Best and Worst Places

Want to outsmart a burglar who, despite your precautions, does get inside your house?

Then hide your valuables!

But be smart about it: approximately 95 percent of a group of inmates polled about their criminal behavior said they always headed for the master bedroom first--where they checked all the drawers, the closets, and between the mattresses.

The best places to hide valuables:
• In packages of food in the refrigerator or freezer
• In a hollowed-out book on a crowded bookshelf
• In a bag of dirty laundry
• In the washing machine under dirty clothing
• In the clothes dryer under clothing
• In an inconspicuous container in a cluttered attic, basement, or garage
• In a floor safe installed in the floor (portable safes don't work--a burglar will simply take the safe)
• In a drop ceiling
• Behind an electrical outlet
• Behind an extremely heavy piece of furniture
• In a plastic bag in a garbage can surrounded by garbage
• In a canister buried in the yard

The worst places to hide valuables:
• Anywhere in the master bedroom
• In a desk
• In a drawer
• In a closet
• In the medicine cabinet (burglars check there for drugs)
• In a jewelry box
• Under a rug

wood or metal ones. Hollow-core doors can be easily kicked in or torn off the hinges. Door frames, too, should be either metal or solid wood. Make sure to remember "secondary doors," such as doors leading from the garage into the house; they need to be just as secure as a front door.

If your exterior door is flimsy and you can't afford to have it replaced right away, you can purchase thick rubber door stops at a reasonable price. Jam these under or against your closed door to provide some added resistance.

If your outside door has a window in it, it should be double-glazed or shatterproof glass. If there is no window, you should equip the door with an eye-level wide-angle peephole so you can identify visitors without opening the door.

All exterior doors should have interlocking hinges.

Take extra precautions with French doors and sliding glass doors--both favorite targets of burglars. New clear breakresistant plastic sheeting looks like glass but can't be broken; you can use it in all the panes within reach of a lock. Sliding glass doors should be equipped with bolt locks so they can't be lifted out of the track; most of these screw into the frame at the top of the door. You should also use a jamming bar in the lower track or a hinged bar that swings down and jams across the doorframe at mid-height.

Every window in your house should have at least a simple spring lock; you should provide additional protection with some other kind of locking device. For little expense, you can secure windows by pounding a nail or drilling a bolt into the frame so the window can't be opened enough to permit access.

Basement windows should be equipped with a bar on the inside to keep them secure--but make sure the bar can be quickly removed from the inside in case of fire or other emergency.

Finally, if you can afford it, install a good alarm system. (Most homeowner's insurance companies will lower your rates if you have an alarm system.) Alarm systems come in a variety of styles at a wide range of prices. For the best protection, you need an alarm at every door and window on the ground level. All but the most determined professional burglars will be scared off by an alarm system.

Don't, however, think you can fool a burglar with a phony alarm system decal mounted in your window. Burglars who know their business know the fakes from the real McCoys.

HOW TO KEEP YOUR CAR FROM BEING STOLEN OR STRIPPED

Protecting your car is a lot like protecting your house: you need to discourage a thief from approaching in the first place, and you need to follow up with some extra security measures as a backup.

To discourage a thief from picking your car out to begin with, avoid parking it in one place for long periods of time. Commuter parking lots where people meet to join a carpool and long-term parking lots at airports are favorite haunts of car thiefs. If you're catching a plane, have someone drive you to the airport--or take public transportation. Get together with others to travel to the commuter lot. If you're going to be shopping for a long time, come out and move your car several times if it is not in a secured lot.

Again, the most critical safeguard is free of charge: lock your car whenever you leave it. Even if you think you'll be back quickly, lock the doors. Don't forget to roll up the windows--plenty of car thieves have reached through a partly open window and unlocked a door. Regardless of your circumstances, **never leave engine running or the keys in the ignition while you leave the car--even for an instant.**

As an added precaution, you can do something simple to temporarily disable your car if you have to leave it parked. Your mechanic can show you how to remove and replace some small but essential part. Make sure you take the part with you--don't leave it in the car!

If you have a car stereo or CB, take some extra precautions to protect against theft. If you're purchasing new units, ask for models that are portable; if you'll be parking the car for more than a few minutes, you can remove the stereo or CB and lock them out of sight in your trunk. If not, visit an auto-parts store and get special heavy-duty fasteners that require odd-shaped tools for removal. If you live in a high-crime area, invest in an alarm system to protect your CB or stereo.

You should also take extra precautions with your trunk if you usually carry valuables or if you travel and lock suitcases in your trunk. For a modest price, a locksmith can harden your trunk lock with a heavy-duty antitheft lock assembly and plate. You should also install a lock on your hood to prevent thieves from stripping out engine parts.

If you live in a high-crime area or an area where auto stripping is a problem, you can invest in locking stud nuts that will prevent your wheels from being removed.

As a final precaution, you can purchase several different kinds of auto burglar alarms. The best kind are motion-sensor or motion-detector alarms--they sound off not only if a door or trunk is opened but also if the car is pushed or jacked up.

You've Been Burglarized: What Now?

If, despite your precautions, your home is burglarized, what should you do to boost the odds of catching the thief and getting your possessions back?

As stated elsewhere in this chapter, don't go into your house if you suspect that you have been burglarized. If you go inside without realizing a burglary has occurred but you immediately see that something is missing, do not touch anything. *Leave the house immediately, call the police, and don't go back inside your house until the police have arrived and searched your home thoroughly.* Why? Someone could still be inside.

Give police a complete description of everything you know was taken. The better you can describe an item, the better your chances of eventually recovering it. All valuables should be inscribed with your driver's license or Social Security number. For insurance reasons, you should keep a complete inventory of your household possessions in a safe place (such as a bank deposit box); list serial numbers and take photographs if you can. You can help police recover your things and will speed insurance claims if items are not recovered.

If you know the serial number of stolen property, it is worth at least $500, and you think it may be taken into another state, you can register it on the National Crime Information Center computer (your local police department will assist you). Then police in any state can identify your property and return it to you.

If you are burglarized, ask your local police department to do a "security check." A policeman will come to your home and analyze where your weak spots are, and can give you advice on how to better secure your home in the future. The service is free of charge. Some police departments even offer discounts on items like dead-bolt locks and window bars.

PARKING LOT SAFETY

Parking lots are often considered the "perfect" place to commit a crime. Why?

Plenty of reasons. They're huge. They're isolated. They're often dark. Few are secured or guarded. They have built-in hiding places (other parked cars) that criminals can hide behind for hours, watching for the ideal victim. And potential victims are usually distracted in parking lots--they are hurrying to or from an appointment. Many are carrying packages, so their hands aren't free to defend themselves. And some are so burdened down with packages that they can't move quickly enough to get away.

There are things you can do to protect yourself, though. Whenever you park in a lot, park as close to the entrance to the building as you can. If you can, park directly beneath a parking lot light (or as close to one as you can). Avoid parking next to a truck, a large van, or shrubbery that will obstruct clear view of your car.

Before you park, be alert to your surroundings. Is someone loitering in the parking lot? Are there people sitting in a car? If so, park elsewhere. As soon as you get out, check to make sure all windows are rolled up; lock your car.

Try not to walk through a parking lot alone, especially at night. If you need to return to your parked car, ask a security guard, a police officer, or a store security officer to accompany you.

Don't let yourself get burdened with too many packages. If you're shopping, make several trips out to your car throughout the day, carrying only a few packages at a time. Lock packages in your trunk, out of sight. If you have done alot of shopping at one place or have something bulky to carry to the parking lot, ask a store attendant or security officer to help you.

Before you leave the building, get your keys and hold them tightly in your closed palm with the door key poking out between two fingers. Rapists have often victimized women who were standing at their locked cars, struggling to find keys.

Keep alert, and walk confidently and purposefully through the parking lot. If you feel uncomfortable or think someone might be following you, immediately walk back to a well-populated area (such as a store, a doctor's office, or an office building) and ask for help.

Before you get into the car, check the floor and the back seat to make sure no one is in your car. As soon as you get in, lock the door again; don't leave the door open or unlocked while you arrange packages, situate yourself, fasten your seatbelt, and so on.

Obviously, you should never let someone you don't know get in your car **for any reason.**

STAY ON THE DEFENSIVE: HOW TO AVOID GETTING MUGGED

Unfortunately, you can get "mugged" (assaulted) just about anywhere--at home, in a public place, as you walk down a sidewalk, or even while you're driving your car. But you can take some precautionary measures to protect yourself. Here's how:

Obviously, there will be times when you have to go somewhere alone--we all do. But whenever you can, go places with at least one other person; a mugger thinks twice before taking on a pair.

When you're driving, even if it's just around town, keep your windows rolled up and your doors locked. If you don't have air conditioning and you're caught in the heat of the summer, roll windows down just a few inches--test to make sure you can't get your hand through the opening.

Muggers have been known to wait at traffic intersections until someone is stopped--at which point the mugger strikes. Whenever you stop at an intersection, stop a short distance back from the car in front of you. If someone approaches your car or tries to get inside, you can accelerate quickly (even if it's just a few feet) and honk the horn to attract attention.

Drive defensively so you can head off problems before they exist. Keep your car in good condition to prevent breakdowns or other problems on the road. And always check your gas tank before you go somewhere--running out of gas can be dangerous if the wrong person stops to help you.

Never pick up a hitch-hiker, no matter how innocent or well-dressed he looks.

Don't stop to help stranded motorists; rapists and murderers have been known to pose as helplessly disabled by a flat tire or car problems. If you want to be of assistance, stop at the next exit or pay phone, call police, and report that a motorist needs help.

By the same token, don't let someone help you if you run out of gas, get a flat tire, or have engine problems. Get in your car, roll up the windows, and lock the doors. If someone stops and offers help, ask him to take the next exit and phone for help. If he sincerely wants to help, he'll do as you ask.

Anyone can be rear-ended innocently, but a recent trick by armed robbers is to "bump and rob." The robber will follow a victim and bump the victim's car with his. When the victim gets out to inspect the damage and exchange insurance information, the robber pulls out a gun or knife instead of a driver's license.

If you become suspicious that you are being followed, **don't go home.** Instead, keep your hand on the horn and head for the nearest police station. If you don't know where the police station is, try some other occupied place where you can attract attention without getting out of your car--a fire station, twenty-four-hour convenience store, hospital emergency room entrance, gas station, laundromat, and so on.

If you're walking, employ some common-sense strategies to protect yourself. Start by looking ordinary: muggers always watch for well-dressed people who are wearing expensive jewelry. Tuck gold chains or other jewelry inside your clothing until you reach your destination.

Similarly, it's best to keep your purse as out of sight as possible; you should tuck a small purse securely under your arm **inside** your coat. If your purse is larger and has a shoulder strap, the safest strategy is to wrap the shoulder strap repeatedly around the purse and tuck the purse securely under your arm, clutching it firmly with your hand. A wallet is best in a front pocket--not as easily accessible to pickpockets as a rear pocket.

Whenever you're walking, stand tall and act confident; many muggers select their victims because they look vulnerable. Stand up straight, keep your head erect, walk with a comfortable but confident stride, and maintain eye contact with others (it shows that you're not afraid).

Stay constantly alert as to what is going on around you, even if you are walking with someone else. Walk on the side of the sidewalk that offers the fewest places for a mugger to hide: in building doorways, in alleyways, or in shrubs. If you're in a city, the best tactic is to walk down the middle of the sidewalk, not too close to the street (where passing bicyclists or motorcyclists could grab you) and not too close to buildings and shrubbery. If you're in a residential area and have to walk at night, the best tactic is to walk down the middle of the street.

Whenever you can, keep your hands free when walking; you'll be able to react more quickly. Carry a shrill whistle, electronic shrieker, or other **loud** noisemaker that will help you get noticed if you run into trouble.

When you are walking on streets or sidewalks, wear the most comfortable shoes you can--you should be able to run if you need to.

Finally, take defensive action. If you're walking down the street and see someone suspicious or unsavory walking toward you, cross the street to the other side. If you even **feel** threatened, do something. It's a lot better to be wrong and a little embarrassed than to risk getting attacked.

If you're at home, try to keep a locked door between you and any potential assailant. Look through a window or peephole before opening your door to anyone, and don't open your door to a stranger if you are home alone. If you have called for a repairman, insist that he produce identification for you and look at it through the window or peephole **without opening the door,** even a crack. **Be suspicious of any repairman or utility person who does not have a truck parked outside.** As a general rule, don't open the door until you're comfortable; talk to the person from behind a closed door until you feel secure in opening it.

Always close your drapes and shut your blinds at night. Some attackers simply travel through neighborhoods at night, selecting their victims by what they can see through the window.

If you live in a condominium or apartment building, be cautious about elevators--they are soundproof and can be stopped between floors. Simply don't get on with someone who looks suspicious. If you do ride the elevator alone, always stand near the control panel so you can immediately grab the emergency button if you are threatened and so it will be more difficult for the other person to stop the elevator.

If you are in the process of finding a place to live, you can take some preventive measures then. Choose a condominium or apartment that has a front entrance along a well-traveled street. Paths, corridors, hallways, and stairways should be easily visible to other tenants and to passersby. Choose a building with a well-lighted lobby that is visible from the street and a well-lighted, closely guarded parking lot.

IF YOU DO GET MUGGED: TO FIGHT OR NOT TO FIGHT?

That is the question!

Remember that an armed robber who attacks or threatens you is probably very nervous and excited--and, chances are, **he really doesn't care about your personal well-being.** You can increase the odds of surviving unharmed by doing a few smart things.

Ex-convicts and former criminals tend to agree: don't fight back. Don't panic. Don't get angry. Keep cool, and listen to the attacker's demands. And never, never argue or try to bargain with him. Your best and safest tactic is to quickly give him what he wants and then let him go. Follow directions promptly; the longer you face a gun or knife, the higher your chances of getting hurt.

During your encounter, be extremely observant. You'll be calling the police after this is over, so look at the attacker carefully. Notice estimated height, weight, hair color, eye color, skin color, unusual marks or scars, unusual mannerisms, speech patterns or accents, distinctive features (such as a missing eyebrow or a beard), and what the person is wearing. The more complete description you can give, the better the chance of the attacker being apprehended.

Listen very carefully to an attacker's demands, and then do exactly what he tells you. Don't do anything unexpected. If he tells you he wants your wallet, let him know what is happening: tell him where your wallet is and that you are getting it. Slowly and carefully remove your wallet and hand it to the attacker, holding it between your thumb and your index finger.

Once your have surrendered your wallet, jewelry, and other requested valuables, wait quietly for the attacker to leave. **Never try to grab his weapon.** If he gives you further instructions, follow them quickly and quietly. The most dangerous moment in a robbery is just after the robber has received what he asked for--now he's faced with the dilemma of how to keep you from following him. Show that you're going to cooperate with what he asks you to do. . .and, above all, **don't try to follow him.**

As soon as the attacker is well out of sight, walk quickly toward the closest populated place and call the police. Wait in a safe place for the police to arrive. Make a full description of your assailant and the incident, and let the police do the investigation.

H oliday time is such a happy time--*if* you take some common-sense precautions to make sure it's a safe time! Knowing a few basics--from how to boil Easter eggs to how many decorations your Christmas tree will safely hold--can keep your holiday celebrations cheerful and safe.

EASTER CELEBRATIONS:
DON'T TAKE A BAD EGG

If you think nothing seems as innocent as a brightly colored Easter egg, think again!

In their natural state, eggs have a thin protective coating on their shells. When eggs are washed, cooked in boiling water, or dipped in dye, that protective coating dissolves--and bacteria are free to enter the porous egg shell, even if it's intact.

To avoid a nasty case of food poisoning, take some simple precautions when you prepare your eggs. Wash your hands with soap and hot water before you handle the eggs. Cook them in a clean pan in boiling water for the recommended length of time (see information in the Eggs recipe section for details).

When the eggs have finished cooking, rinse them with cold water and put them in the refrigerator immediately. Keep them refrigerated until you dye them, color them, or apply decals. Then return them to the refrigerator and keep them refrigerated until they are ready to be eaten.

Want a fun, multi-colored egg? It's fast and easy! Prepare several different colors of dye in separate bowls: use half a cup of hot water and the desired amount of food coloring in each. Then stir 2 T. vegetable oil into each bowl. Dip the egg in the first color until you get the desired shade, dry with a paper towel, dip in the next color, dry, and so on. Repeat the process until you have dipped the egg in all of the colors. The vegetable oil in each bowl leaves "blank" spaces on the eggshell for the next color, and the result is a wonderful marbling of multiple colors!

HALLOWEEN FUN: GET TREATS, NOT TRICKS

To make your Halloween celebration fun *and* safe, start at the top--with the costume, of course! Whether you are trick-or-treating yourself or helping a child, keep the night's activities safe by following these guidelines:

- Use only makeup appropriate to the age of the trick-or-treater; Halloween makeup kits list a recommended age limit on the package. Follow package directions carefully for both applying and removing the makeup.
- Avoid using makeup that contains spirit gum adhesive--it's flammable and could ignite around candles or pilot lights.
- If you are purchasing costumes, wigs, beards, or other items, make sure they are labeled as being "flameproof" or "flame resistant." These can still catch on fire, but burn more slowly and are easier to extinguish. If you have questions about any item, you can call the Consumer Product Safety Commission toll-free, 1-800-638-2772.
- Wear a light-colored costume to increase your visibility after dark.
- Use reflective tape (available at hardware or sporting goods stores) to trim your costume and your trick-or-treat bag.
- Wear shoes that fit properly. Oversized shoes or high heels limit your movement, increase the chances for accident, and prevent you from getting away quickly in case of trouble.

- Avoid oversized clothing that is hard to manage--it can get caught in doors, caught on shrubbery, or may brush against a candle without you knowing it.
- Make sure all wigs and beards are securely attached so they won't slip and obscure your vision. If you wear a mask, make sure it fits securely and that the eyeholes are large enough to allow full vision.
- If the weather is cold in your climate, layer cold-weather clothing beneath your costume. Make sure the costume is large enough to fit over your cold-weather clothing, but not so large that it is cumbersome.

For safety's sake, a young trick-or-treater should always be accompanied by an adult or a responsible older child. Younger children should leave and return home while it is still light; older children who trick-or-treat after dark should carry a flashlight. (*Never* let a child carry a candle or other flame.)

If a younger child is going out with a group of older children, attach a label to his costume that gives his name, address, and telephone number. If he gets separated from the gorup, he can find help in getting home.

To help older children stay safe, follow these guidelines:
- Give the child a small bag that will fill quickly; the sooner the bag gets filled, the sooner he'll return home.
- Review the "rules of the road." Your child should walk on sidewalks, not in the road, and should cross streets only at corners or in designated crosswalks. Obviously, children should obey traffic signals and should cross a street only after looking in both directions.
- Insist that your child visit only the homes of people he knows. You might agree on which homes he can visit, or you might even draw a simple map outlining where he may go. A child should *never* enter a stranger's home or apartment unless he is accompanied by an adult.
- Tell your child that he may not eat anything until you have inspected it. To cut down on the temptation to nibble along the way, don't send a child out trick-or-treating if he's hungry. Have him eat dinner before he leaves--and, if you need to, send some treats from home that he can eat along the way.
- Tell your child not to accept candy from strangers.
- Tell your child not to accept homemade treats, unwrapped candy,

or unfamiliar candy.

- Inspect all candy before you let your child eat it. Look for strange odors, questionable appearance, torn wrappers, or pinholes that have been poked in the wrapper. Wash all fruit thoroughly and slice it into small pieces before you let your child eat it. If you have doubt about any piece of candy or fruit, destroy it so it can't be retrieved and then throw it away. If you need help ascertaining the safety of your child's candy, contact the local police, local poison control center, or your local hospital (many hospitals now offer the use of x-ray equipment to detect hidden razor blades, pins, or other metal objects).
- If your child has received toys or tokens instead of candy, inspect the toys to make sure there are no toy parts that could be harmful to your child.

Keeping teeth in tip-top shape. Let's face it: no one is going to be diligent about brushing after every Halloween snack. But there is hope. Experts with the American Dental Association have some great advice for keeping dental decay to a minimum: what you eat and when you eat it can help protect your teeth.

How?

Eating candy after a meal instead of between meals is a safeguard--the saliva you produce while chewing your meal will help wash away the sugars from the candy.

And candy that keeps sugar on your teeth for extended periods is always a poor choice. Sticky candy--like caramel or toffee--is worst; lollipops and other hard candy that has to be sucked is also bad.

The best option? Candy that you or your kids can chew and swallow quickly!

Crispy Jack-o-Lantern Treats. Want a fast, easy, yet festive treat for your own trick-or-treaters? Try these:

1/4 C. butter or margarine

1 10-oz. pkg. marshmallows (or 4 C. miniature marshmallows)

5 C. crisped rice cereal

In a large saucepan, melt butter over low heat. Add marshmallows, and stir until completely melted. Cook over low heat 3 minutes longer, stirring constantly; remove from heat. Pour in cereal and stir until well coated. Form into five pumpkins with stems. Decorate with gumdrops, candy corn, licorice, chocolate drops, or other Halloween candy.

KEEPING CHRISTMAS SAFE

For most of us, Christmas is a time of cheer--but fewer daylight hours, increased traffic, more drinking drivers, and potential severe weather conditions can lead to more traffic accidents. Unfortunately, you don't even have to leave your own home to face a hazard--Christmas decorations, plants, and other holiday objects can pose safety problems, too.

To keep your holiday season safe, follow these tips:

* Keep your car in good mechanical condition to avoid getting stranded.
* Be especially cautious while driving; be aware of what drivers around you are doing, and be on the lookout for an increased number of pedestrians. (Many pedestrians are carrying bundles at this time of year, and some can't clearly see where they are going.)
* If you have snow and ice in your climate, keep your steps and walks cleared and well lighted; wipe up tracked-in snow promptly to avoid slipping. Wear appropriate shoes or boots with enough traction to keep you sure-footed.
* Keep holiday plants--such as poinsettias, holly, and mistletoe-- out of the reach of children and pets. Poinsettia causes nausea and diarrhea if eaten; holly berries and mistletoe are poisonous if ingested in large amounts.
* If you purchase batteries for toys or games, keep them out of reach until they can be inserted. Small, shiny batteries appeal to children, who may chew on them, swallow them, or lodge them in their noses or ears.
* Never throw an old battery into the fireplace; it could explode.
* Keep gift wrapping supplies out of the reach of children. A small child could try to chew and swallow plastic packing pellets, ribbons, or other decorative items.
* Be especially diligent in promptly removing plastic bags, plastic sheeting, or the plastic that covers gift wrapping paper.
* Never leave extension cords plugged into a wall outlet if it is not in use. A child could chew on the cord or try to insert something into the end, leading to possible electrical shock and death.
* Be on guard for dangling cords from appliances.
* Keep liquor, cordials, and rum-laced candies or cakes out of the reach of children.
* Choose toys appropriate for your child's age; follow age guide-

lines on the package. Avoid toys with loose parts, small parts, or sharp edges. Toys should be nonflammable and painted with non-toxic paint. Brief your child on how to use any unfamiliar or new toy.

- Stay especially alert for fires from fireplaces, trees, candles, or carelessly handled cigarettes.

EVERGREEN SAFETY: THE CARE AND FEEDING OF YOUR CHRISTMAS TREE

For many, the twinkling lights and shiny ornaments on the Christmas tree are the center of holiday decorations. Keep yours safe by following these guidelines:

- If you want a fresh tree, make sure it's really fresh. Before purchasing a tree, shake and bounce the tree base on the ground; watch for falling needles. Stroke the branches to see if they feel dry or brittle. The tree should have a bright green color, and needles should remain tightly attached to the branches when you pull gently on them.
- As soon as you get a fresh tree home, cut the base at an angle to expose as much new surface as possible. Stand the tree in a bucket of water, and place it where it will be sheltered from wind and the winter sun. Make sure the tree is sheltered so that the water in the bucket doesn't freeze.
- When you bring a fresh tree indoors, cut it again at a slant to fit it into the Christmas tree stand. If you can, drill two or three holes in the base to help the tree absorb more water. Use only stands that

will hold water, and keep them filled--an eight-foot tree will absorb up to a quart of water a day.

- Keep a fresh tree in the coolest part of the room, away from the fireplace, heat stoves, heat vents, radiators, television sets, or sunny windows. The tree should not block exits, stairways, or walkways.
- Don't run an electric train around the base of a fresh tree; possible sparks could ignite the tree, causing a tragic fire.
- If a fresh tree gets really dry, discard it. That may seem difficult to do if your holiday celebrating isn't finished, but it's not worth risking a fire.
- Promptly sweep or vacuum up dry, fallen pine needles. Children or pets can choke if they try to eat them.
- Decorate your tree only with electric lights that have the safety seal of Underwriters Laboratories. Carefully inspect all strings of lights before you put them on the tree; don't use light sets that are frayed, cracked, or have broken insulation on the wires. Don't use light sets that have cracked sockets or loose connections, either.
- Always disconnect a string of lights before you try to replace a bulb. Your replacement should be of equal size and wattage to the bulb you remove.
- Never use electric lights on metal trees.
- If you have toddlers or pets in your home, leave the bottom branches unlit and undecorated. Small or fragile ornaments should be hung on top branches. Bubbling tree lights that contain methylene chloride (a poison) should not be used around young children, who could bite them and swallow the contents.
- Never leave tree lights plugged in overnight or when you are leaving home.
- Don't overload your tree with lights, garland, or other ornaments. According to the National Ornament and Electric Lights Christmas Association, you can safely put the following number of lights and ornaments on your tree:

   Two-foot tree: 35-50 miniature lights, 10 feet of garland, 25-35 other ornaments.

   Three-foot tree: 70-180 miniature lights, 24 feet of garland, 35-50 other ornaments.

   Four-foot tree: 100-240 miniature lights, 40 feet of garland, 50-75 other ornaments.

   Six-foot tree: 200-280 miniature lights, 75 feet of garland, 100-

150 other ornaments.

Seven-foot tree: 315-450 miniature lights, 90 feet of garland, 150-200 other ornaments.

Seven-and-a-half-foot tree: 400-650 miniature lights, 100 feet of garland, 175-275 other ornaments.

- If you choose a living tree (one that you can plant outdoors after Christmas), place the tree in a large container with handles so it will be easier to move around. Live trees must be handled very carefully; don't put electric lights on a live tree, since they can dry out and scorch the branches.

    Keep a live tree watered well. It should only be kept in the house for about five days to prevent it from breaking its winter dormancy. Keep a live tree in the coolest place in the room, away from any sources of heat.

    Once you've had a live tree in the house, "harden" it gradually by moving it outside in stages--first to an unheated garage or porch before putting it in the yard.

    If you plan to use a living tree, you need to dig and prepare the hole well ahead of time--obviously, before the ground freezes. Dig a deep hole and line it with mulch or peat moss; cover the ground around the hole with leaves, mulch, or sawdust. Cover the hole with plastic or canvas to keep the soil from freezing before you plant the tree.

    Sneezing at Christmas? Don't blame the common cold! If you always seem to start sneezing and sniffling at Christmas time, you're probably not being plagued by a cold.

    Why?

    You might be allergic to your Christmas tree! Fresh trees are often covered with mold spores, and some even produce pollen when brought inside.

    Look for common plant allergy symptoms: a stuffy nose, sneezing, and red, burning, itchy eyes. Over-the-counter antihistamines might help, or your doctor might be able to prescribe medication to ease your symptoms. (Be careful that you never mix alcohol and antihistamines.) If the problem persists, you might consider switching to an artificial tree.

CHOOSING AND CARING FOR POINSETTIAS

If a poinsettia has always symbolized Christmas for you, you've got more choices than ever! Poinsettia growers have developed some innovative varieties: you can choose any size from a tiny six-inch plant to a five-foot tree, and colors range from cream to deep red, with marbled and speckled varieties available.

Protect your poinsettia from cold during the trip home; chilling will cause leaves to drop. Keep your plant at a constant, moderate temperature to keep color at its brightest; during the day it should be less than seventy-two degrees, and at night less than sixty. Your poinsettia should have about six hours of bright, indirect light every day, but be careful--strong direct light will fade its color.

Keep your poinsettia moist, but guard against overwatering. You should water it thoroughly and let it dry out before you water it again.

To preserve your poinsettia for another season, prune the top as soon as the flowers are gone. Keep the plant compact with regular pruning, keep it watered, and fertilize it often. To prepare for Christmas blooming, keep it in total darkness after 5 p.m. every day beginning in mid-September.

PACKING AWAY TREE TRIMMINGS: PLAN FOR NEXT YEAR

To keep your tree trimmings in top condition, take some extra care as you pack them away for the season. Consider these tips:

- Each ornament should be cleaned and individually wrapped before you pack it away. Fragile ornaments should be wrapped in several layers of tissue and surrounded by crumpled tissue.
- Pack fragile ornaments, surrounded by crumpled tissue, in small individual boxes; pack small boxes into a larger box filled with plastic packing pellets or crumpled newspaper.
- Pack all ornaments, lights, and other decorating items in heavy cardboard boxes with lids. The type of boxes used to pack apples and other fruit are good; you can usually get them (sometimes for minimal cost) from your local grocery store.
- Group like items in the same box and clearly label the boxes. You'll avoid tossing a heavy box on top of one that contains fragile items, and you'll be able to unpack next year in logical order.
- Pack "edible" ornaments (such as bread-dough ornaments or popcorn garlands) in containers that household pests can't nibble through. (Cardboard alone won't do the trick.)

- Store Christmas decorations in a cool, dry place protected from any extremes in temperature. Too much heat or cold can crack crystal, melt candles, and break delicate glass.

SPREADING CHRISTMAS CHEER: HOW MUCH SHOULD YOU TIP?

Christmas is a great time to thank people who serve you throughout the year--but how much is a customary tip? According to etiquette expert Emily Post, the following are acceptable:

- Newspaper carriers, $5 to $15 (tip more if you have received unusually good service or if the carrier has to make special accommodations to deliver your paper)
- Hair stylist, a small gift (something edible is the ideal), $5 over your regular tip, or $10 for a shop owner whom you don't regularly tip
- Teen-aged baby-sitter, a small gift or a tip that equals double an average night's wage
- Adult baby-sitter or cleaning help, one week's pay
- Delivery person (anyone who delivers regularly for a dry cleaner, drugstore, dairy, or so on), $5
- Garbage collectors, $5 to $15 (if your city has municipal garbage collectors, check to make sure compensation is not against the law)

PROTECTING AGAINST HOLIDAY PICKPOCKETS

Unfortunately, the holiday season is prime time for thieves and pickpockets. Follow all general suggestions for protecting yourself listed in the crime prevention chapter. In addition, follow these guidelines for preventing holiday theft:

- Never leave your wallet, checkbook, or handbag in your car--not even if you have it locked in the trunk.
- If you must leave packages in your car, lock them in the trunk. Never leave packages where they can be seen through a window.
- Park in as open an area as possible; avoid parking next to vans or trucks. Make sure you park where parking lot security personnel can have a clear view of your car. Even during daylight hours, park immediately beneath parking lot lights--if your shopping runs longer than expected, you'll be protected.
- Carry your handbag tucked securely under your arm; if it has a

shoulder strap, use the shortest length looped over your shoulder for added security. Hold your handbag with the pockets against your body, and keep all valuables zipped securely inside compartments within the handbag.

- Keep your hands free; carry packages in collapsible, expandible canvas tote bags that can be carried over your shoulder. When bags start filling up, make a trip to your car and place packages in your locked trunk.
- As much as you can, avoid crowds; pickpockets do their best work by bumping into people in crowds. Stay aware of where bottle-necks occur in stores and shopping centers, and avoid them.
- Before you start for the parking lot, get your car keys out and have them ready. Many thieves grab packages while people are fumbling for keys.
- As soon as you get in your car, lock your doors. Don't leave doors open or unlocked while you arrange packages.
- Make an effort to make your home look occupied while you are gone. Never leave Christmas tree lights on while you are gone, but do leave random lamps or room lights on. You might also leave a radio on to give the impression that you're home. Obviously, keep all windows and doors securely locked.

HOLIDAY EXPENSES: HOW TO AVOID GETTING IN OVER YOUR HEAD

You've undoubtedly seen the cartoons and heard the jokes about January--the miserable month following all the festivity when the bills start pouring in. To avoid ruining a wonderful holiday by getting too far in debt, follow some of these suggestions:

- If you love sending Christmas cards but find your list growing longer every year, keep your eye out for festive postcards. They're available in many different designs; some even feature art reproductions of antique Christmas cards. They are about one-fourth the cost of Christmas cards, and the postage is less expensive, too!
- Before you begin your holiday shopping, determine how much you can spend on holiday gifts. Make a list of the people you want to buy gifts for. Then decide on what you're going to buy; try putting a great deal of thought into the gift, but stay within your budget. Take the list with you when you go shopping, and check

off items as you purchase them. Following a list will help you avoid impulse purchases that can break your budget.

- If you use credit cards, try making all your purchases on one major card; it's easier to lose track of how much you're spending if you spread your purchases out among several cards.

- If you use a credit card, clip half an index card to the back of it; keep a running total of everything you charge. You'll be aware of what you're spending and will be less likely to go above your limit.

- Make a concerted effort to pay off any balances on your credit card *before* you start shoping for the holidays. Most credit card companies offer an interest-free grace period on initial bills, so you might be able to pay off your Christmas purchases before interest begins accumulating.

- If you use a credit card for convenience instead of as a "loan," keep track of purchases by deducting them from your checking account as though you were writing out personal checks. Then when your credit card bill arrives, simply write out a check and mail your billing--the amount has already been deducted from your checking account.

- If Christmas is traditionally a difficult financial period for you, plan ahead. Tuck any bonuses, income-tax refunds, dividends, cash gifts, or other unexpected money away in a separate interest-bearing account throughout the year. When Christmas arrives, you'll have a cash resource with which to meet holiday expenses--and, with discipline, you can stay within your budget.

- If you are on a tight budget year-round and can't spare the money for Christmas expenses, work throughout the year to mobilize additional resources. Hold a garage sale; you'll find tips on how to make one a success elsewhere in this book. Sell personal possessions you no longer need or want. Put hobbies or skills to work; you might teach piano lessons, teach dance classes, or take care of pets for vacationing neighbors.

- Instead of buying many individual gifts, you might decide on one major family gift (such as a video cassette player, a trampoline, or a special vacation). You might also try giving a single gift to other families on your list instead of buying smaller individual gifts for each family member.

OVER THE RIVER AND THROUGH THE WOODS: GETTING TOGETHER WITH FAMILY FOR THE HOLIDAYS

Everyone wants to be with family for the holidays, right?

Maybe so, but it can be a big strain if family members have to travel from distant places for a holiday reunion. To avoid hurt feelings and other potential problems, keep the following in mind:

- Well in advance of the holidays, openly discuss plans. Decide on who will travel, where people will stay, and how long the visit should be.
- If accommodations are cramped, consider staying in a hotel instead of at a relative's house; discuss it ahead of time to avoid any hurt feelings.
- If you do end up staying at a relative's home, plan short outings that enable you to get out of the house. You'll need the time by yourself, and your hosts will appreciate some private time, too.
- If traveling to be with family *and* buying gifts puts a real strain on your budget, discuss the situation with family members. You might agree to exchanging inexpensive gifts, exchanging hand-made items, or come to some other conclusion that will be less difficult for everyone.
- If distance, budget, or other considerations prevent you from getting together with your family, plan carefully to spend the day with close friends. Instead of feeling lonely, invite friends to your home for a cozy get-together.
- Plan ahead to make phone calls to members of your family. Agree on a time when you should call; you'll avoid reaching people who are frantic, in the middle of chaos, or just on their way out the door. A little advance planning can result in a relaxed, happy conversation.
- If a family member can't join the rest of you, plan to make a tape or videotape of your celebration. Send it off as quickly as possible after the holidays to help spread the cheer!

INDEX

required prior to making
funeral arrangements, 25
deeded time-share, 83
defensive driving, 260-268
dehumidifier, 249
dental decay, preventing, 302
Depression glass, as used
merchandise, 15
desserts
in Dutch oven, 171-173
in lunchboxes, 112-117
Mexican, 191
deviled eggs, 99
dip
dill, 110
for fruit, 109, 110
grilled, 154
Mexican, 186
shrimp, 217
direct flight, 74
discount rate, 28
discounts
travel, 69
tickets, 70
dishwasher, overflowing, 244
divorce records, how to get
copy of, 23
doors
deterioration of, 231
how to paint, 239
door-to-door sales, 3-4
down payment, as appears on
a contract, 8
dressers, as used merchandise,
17
dried fruit, in lunchboxes,
109, 113
drill, electric, variable-speed,
250
drinks (see beverages)
driving
how to stay awake while,
268-269
in hot weather, 270-271
in ice and snow, 271-274
in rain, 272
rules, 264-265
to avoid accidents, 260-268
Dutch oven
beans, 166, 167
beef, 163, 164
breads, 169, 170
candy, 173
chicken, 164
chowder, 165
desserts, 171, 172, 173
equipment for, 165

fish, 165
how to season, 166
pits for, 168
pork chops, 163
stew, 164
yams, 167

E

earnest money, 28
Easter egg
decorating, 300
safety of, 299-300
economy bedrooms on
trains, 78
eggnog
banana, 112
chocolate, 90
cranberry, 90
easy, 91
orange-grapefruit, 90
strawberry, 85
eggs
casseroles, 103
deviled, 99
Easter, 299-300
fried, 98
grades, 97
hard-cooked, 102
how to buy, 97
how to store, 101
Huevos rancheros, 194
omelets, 100, 101, 102
poached, 99
quiche lorraine, 102, 103
sandwiches, 106, 123,
130, 135
scrambled, 98, 100, 103
stuffed, 97
egg-salad sandwich
bacon and, 135
Caesar, 130
crunchy, 123
variations of, 106
emergency fund
for travel, 70
how to establish, 37-38
employee
benefits, 58
how to excel as, 59-61
enchiladas
beef and bean, 183
beef and cheese, 185
cheese, 187
chicken, 187, 196
epoxy, 251
estate auctions, 15-16

executor of will, 24
express warranty, 5-6
exterior doors, deterioration
of, 232
exterior siding
deterioration of, 232
how to paint, 240
foundation walls,
deterioration of, 231
exterior wood stain, 242
eyeglasses, packing for
travel, 69

F

fajitas, beef, 191
family, celebrating holidays
with, 311
family bedrooms on trains, 78
family-plan fares, train, 78
Fannie Mae, 28
fares
air, 74-76
train, 78-79
Federal Fair Credit Billing
Act, 14
financial records, how long
to keep, 51
fireplace, deterioration of, 231
first-class seats, airline, 74
fish
baked, 205, 206, 208, 211, 212,
213, 214, 215, 216
broiled, 210
casserole, 205, 211, 214
chowder, 165, 208, 210
dip, 217
Dutch oven, 165
fatty, 207
fried, 213
how to buy, 209
how to determine doneness
of, 206
how to marinate, 218
how to store, 209
lean, 207
loaf, 206
marinades for, 218, 219
stew, 210
fish, Dutch oven
roll-ups, 165
flat paint, 236
flat tire, how to change, 269
flatware, silver, as used
merchandise, 15
flauta, 184
flight

ASPEN WEST
PUBLISHING & DISTRIBUTION

"Where's Mom Now That I Need Her?" Surviving Away from Home. Frandsen, B.R. 356 pages of hints on nutrition, grocery shopping, laundry and clothing with a stain removal guide, first aid and recipes for quick, easy meals, plus lots more.

0100 Vinyl 3-ring ISBN 9615390-0-3 cost $22.95
0101 Paperback ISBN 9615390-1-1 cost $13.95

"Where's Dad Now That I Need Him?" Surviving Away from Home. Frandsen, B.R. 350 pages of hints on budgeting, credit cards, buying and maintaining cars, home maintenance, crimes prevention and more. Also includes recipes such as Dutch-oven, BBQ, fish, beverages, soups and pancakes!

0102 Vinyl 3-ring ISBN 9615390-2-X cost $22.95
0103 Paperback ISBN 9615390-3-8 cost $13.95

"A Pinch of This A Dash of That" Conversations with Cook. Johns, K. Treasured recipes passed down from one generation to another.

0106 Vinyl 3-ring (tabs) ISBN 9615390-5-4 $24.95
0107 Paperback ISBN 9615390-6-2 $14.95

"After the Wedding" A guide for the Bride. Collins, S. Information to the newly married couple on communication, physiological insights, social etiquette, entertaining ideas, and easy recipes.

0113 Hardback ISBN 0-96275260-6 cost $22.95

"Financial Survival" Personal and Financial Organization. Weinrub, R. A workbook for information on insurance, investments, taxes, probate, cash flow, wills, trusts, medicare and social security. Never again will you be the one who doesn't know…

0118 Vinyl 3-ring (tabs) ISBN 1-885348-18-5 $19.95
0116 Paperback ISBN 0-9615390-8-9 $8.95

"Me Mum Sez…" Outrageous truths about Life and People. Salty, M. Pages full of thoughts and illustrations. No amount of expertise can substitute for the intimate knowledge of our Mums. So, when Me Mum Sez it, we better listen up!

0117 Paperback ISBN 09615390-9-7 $5.95

Bestsellers from #1 Cleaning Expert, Don Aslett collection.

0120 Clean In a Minute cost $5.50
0121 How to be #1 with your Boss cost $6.50
0122 Painting without Fainting cost $5.50
0123 Who Says It's a Woman's Job cost $6.50
0124 Office Clutter Care cost $10.95
0125 Pet Clean-Up Made Easy cost $9.95

"Teaching Truths to Tiny Tots" My Everyday Book. White, E. Through Grandma Erma's stories, pictures, rhyme and poetry are used to teach children ages 2 to 6 years proper manners in everyday life. The magical voice of Grandma Erma is captured on the cassette tape.

0130 Book and cassette tape cost $10.95

"How to be a Successful Bachelor" A Humorous Guide To Your New Life. Ratchford, W. This is the first book written to help men cope with single life with a twist of laughter at oneself.

0119   **ISBN 0-9640027-0-1**   **cost $16.95**

"How to Hire an Honest Lawyer and Other Oxymorons" Martin, M. Mel Marten's definitive and hilarious guide for when you do have to hire a lawyer. A genuinely funny book to read-this one is for you. Pick it up and start laughing!

0138 Paperback ISBN 0-9642951-0-5   cost $9.95

"Deliciously Healthy Favorite Foods Cookbook" Castle, S. Over 250 mouth-watering recipes. Low fat, sugar free, quick & easy, physician endorsed. Adapt your own recipes for meals that are both healthful and delicious.

0137 Paperback ISBN 0-9647423-2-2   cost $15.95

"Laundry 101"   Where do I start? A simple "How To" book for anyone doing laundry. A 6 x 9 booklet with 22 pages.

0112   **ISBN 09615390-7-0**   **cost: $3.95**

 Hugs pick you up when you are down. Hugs show my love when I'm not around. Hugs can replace candies, rings and material things. Now, here's a thought that's true A Great Big Hug, From Me To You!

0057	Hug Assorted Fabric (Includes Box)	cost $19.95
0058	Hug Natural Fabric for Autographing (Includes Box)	cost $19.95
0059	Light Pink Fabric for Autographing (Includes Box)	cost $19.95
0021	Fabric Marker Assorted Colors	cost $1.00 ea.

TOLL FREE ORDERING DEPARTMENT
1-800-222-9133 *ORDER NOW!*

LAUNDRY BAGS

Bonus: Includes Laundry 101 Booklet!

LAUNDRY 101
PILE #1 WHITES
PILE #2 DARKS
PILE #3 COLORS
1559

HI MOM IM HOME!
1501

WHERE'S MOM NOW THAT I NEED HER?
1506

HELP WANTED
Looking for the right person to assist in the following: *sorting, washing, drying, and folding* the contents of this bag. Pay negotiable. *MUST BE RELIABLE!*
1503

C.O.D. CLEAN ON DELIVERY
OPEN IMMEDIATELY
CONTENTS RECYCLABLE
To:
From:
1574

TO BLEACH OR NOT TO BLEACH... THAT IS THE QUESTION?
1556

LAUNDRY INSTRUCTIONS
IF A CRISIS OCCURS... CALL 1-800-HOME
1577

Yellow Fabric

CAUTION
WEAR YOUR RESPIRATOR
1553

Large Laundry Bags- 24"X30", Natural with sewn cash pocket   **$15.00 each**

PILLOWCASES

P.S. I Love You!
4201

Make me late for work.
4573

Have I Told You Lately That I Love You?
4203

this is MY pillow
4189

P.M.S. PLEASE MORE SLEEP
4514

Please, Make Your Bed
Love Mom OXOXO
4246

YOU SNOOZE YOU LOSE
4241

Osmosis
Do your thing.
4519

DO NOT DISTURB
4219

Pillow Cases - Percale/ STD, Queen size   **$12.00 each**

Ask your local retail Gift or Bookstore about our other fine products!

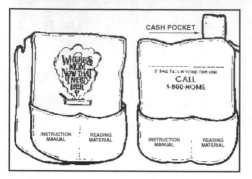

CASH POCKET

WHERE'S MOM NOW THAT I NEED HER?

IF BAG FILLS BEYOND THIS LINE CALL 1-800-HOME

INSTRUCTION MANUAL · READING MATERIAL

INSTRUCTION MANUAL · READING MATERIAL

Extra Large Laundry Bags with Pockets

Available in blue or white cotton twill. Size- 20" x 30" with a 6" gusset and pockets for laundry essentials. All bags have a strong nylon draw-cord at the top. Available stock, or blank for custom printing. Order in multiples of 6.

2000	Where's Mom?	XL	white	$22.00
2001	Where's Mom?	XL	blue	$22.00
2002	CALL 1-800-Home	XL	white	$22.00
2003	CALL 1-800-Home	XL	blue	$22.00

ORDERING INFORMATION

Sold to:_____

Date: _____

Customer rep. _____

Day phone # _____

Eve phone # _____

ITEM DESCRIPTION	PRICE	QTY	TOTAL

Shipped via UPS. Figure shipping rates according to the following schedule:

If your order totals up to $10.00 ADD	$3.95
$10.01 - $25.00	$4.95
$25.01 - $40.00	$6.50
$40.01 - $55.00	$8.90
$55.01 - $75.00	$10.50
$75.01 - $200.00	$12.50
$200.00 + additional charge	
Outside the Continental U.S. Special Quote	

Total for Merchandise	
Sales Tax (UT x .0625)	
Shipping/Handling *	
TOTAL ENCLOSED	

MY METHOD OF PAYMENT IS:

❏ CASH ❏ CHECK NO. _____ ❏ MASTERCARD ❏ VISA

* ALLOW 10-15 DAYS FOR DELIVERY

Credit Card No._____ Exp. Date _____ Home Tel. _____

I agree that I have ordered the above items and have approved the above method of payment for the merchandise purchased. This form must be filled out completely for the order to be processed. All sales are FINAL. Prices subject to change without prior notice.

Customer Signature   Print Name   Date

ASPEN WEST PUBLISHING CO. INC. • TOLL FREE 1-800-222-9133

P.O. Box 1245/8385 Allen Street No. 129 • Sandy, UT 84070 • 801-565-1370 • FAX 801-565-1373

All designs copyrighted and/or trademarked   © 1996 Aspen West Publishing Co. Inc.   All products made in the U.S.